MOUNTBATTEN

MOUNTBATTEN

The Private Story

BRIAN HOEY

First published 1994 by Sidgwick & Jackson Limited
This new edition published by

The History Press
Cirencester Road, Chalford,
Stroud, Gloucestershire, GL6 8PE
www.thehistorypress.co.uk

British Library Cataloguing in Publication Data.
A catalogue record for this book is available from the British Library.

ISBN 978 0 7509 5036 7

Typesetting and origination by The History Press Ltd
Printed in Great Britain by Ashford Colour Press Ltd., Gosport, Hants.

Contents

AUTHOR'S NOTE

This is not a biography of Earl Mountbatten of Burma. Other writers have already successfully completed that project so there is no need of another chronological account of his life and times. What I have attempted to do with this book is to look for the private man behind the public face. It is intended as a portrait of certain, by no means all, aspects of Mountbatten's character, and as such the reader may find large gaps where I have not felt it necessary, or desirable, to go over territory which has been explored so thoroughly elsewhere.

Where this book differs from any of the others is that I have been able to use the words of those who knew Mountbatten best. His two daughters have been refreshingly honest about their father's behaviour, the last of his serious girlfriends talks about their affair, and King Constantine, Prince Philip and Prince Michael of Kent speak for the first time about their feelings for, and attitude to, this patrician figure in the Royal Family.

I have been able to examine in some detail Mountbatten's troubled marriage, his love affairs, his attitude to money and his fascination with all things royal.

Apart from the quoted sources, all the information I have used has come from the Mountbatten Archives at the Hartley Library at Southampton University where every fact can be verified. For this reason I have not included footnotes.

BRIAN HOEY

ACKNOWLEDGEMENTS

Among the many people who have been kind enough to talk to me or allow me access to their private papers are the following to whom I am glad to be able to record my appreciation: His Majesty King Constantine of The Hellenes, HRH The Duke of Edinburgh, HRH Prince Michael of Kent.

Lord Mountbatten's daughters, Patricia and Pamela, the present Countess Mountbatten of Burma and Lady Pamela Hicks, have been the prime source of information, and I am very grateful to them for sharing with me their memories of their father. I am also indebted to Mountbatten's sons-in-law, Lord Brabourne and David Hicks, and his grandchildren, Norton (Lord Romsey), Joanna (Baroness du Breuil), Lady Amanda Ellingworth, Philip, Michael-John and Timothy Knatchbull, Ashley and India Hicks, Edwina Brudenell and Mountbatten's granddaughter-in-law, Penelope (Lady Romsey).

My thanks also go to the Duchess of Abercorn, Lady (Gina) Kennard, Lord Charteris of Amisfield, Sir Ian Scott, Sir Brian McGrath, Douglas Fairbanks Jr, Ronald Allison, Lt-Col Peter Gibbs, Philip Zeigler, Dr Richard Wallace and Dr Brian Best, Mr and Mrs Richard Wood-Martin, Charles and Kathryn Pierce, Peter Nicholson, Derek Hill, Vanessa Adamson, Vice Admiral Sir Ronald Brockman, Mrs Charles Collins, Rocky Wilkins, James Mooney-Boyle, William Evans and Alan Warren. My Chief Researcher Marc Cole-Bailey and Dr Chris Woolgar provided invaluable help at the Mountbatten Archives in Southampton University, as did Helen Gummer, Deborah Adams and Hazel Orme, who edited the manuscript and Ingrid Connell, who researched the pictures. William Armstrong was the man who had the original idea for the book.

Finally, I must mention the late Aideen Gore-Booth and the late

Acknowledgements

John Barratt, both of whom were very close to Lord Mountbatten in his lifetime, and who sadly died before they could see their contribution to this book in print.

BRIAN HOEY
1994

INTRODUCTION

When I was asked if I would write a book about Lord Mountbatten my initial reaction was less than enthusiastic. I knew there had been at least two major biographies, one of which had been the authorized version, with all the co-operation and access to family, friends and private papers that that implies, so what on earth more could there be to say?

I then read all the books I could find, including the edited Mountbatten diaries, and realized, without wishing to be hyper-critical, as I would have done the same thing myself, that each of these well-written, thoroughly researched works of scholarship was highly selective. This is not to suggest that the authors have deliberately omitted unpalatable facts in order to portray their subject in any particularly favourable light. It is simply that this man's life and career offered so many fascinating aspects that pressure of space had forced the writers to concentrate on the more public side.

My own researches then revealed that perhaps there was a little more to be told to complete the story of what was undoubtedly a great man and one of the most influential figures in the world in the middle part of the twentieth century. He was nowhere near as powerful as he himself believed, or would have others believe, but there was a time when he had the ear of every leader of every country that counted, and his close relationship with the Royal Family opened many doors that would otherwise have remained firmly closed.

His list of achievements reads like the script of a Hollywood movie that's gone way over the top. Born a Serene Highness, bullied at naval college, forced to change his name in the First World War because of his German background, Second World War hero who had his ship blown from under him, Chief of Combined Operations at the age of forty-one, married to one of the richest women in Britain, the last Viceroy of India and its first Governor General, Chief of the Defence Staff, Admiral of the Fleet, First Sea Lord, a Knight of the Garter, holder of the Order of Merit and dozens of other honours and decorations, and finally, blown up by the IRA on board his own boat at the age of seventy-nine. All the ingredients of a score of lives were packed into eight decades by this one remarkable man.

Several million words have already been written about Mountbatten. What attracted me to the subject was the possibility of learning at first hand something about his character from those who knew him best, but had not spoken publicly before. So I was delighted when Prince Philip agreed to give his very personal assessment of the man – not all of it complimentary. How Mountbatten gave him a home as a young man, introduced him to the game of polo and helped him in his early years as a member of the Royal Family. And also how he manipulated people to get his own way.

Then King Constantine of The Hellenes provided a number of anecdotes about his personal relationship with 'Uncle Dickie' which showed Mountbatten's fascination, almost an obsession, with all things royal. How Mountbatten's attitude to him changed overnight when Constantine became King, and the lengths to which he would go to obtain another honour. Prince Michael of Kent showed another side to Mountbatten's character when he told me how Uncle Dickie had acted as intermediary between the Kents and the Queen when Prince Michael wanted to marry a Roman Catholic divorcee.

Members of the Royal Family do not like talking about their relatives, particularly when it involves expressing personal opinions, so I am grateful to those who made an exception and spoke to me on this occasion.

Similarly, past and present members of the Royal Household do not normally give private interviews, so when Lord Charteris of Amisfield, a former Private Secretary to the Queen, spoke to me in the House of Lords about his long association with Lord Mountbatten, he was able to shed some light on the reasons why the Household disliked him so much. Charteris, who was one of the few courtiers who got on with Mountbatten, also gives an insight into his unique relationship with the Queen.

It was another former member of the Royal Household who told me of the way Mountbatten acted as a conduit between the Queen and the Duke of Windsor and how the efforts to get the Duke to give away Princess Margaret on her wedding day were thwarted.

Another former senior royal aide, Ronald Allison, who was Press Secretary to the Queen for five years, was able to illustrate Mountbatten's legendary attention to detail, when he described some of the preparations Mountbatten involved himself in when planning his own funeral.

One of the contributors to this book is Sir Ian Scott, a former distinguished Indian civil servant who worked with Mountbatten when he was Viceroy. Scott admired Mountbatten's energy but disliked him intensely as a person, saying he was the vainest man alive and giving examples to back his claims. He also says that much of what Mountbatten achieved was because 'he had no principles' and justifies his opinions with stories of actual events.

I first met Lord Mountbatten in the 1970s, by which time he had relinquished all his most influential roles. He was then President of United World Colleges and I was working as a television reporter with BBC television in Wales. The first United World College had opened at St Donat's Castle in the Vale of Glamorgan and Lord Louis was making the first of what were to become many regular visits. Before he arrived he had telephoned one of the BBC governors, the late Christopher Cory, who was an old friend, to suggest that it would be appropriate for a television crew to be on hand when he arrived to interview him about his plan for the college. I was detailed to conduct the interview and I soon found that a suggestion from Mountbatten amounted to a command.

When we met he told me where he wanted the interview filmed, how the lights should be placed, which side he was to be filmed from, and not only the answers he intended to give but also the questions he was to be asked. He told my lighting cameraman that it was important for him to be shot from six inches above his eyeline. In an aside to me he explained that his old friend Cary Grant had given him this tip, saying, 'When you're over fifty never let them photograph you from below. It shows all the wrinkles.' Mountbatten asked the length of the programme I was working on, the context into which the interview was to be placed, and consequently he was able to tailor his comments to fit exactly. It was the first of several interviews I recorded with him on both radio and television and the format never changed. He was in complete control, knew precisely what it was he wanted – and was determined to get it right. The strange thing was that neither the camera crew, who were all very experienced professionals, nor I – and I had been in the business over twenty years at the time – felt any resentment at being ordered about in this manner. He was obviously used to having his instructions obeyed to the letter without question; the idea of any of us not complying with his orders simply never occurred to him – or to us.

Before we started Mountbatten gave us a lecture on St Donat's Castle, which had belonged to the late American press baron William Randolph Hearst, and he regaled us with tales of the wild parties that were held there in the thirties when stars such as Bing Crosby and Bob Hope would arrive in the middle of the night and Hearst would wake the servants to prepare a five-course banquet at two or three in the morning. Mountbatten found nothing unusual in this; he had been used to being waited on hand, foot and finger ever since he had married the wealthy Edwina Ashley in 1922.

In the course of that first meeting of perhaps an hour and a half I heard the names of more world figures mentioned than in the previous two years. Mountbatten, it appeared, was the consummate name-dropper. He knew everyone and everyone knew him. He also had recently finished filming a television series based on his life, which was subsequently shown with great success in many countries, and as a result he had become a self-appointed authority on the making of television programmes.

One other thing I learned about him at that first meeting was that he never forgot a name. After I had introduced myself he repeated my name several times – he said this was a trick he had learnt in Hollywood in the twenties – and thereafter, whenever we met, he always called me by my Christian name. It was very flattering to me and I saw him do it with many people. He was even able, after meeting a roomful of men and women for the first time, to reintroduce each one by name immediately. It was a formidable accomplishment and one of which he was justly proud.

The last time we met was on the day he handed over the presidency of the United World Colleges to Prince Charles. For such an occasion a mere interview wasn't going to be nearly long enough so he persuaded the BBC to record a half-hour documentary featuring himself and the Prince of Wales. As usual he took over the entire project, coaching Prince Charles in how he should act in front of the cameras, what he should say and how it should be said.

It was the first, and only, time I saw Mountbatten with Prince Charles, who was to describe himself as 'Honorary Grandson' on the wreath he placed on Mountbatten's grave. What became immediately apparent was the proprietorial way in which the older man acted towards the heir to the throne. Other, closer members of the Royal Family have invariably, in my presence at least, referred to each other by their titles; the Princess Royal is always formal when she talks about her brothers or parents. Even the Princess of Wales, if she is discussing her husband in conversation, will refer to him as His Royal Highness or the Prince of Wales. Never do they use just the Christian name. Lord Mountbatten was openly affectionate and informal with the Prince of Wales throughout the day we spent with them, whereas Prince Charles always referred to him more formally as Lord Mountbatten, except when they spoke privately and then it was 'Uncle Dickie'.

There was obviously a great deal of mutual affection between the two men and I think Prince Charles was slightly in awe of Mountbatten. It would have been difficult not to be; he was an impressive figure right until the time of his death in 1979.

On some of the other occasions I met Mountbatten I had the opportunity of talking to him about his life and listening to him discussing the problems of facing the world and how he would solve them. It seemed to me that here was a man who was totally at ease with himself. He never appeared to have a moment's doubt about his ability to do anything, or that his way was the right way. He even admitted that his one congenital weakness was the belief that 'I can do anything I set my hand to, usually better than most other people.' In fact, he never saw this as a weakness; he regarded it as a strength and who is to say he was wrong?

When I watched him with the young sixth-formers at Atlantic College I was struck by the remarkable ease with which he could converse with boys and girls a quarter of his age, of all colours, races and creeds. If he tended to dominate the gatherings he still did not appear to patronize his listeners. He was prepared to listen to their point of view, even if it was obvious that nothing any of them could say would get him to change his opinion one iota.

When I later spoke to several of the students they revealed that while they acknowledged his achievements in the Second World War, and in India during the independence negotiations, many of them regarded him as a 'Colonel Blimp' figure. He was a typical example of the old

British Raj, believing that to hold a British passport was the best and only qualification one needed. He could not possibly understand their attitudes today and the problems they would have to face in the future. And while they recognized that he had done great things in the past, those achievements were all very much in the past. He was part of a history about which they cared very little, being much more concerned with their own immediate future. And where I felt he was at heart a kindly person with a genuine rapport with young people, one or two of them said he was an arrogant old man whose ideas were totally out of date and even when he explained that he had persuaded Prince Charles to take over from him because he felt he was getting too old for the job, they were not satisfied. By imposing Prince Charles on them, many felt that Mountbatten was merely using his honorary grandson as an extension of his own Establishment views. They were proved wrong in this as Prince Charles, since he became President, has introduced a number of ideas to which Lord Mountbatten would almost certainly have taken exception.

Rumours surrounded Mountbatten throughout his life, the most common being that he was bisexual and had extra-marital affairs which were carried on regardless of gender. He was certainly a most tactile man. He loved to touch people, male and female, on every occasion. I found it strange on our first meeting when he put his arm around my shoulder to illustrate a point he was making and I saw him take others by the arm if he wanted them to look at something special or listen with particular care to something he was saying. The strangeness to me was probably because of his association in my mind with the Royal Family, who go to extreme lengths to avoid physical contact.

There is no doubt that Mountbatten gave the appearance of being an arrogant man. Many people with his natural good looks, aristocratic background and glamorous lifestyle share this characteristic and as one of his naval contemporaries said of him, 'He had to have a streak of the "bastard" in him to get on in the way he did.' He was also said to be a fearful snob, referring, in letters to his mother when he first joined the Navy, to certain of his shipmates being 'not our type'. And yet, coming from a background and social class which could not have been more different from his, I found him to be kind, friendly and courteous, without the slightest hint of condescension.

He was an admitted avid collector of decorations – from any source – and in his edited diaries one gets the impression that though he was fond of his nephew, Prince Philip, having provided him with a home as a young man, he was also slightly sensitive about Philip's more senior position within the Royal Family and the many superior (though honorary) ranks he held in the other branches of the armed forces. A story is told that when Mountbatten had been promoted to Admiral of the Fleet he arrived at Buckingham Palace to be greeted by Prince Philip, also wearing his uniform of the same rank. Apparently a mischievous member of the Royal Family asked them, 'Who salutes whom when you two meet as Admirals of the Fleet?' The reply came: 'We salute each other – but only one of us means it.' The punch line has been attributed to both men.

It is fairly common knowledge that much of Mountbatten's motivation in life came from the feeling of having to restore the family name following the forced resignation of his father, Prince Louis of Battenberg, from his position as First Sea Lord during the First World War. Prince Louis never recovered from the humiliation and his son was determined that the adopted name of Mountbatten would become associated with the highest honours in the land. He only ever admitted this once and that was to his elder daughter, Patricia, late in his life. That he achieved his ambitions has been proved beyond all doubt. What is not so apparent is the cost to him of doing so.

His marriage to Edwina Ashley was the social event of the year, the Prince of Wales acting as his best man and the cream of European royalty among the guests. From then on he never had a moment's anxiety about money for the rest of his life (though in his later years he developed what amounted to a phobia about being poor) and he was able to concentrate on fulfilling his ambitions without the usual domestic worries that any other naval officer might have encountered. He also had the distinction at one time of being the only serving officer in the Royal Navy who drove himself to work each day in his own Rolls-Royce, behaviour not guaranteed to attract unqualified admiration among his contemporaries.

He felt that what other people might regard as his advantages were exactly the opposite. In 1970 he wrote: 'To have Royal connections and private means and to be married to a very rich wife is a devastating disadvantage in the Navy up to the rank of Rear-Admiral... As a result, to overcome this automatic suspicion, no single person worked harder than I did.'

That he was an affectionate husband and doting father has never been in doubt. The amount of time and personal attention he was able to devote to his family is another matter, and this will be examined in later stages of this book.

Very little of the private Mountbatten has been revealed so far. Who were his closest friends, apart from the Royal Family? What did his daughters think of him as they were growing up? Was he regarded as an 'absentee father' because his commitments took him away from home so often and for such long periods? And what about the dark side of his public life? Was he, as some have claimed, a sinister figure who was willing to sacrifice an empire, causing untold misery to millions and death to thousands, because of his stubbornness and vanity? All of us have blind spots. Most of us prefer to ignore them and when we do it rarely causes grief on a grand scale, as happens when a world leader makes the wrong decision. Did Mountbatten rush India and Pakistan into Partition with foreseeing the disastrous consequences? Or was he warned of the likely results – and simply ignored all advice?

His enemies, and there were many, claimed that he was an opportunist who would sacrifice anyone and anything to further his career, and there's little doubt that from time to time his ambition clouded his judgement. But many of the criticisms that were levelled at him came from people who were jealous of his success; he never seemed to fail at anything, except perhaps his marriage, and the relationship with his wife foundered mainly because of her infidelity. He began his affairs only after she refused to remain faithful.

The explosion which caused his death in Ireland was the work of the IRA. They not only admitted it but proudly claimed the credit, saying he was a 'legitimate target'. It has also been suggested that, again, Mountbatten was not entirely blameless, as he had been warned many times that this was going to happen, the last time just a few weeks before the explosion. He was a prominent figure who should not have put himself and – more importantly – his family, at risk by being in such a vulnerable position. One highly placed contributor to this account of Mountbatten's life claims to have evidence that the authorities knew the names of the men responsible for the murder, and that they were quietly 'disposed of' with the knowledge of their IRA masters, in order to satisfy the British and American governments and to prevent a massive 'backlash'.

In preparing for this book I have been fortunate in being able to talk to the present Countess Mountbatten of Burma, Lord Mountbatten's elder daughter, and Lady Pamela Hicks, his younger daughter, both his sons-in-law, Lord Brabourne and David Hicks, and his nine surviving grandchildren. So this account is partly theirs: *Mountbatten – The Private Story*.

MURDER AT MULLAGHMORE

August was always a special month for the Mountbatten family for it was then that the entire clan gathered for their annual summer holiday at Classiebawn Castle in Ireland. The ten-bedroomed castle, which is really a misnomer, as it is more a turreted manor house, was on land that had originally been acquired in the seventeenth century by the ancestors of the nineteenth-century prime minister Lord Palmerston, whose wife was an ancestor of Edwina Mountbatten.

Palmerston started to build the castle in the mid-nineteenth century and it was completed by his heir, his stepson William Cowper-Temple. The estate had descended to the Mountbattens through the wife of the seventh Earl of Shaftesbury, who was a stepdaughter of Palmerston. Shaftesbury's second son was Edwina Mountbatten's grandfather, and the castle came down through the Ashley family until it came to Edwina on the death of her father in 1939. He had closed Classiebawn in 1922, when Sligo became part of Eire, and he refused to set foot in the place for the rest of his life.

The castle had been empty for over twenty years when Edwina Mountbatten visited it in 1943. It was practically derelict, with an inadequate water supply and only one bathroom; the whole house needed attention.

In 1946 the Mountbattens took their daughters Patricia and Pamela, and their son-in-law to be, John, to see the castle but it was obviously not in a fit state for them to stay so they spent five days at the village inn. But Edwina had fallen in love with the place once again, and when she returned to Broadlands she sent their own electrician to Ireland to supervise the castle's modernization. He rewired it and arranged for extra bathrooms to be built and a new water system installed. Unwanted furniture, pictures and carpets were taken from their various homes in England and once again Classiebawn came to life.

When Edwina died in 1960 a life interest in the castle was willed to Lord Mountbatten (and the estate subsequently passed to his daughter Pamela). Mountbatten adored the place. He told his private secretary John Barratt that he felt more relaxed at Classiebawn than anywhere else in the world. He made valiant efforts to make the estate of 1,500 acres pay its way, but the only part of it which was in the least bit profitable was the woodland. There was excellent timber and the late Miss Gabrielle Gore-Booth of Lissadell House, who was employed as Mountbatten's agent at Classiebawn, was an expert in managing forestry. She helped enormously in trying to keep Classiebawn out of the red. She also arranged the summer lettings, mostly to wealthy Americans, who paid substantial sums for the privilege of staying in the Mountbatten home; in turn, Mountbatten co-operated in trying to provide extra facilities for his paying guests. In one letter to Miss Gore-Booth, replying to her suggestion that they buy a pony so that any children of their tenants could learn to ride, Mountbatten wrote, '. . . Yes, by all means look into the costs of buying a pony, but do not spend more than £50 and make sure the pony is a quiet one. I don't wany any claims for damages and you know what Americans are like for litigation.' Miss Gore-Booth also did her share of trying to keep costs down, telling Mountbatten that at one time the domestic staff were eating too many eggs and too much bacon for breakfast. There is, however, no record of his reaction to this news. Nevertheless, in the latter years of Mountbatten's life the estate was constantly showing a loss, usually around £1,800 a year, and he considered the possibility of selling it outright.

Eventually, a local self-made millionaire, Mr Hugh Tunney, took over the lease of the estate in 1976, with a clause that allowed Mountbatten to occupy the castle for the month of August every year. That it became merely a holiday home made no difference to Mountbatten's style of living. He employed a staff of ten including a butler, Peter Nicholson, a slim, shy Sligoman who had been recruited into the Mountbatten household from the farm where he grew up nearby, and who was taken to England to be trained as a butler at Wilton Crescent, Mountbatten's London home. Peter Nicholson wore a special livery designed by

Mountbatten himself, of dark blue battledress with silver buttons and bearing the Mountbatten coat of arms.

He remembers that His Lordship brought to Classiebawn a characteristic that was completely foreign to the Irish way of life: punctuality. He says, 'If breakfast was timed to start at eight o'clock in the morning, then at precisely eight o'clock and not a second before or after, it had to be on the table. It was the same at lunch and dinner, whatever time was arranged everybody had to be seated, one fifteen for lunch and eight o'clock for dinner. His Lordship hated anyone to be late and he would let them know his displeasure in no uncertain terms if they were not there on time.'

Mountbatten ran his holidays in exactly the same way that he organized the rest of his life. There had to be a prepared programme for every day and he hated the idea of any disruption. His grandson Tim Knatchbull, who was to suffer horrific injuries in the bomb explosion that killed his twin brother Nicholas, along with his grandfather, paternal grandmother and a fifteen-year-old local boy, said that his grandfather naturally assumed command wherever he was and whatever he was doing. If they were going shrimping or building a dam across a stream or out in the boat for a fishing trip, he would arrange everything and all the timings were listed using the twenty-four-hour clock; even at eight years old the children soon learned that 15.30 meant half past three in the afternoon. He made no concession for age or lack of experience. On one occasion on the boat Tim was handling the engine and Mountbatten shouted out for him to move the controls 'Full astern'. His nine-year-old muscles weren't sufficiently strong to turn the handle quickly enough and Mountbatten immediately shouted, 'You bloody fool, don't you know astern from ahead?'

When the family gathered at Classiebawn they filled the castle. As well as Mountbatten himself, there were usually his two daughters Lady Brabourne (Patricia) with her husband Lord Brabourne (John) and their seven children, and Lady Pamela Hicks accompanied by her husband David and their three children. Occasionally friends of the children would also be invited but, in the main, Mountbatten preferred Classiebawn to be reserved for the immediate family. They used to say, 'We didn't really need any outsiders, there were so many of us.'

When the family moved to Classiebawn they invariably took the ferry from Liverpool to Dublin and drove the one hundred and thirty-five miles across Ireland to the wild, untamed north-western coast of Sligo. In those days the small airport near the town of Sligo had not been opened but, anyway, they needed transport while they were there and as they travelled carrying 'everything but the kitchen sink', road and sea were the means they all chose.

The Garda, the Irish police force, would have preferred Mountbatten to use a less open form of transport as he had been warned several times that he was considered by the IRA to be a possible target. He took the threats seriously enough to let the police know when he was arriving and his proposed movements during the holiday, but, like other members of the Royal Family, he had always refused to allow such threats to influence his lifestyle. He once said, 'I am not going to live my life surrounded by armed guards, with someone telling me where and when I can go.' And as the years went by he used to say, 'Who the hell would want to kill an old man anyway?' A more realistic threat in his view was that either he or one of his family might be kidnapped. He wasn't particularly worried for himself but the thought of one of his daughters or grandchildren being taken as a hostage filled him with dread.

When Mountbatten arrived in Dublin for his annual holiday in 1979 he was met by the then British Ambassador to Ireland who told him that they had received a threat and that there was a real possibility that something might be attempted during the coming weeks. Mountbatten took the warning seriously but declined to alter his plans.

As soon as he landed on Irish soil he became the responsibility of the Irish Special Branch, who provided him with at least four armed bodyguards for the duration of his visit. One of them was with him at all times, when he left the castle and even though Mountbatten found their presence an irritation, he was realistic enough to understand their position and did not try to make their task any more difficult than it already was. He never tried to give them the slip and one sometimes accompanied the family when they went out in *Shadow V*. No policeman was on board on the fateful day of the explosion and Mountbatten had not thought it important for what was supposed to be a short, uneventful fishing trip when they would always be in sight of the shore.

Edwina, Mountbatten's granddaughter, is arguably the most sensitive of all his family. She gives the impression of extreme vulnerability and sometimes appears to hesitate before answering any questions, weighing her words carefully to make sure that nothing she says will be hurtful to anyone. Married to the actor Jeremy Brudenell, of whom she is fiercely proud and protective, Edwina lives in a modest but comfortable home in south-west London. Like all those who were closely involved with the events surrounding Mountbatten's murder, she retains vivid memories of the occasion. 'Two days before it all happened I was alone with Grandpapa in the house because the cousins were en route from their fishing lodge in County Mayo, and were due back that evening. I was up in my bedroom in the tower right at the top of the castle revising for my A level examinations. I heard these thumping footsteps trudging up the stairs and I knew it could only be him. He came into my room and he was completely exhausted after the long climb so he lay down on my bed and stayed there for an hour or so, and we had a long, cosy conversation about everything: love, school, boyfriends, mine and Amanda's, who he was rather worried about at the time because one of them had long hair. We just about covered everything and it was lovely. Afterwards I was so glad we'd had the chance to talk in this way. Later that day we went riding together and he kept falling asleep in the saddle, so I had to guide him and make sure his horse didn't step on any of the young trees that were growing. He was very concerned about them and if he'd damaged any he would have been furious.'

On the evening before the bomb went off, Aideen Gore-Booth, who had taken over as Lord Mountbatten's agent on the death of her sister Gabrielle, had been invited to dine at Classiebawn. Miss Gore-Booth was a gentle Anglo-Irishwoman whose family had owned the huge Lissadell estate, about eight miles from Classiebawn, for two hundred years. A succession of personal misfortunes had reduced the estate to a mere four hundred acres and when first her sister, and then she, had been offered the job of agent to Lord Mountbatten, she said, 'He became not only a benefactor but a good friend.'

A woman of immense charm, quiet humour and vivid imagination, she said she approached the dinner at Classiebawn with a sense of deep foreboding. 'I don't know what it was. There was nothing I could put my finger on, but I knew that something awful was about to happen. I had only experienced a feeling like this once before in my life and that was when my brother Brian was killed in the Second World War. During the dinner I could not touch a single thing to eat or drink and I'm told that I hardly spoke a word. Which was most unlike me.'

Lady Pamela Hicks and her three children had been staying at the castle for most of August and their holiday was due to end in two days' time. Her husband David had already left for England as he was due to fly on to Japan on business the following day. Mountbatten's son-in-law John, and his wife, Patricia, had come over from their holiday home, Aasleagh Lodge in County Mayo, and as Pamela recalls: 'It was a lovely end-of-season family occasion.'

Mountbatten himself was in excellent form, even joking about what he hoped the mourners at his funeral would do to enjoy themselves, at some distant date. That very evening a pre-recorded interview was shown on BBC2 in which he discussed his plans for his funeral in some detail, saying he wanted it to be 'a happy occasion' and that he had chosen the hymns to include Rudyard Kipling's 'Recessional', 'I Vow to Thee My Country', 'Jerusalem' and at least one verse from the naval hymn 'Eternal Father Strong to Save (For Those in Peril on the Sea)'.

Privately, though, he acknowledged that time was catching up with him and earlier that day in a conversation with his granddaughter Amanda (now Lady Amanda Ellingworth), he admitted that one of the things he dreaded was the thought of growing old and senile and not being able to do the things he had always done. He could feel himself getting old and crotchety and had seen the way his own mother went in old age and didn't want to get like that himself.

And another of his grandchildren, Michael-John Knatchbull, known as Joe in the family, who was not at Classiebawn that day but who had been there on many other occasions, recalled that 'Grandpapa went to extraordinary lengths to try to maintain his fitness. His bedroom and bathroom were immediately over the dining room at the castle and if we happened to be down before him in the morning we would hear these thumps as he religiously carried out his Canadian Air Force exercises. They had been designed for men fifty years his junior but he insisted on doing them every day, even at seventy-nine. In some ways it was rather pathetic, how he couldn't accept growing old, in other ways it was rather endearing.'

The morning of 27 August 1979 dawned clear and beautiful; it was Bank Holiday Monday. The previous day Mountbatten had been out in his boat laying lobster pots and today he organized his team to lift them, in what was intended to be the last trip of the season. Shortly after breakfast he asked which members of the family wanted to join him. Amanda and her brother Philip decided to remain behind and sunbathe on the terrace at the front of the castle, together with their cousin Edwina. Edwina and Philip also wanted to use the time to work for their A levels. Edwina had an ulterior motive for not wanting to go out in the boat that day. 'A couple of days earlier I had driven Grandpapa's Peugeot to the station and given it a bit of a bang so I intended to take it down to the local garage and get it mended before he noticed it.' As it happened she could not take the car because the family used it to get to the harbour.

Ashley Hicks had intended to join the party because he and his cousin Nicky were extremely close and did many things together. 'He was my closest friend in the family and was more like a brother to me than a cousin. Just before they set off I decided to go into the village. I had started smoking – without anyone knowing – and Amanda offered to drive me down to the shop to buy some cigarettes. Nicky said they would wait for me. On the way back I threw a sweet paper out of the window and Amanda, who was into her 'green' period at the time, stopped the car and made me go back and fetch it. I remember we had a blazing row about it. Anyway, by the time we got back the rest of the family had gone down to the boat so India and I went into the castle and watched a Laurel and Hardy film on television. That's what we were doing when the bomb went off and I should have been on board.'

The Mountbatten boat, *Shadow V* (which the locals called *Shadow Vee*), was not in any way, shape or form a luxury yacht, though the press liked to describe it as such. It was a clinker-built, typical Donegal fishing boat which had been built in an outhouse adjoining one of the cottages in a nearby village, to Mountbatten's order. The family had watched as part of the building was removed to get the boat out. *Shadow V* was ideal for fishing in the Atlantic waters off the Irish coast: sturdy, tough and just twenty-nine feet in length, she was just about coming to the end of her useful life. Mountbatten had spent a certain amount of money in maintaining her and making sure she was seaworthy, and he was thinking of selling her if much more money was needed, and hiring a boat in future. Only the week before, Hugh Tunney had had some work done on her engine on Mountbatten's behalf and she had been repainted green and white (the colours of Admiral's Barges in the Royal Navy). She was also fitted with two-way radio communication with Classiebawn Castle as Mountbatten was never allowed to be out of touch. Rodney Lomax, a local boatman, had looked after the servicing of *Shadow V* for twelve years and, as usual, at the beginning of the season he gave the boat its annual overhaul. The cabin was kept locked but there were several lockers in the cockpit, used for stowing fishing tackle, ropes and lobster pots, which were never locked. *Shadow V* was moored in the harbour at Mullaghmore, just under a mile from Classiebawn, where her hull gleamed in the Bank Holiday Monday sunshine.

Eventually it was decided that Mountbatten would be joined by his elder daughter Patricia, her husband John and his eighty-three-year-old mother, the Dowager Lady Brabourne, of whom the grandchildren said they were much more frightened than they were of their grandfather. He might shout and bellow, but they knew it was all talk with him and he soon forgot what he was shouting about so they took little notice. With Grandmother Brabourne it was a little different. Nicholas and Timothy, the fourteen-year-old identical twins sons of Lord and Lady Brabourne, clamboured on board together with fifteen-year-old Paul Maxwell, the son of a local man, who came along to help with the boat. Paul's family lived at Enniskillen, just over the border in Northern Ireland less than a dozen miles away, and which itself would become notorious as the scene of one of the worst IRA outrages on Remembrance Sunday eight years later. Mountbatten usually employed a Mullaghmore seaman as a seasonal boatman to assist with *Shadow V*, but this year he had been unable to help them and Paul Maxwell, who knew almost as much as any man about boats, was delighted to fill in and earn a little extra pocket money.

Before being driven down to the harbour by his son-in-law John, Mountbatten had greeted the two Garda officers on duty and told them of his plans for the morning. They followed his car down the winding road to Mullaghmore, their watchful eyes missing nothing as they saw how the holidaymakers and local people nudged each other as Mountbatten passed. Everyone knew he was the local lord of the manor; he had been a familiar sight for thirty years, and his distinctive figure, six feet two topped with a shock of white hair, was not the sort you could miss. The Mountbatten features were instantly recognizable; throughout his long life his face barely altered and he exchanged smiles and 'good mornings' with many of the people on the quay.

The two bodyguards, complete with binoculars and revolvers, parked their Ford Escort on the quayside and remained unobtrusively in the background as the Mountbatten family party prepared to leave. The Dowager Lady Brabourne was helped on board by her grandsons, Nicky and Timmy. As it was low tide, the boat was way below the harbour wall and they had to negotiate a steep climb down via a somewhat rickety ladder. Paul Maxwell had already started the engine as Lord

Brabourne was the last to board after taking a few final photographs from the shore.

Lord Mountbatten took command – as usual – and as the senior Lady Brabourne took her seat on the stern starboard side with her daughter-in-law on the opposite side of the boat. Tim sat in his favourite place, on the roof of the cabin, within three feet of his grandfather at the wheel. Concealed beneath the deck barely inches from them was the bomb, said by the IRA later to contain fifty pounds of plastic explosive.

Shadow V released her moorings at 11.30 a.m. and the Garda's car followed her progress as far as they were able along the narrow coast road with one of the bodyguards watching those on board through his binoculars. Also watching through binoculars a little further up the road were another two pairs of eyes, belonging to the murderers, active members of the Provos, the Provisional IRA. They could see clearly the old lady sitting in the stern, the three young boys in the middle of the boat – and their target, Lord Mountbatten, standing at the wheel. One of the assassins held a remote control device with which he was about to detonate the bomb on board *Shadow V*. They could clearly see that there were women and children on board, innocent victims who could not by any stretch of imagination be described as 'legitimate military targets'.

At exactly 11.45 a.m., just fifteen minutes after *Shadow V* had left the harbour, and when she was still only two hundred yards from the shore and half a mile away from the pier, one of the terrorists pressed the button which activated the mechanism. Fifty pounds of gelignite exploded, blowing the boat to pieces.

Patricia remembers having just turned to her mother-in-law and saying, 'Isn't this a beautiful day?' – the last words she was ever to speak to the old Lady Brabourne. As luck would have it, she then began reading the *New Statesman* so her eyes were turned down, otherwise she would have suffered even worse injuries than she did. 'Suddenly there was this enormous explosion and I do remember sensing there was something like a tennis ball with light radiating from it coming from directly under my father's feet. The next thing I remember was being in the water, rolling over and over.'

Lord Brabourne had been standing in the centre of the boat and at the moment of the explosion he had turned away from Lord Mountbatten to look at the lobster pots. This is what undoubtedly saved his life. The blast caught him on one side of his body but missed his face completely.

Seconds before the bomb went off Lord Brabourne had called out to his father-in-law, who was powerfully revving the engine, 'You are having fun today, aren't you?' That must have been the last thing Lord Mountbatten heard before he was killed. The next thing Lord Brabourne remembers was being under water and feeling intensely cold. He was going into and out of consciousness and doesn't recall being pulled to safety. When he came to he was in a small boat, his mother lying alongside without a hair out of place. He felt a movement underneath and found he was lying on top of his wife who was barely alive. Her face was in a terrible mess with blood pouring out of her eyes.

The small boat Lord Brabourne found himself in belong to Charles and Kathryn Pierce, who were on a fishing expedition with a friend, Billy Wilkinson. Their craft was just a twelve-foot Avon dinghy and they were within a hundred yards of *Shadow V* when the bomb went off. Mrs Pierce says: 'Little remained of what had been *Shadow V* except small pieces of hull timbers. We noticed bodies floating in the water and the first one we took into our boat was that of Lady Patricia Brabourne, who had severe facial injuries and was semi-conscious and bewildered. Next we took on board the Dowager Lady Brabourne. She didn't appear so badly injured but was very shocked and stunned. Thirdly, we took Lord Brabourne on board. He was conscious but also quite bewildered. This meant we now had three injured people plus three crew in a small speedboat, ill suited for the task. We then saw Lord Mountbatten in the water, whom we held alongside, but not on board, because space did not permit. Presently another dinghy, belonging to a Mrs Dawson, came alongside and the body of Lord Mountbatten was placed on board his boat and covered. It was obvious he did not survive the initial blast. We set off back to the harbour, moving very slowly as we were low in the water with the extra weight and then another small boat approached and we transferred Lord and Lady Brabourne to it.'

The boat Mrs Pierce refers to was an inflatable crewed by two young doctors, Brian Best and Richard Wallace. They could not have arrived at a more fortuitous moment. They were just about to start water-skiing when they heard the explosion. Richard Wallace says: 'We heard the bang but it didn't even cross my mind that it might have been a bomb, even though I had worked for some time in Belfast where such things were commonplace. When we got to the scene we could see a number of people in the water and our first task was to sort the living from the dead. As doctors we knew that those alive were the ones who needed our attention.' Among the first was the Dowager Lady Brabourne, who was fully conscious. 'She had a very badly broken arm but all she was concerned about was the children. She kept repeating, "Don't bother about me. I'm all right. Look after the children." She was very brave.'

As the only two with any medical experience, Richard Wallace and Brian Best then split up and each took over a different boat. Dr Wallace says the difficulty was that the rescuers did not know how to move the survivors; some thought they should be left, while others believed that speed was of the essence – which it was. Wallace got Patricia Brabourne and her husband into his boat and set off back into harbour, a journey of less than five minutes. 'Lord Brabourne was in considerable pain, but his wife looked the worst. She was bleeding from superficial cuts all over her face and her eyes were in a bad shape. Also it was vital to keep her breathing channel open so Lord Brabourne held her jaw so she wouldn't swallow her tongue.' By the time they arrived back at Mullaghmore Harbour dozens of people were milling about trying to help. A door was ripped off an outhouse to use as a makeshift stretcher and women tore bedsheets into strips for bandages. 'I needed to set Lord Brabourne's leg and his mother's arm, so someone brought a couple of broom handles which I used as splints,' recalls Dr Wallace. 'Then I went back with the boat to bring in the dead bodies. The sea was calm but several of the rescue boats were in danger of being swamped with too many people on board, so we tried to organize them into some sort of order. Brian Best and I persuaded them to leave the dead and concentrate on the living for the moment.'

When Lord Mountbatten's near-baked body was recovered from the water the only recognizable piece of clothing he still wore was a fragment of his old *Kelly* jersey with the emblem still readable. To avoid unnecessary exposure to the public gaze, the body was left in Mr Dawson's dinghy until the ambulances had arrived. Dr Wallace adds an important point: 'When we brought Lord Mountbatten's body back I could see quite clearly that he was not disfigured in any way. There were cuts and bruises on his body and face but no disfigurement – in spite of what the press reported afterwards. And one of the most poignant memories I still have of that occasion was when we carried him up on the beach on an old green door. All the people stood in silent respect for this great man. All, that is, except for a few who used their cameras to record the event. I suppose it's human nature but as I heard the clicking of those cameras I wondered what sort of people they were. The majority were absolutely disgusted by what had happened and ashamed that it had taken place in Ireland.'

Lord Brabourne had broken both his legs – one so badly that the bone was showing through the skin and he also had injuries to his hands, ribs, chest and ears. But he was not considered to be in immediate danger and when the ambulances arrived from Sligo he waited while his wife and mother were given priority treatment. Mountbatten and the boy, Paul Maxwell, had been nearest to the bomb and they were killed outright. So too was Nicholas, Mountbatten's grandson, whose body was not recovered for several hours, and was brought back by an air-sea rescue helicopter which had become airborne within minutes of the disaster. The Dowager Lady Brabourne's injuries were thought at first not to be so serious, but she died the following day, mostly of shock.

Mr and Mrs Richard Wood-Martin were among the local people enjoying the Bank Holiday Monday fine weather. They too had been out in their boat the previous day to place lobster pots and, like the Mountbattens, were setting off to retrieve them when the explosion happened. Mrs Wood-Martin recalls, 'We were about three hundred yards from *Shadow V*, with several other small boats in the vicinity. We were between *Shadow* and the shore because we had decided to pick up our own pots first. Our younger son, Michael, had a couple of pots of his own further out – very close to where *Shadow* was when the bomb went off, so we were lucky we didn't go for those first.' Her husband says, 'There was a tremendous explosion which we heard and could see quite clearly of course, but strangely, we didn't feel the blast. *Shadow* literally disintegrated before our eyes. There was nothing left that looked remotely like a boat. We immediately set off towards the wreckage to see if we could help and my wife saw something that looked like a football bobbing about in the water. When we reached it we could see it was a head. At least that's what it looked like, all we could actually see was a mop of hair.'

Mrs Wood-Martin grabbed the hair and tried to raise the head out of the water. 'But the boy [it was Timothy] was a deadweight and I couldn't lift him on my own. Together Dick and I managed somehow to drag him into the boat and we were very relieved to see that he was in one piece. At first we thought that perhaps his legs had been blown off. Although he was not fully conscious, he did make some efforts to swim when he was in the water, flapping his arms about, but he had been under a couple of times and I believe if we hadn't reached him when we did – about three minutes after the explosion – he would have drowned.'

Tim Knatchbull remembers being blown a great distance and swallowing massive quantities of blood, sea water and oil.

Dick Wood-Martin says that Tim kept asking, 'What happened?' and telling them how cold he was. They didn't have any warm clothing on board as this was probably the warmest August day for years. Tim also kept trying to stand up in the boat. 'It was only a seventeen-footer so there wasn't a lot of room. In the end I shouted at the top of my voice. "Will you lie down." Eventually we managed to get him to lie in the bottom of the boat and we set off back into the harbour.'

Tim was obviously very badly injured and at first the Wood-Martins thought he was blind. 'He had a massive black eye,' says Mrs Wood-Martin, 'and the other one had the sort of glazed look that blind people have.'

By the time they got back to the harbour, the other survivors were being brought ashore and Mr Wood-Martin said that the Dowager Lady Brabourne was the most lucid of them all. 'She kept telling the people who were carrying her to the ambulance to be careful, "as my arm is broken in at least two places".'

When Tim Knatchbull was being transferred to a stretcher Richard Wood-Martin noticed something which in other circumstances would have been highly embarrassing to a fourteen-year-old. 'I could see that he had a neat circle burnt out of the seat of his jeans. Apparently he had been sitting on the roof of the cabin when the bomb went off and his trousers had stuck to the wood with the intense heat, when he was blown overboard.'

Amanda and Philip had been reading on the terrace steps in front of Classiebawn when they heard a loud bang. They knew straight away that it was a bomb. When they got to the cliffs from where they could see where the boat should have been, all that was visible was a load of splintered wood in the water. By this time a crowd had gathered, and one of them, a local doctor, said that Lord Mountbatten's boat had been blown up. In a state of complete shock the youngsters drove back to the castle, fearing that the IRA might still be around and looking for further members of the family. When they got back to the castle they saw Mountbatten's younger daughter Pamela sitting with Hugh Tunney, and told them what had happened.

Peter Nicholson had been in the dining room laying the table for lunch when he heard the explosion. 'I heard the bang and I thought it might be a bomb as the thought was never very far from our minds whenever Lord Mountbatten was there, but for some reason I just carried on setting the table. It was to remain as it was for nearly a week even though we had to serve quite a few meals in that room in the following days.'

When Pamela Hicks told her young daughter India what had happened, the reaction was violent and immediate. 'She let out the most awful scream and ran into the grounds. I was very frightened that in her emotional state she might even run over the cliffs which are very sheer so I asked Amanda and Philip to help look for her – mainly to give them something to do. We also had a small group of Girl Guides staying in the grounds and they set up a search party. As it happened India came back of her own accord shortly afterwards and wondered what all the fuss was about.'

At first Ashley Hicks thought that the engine of *Shadow V* had exploded but then when his mother came to tell the children what had happened and gave them tranquillizer pills, 'I realized it must have been a bomb. When we were given pills we knew things were serious.'

Sligo General Hospital contained only two operating theatres and as Patricia Brabourne and her son Tim were thought to be in the greatest danger they were given priority treatment. Tim remembers short periods when he knew what was happening, but he was heavily sedated for most of the time.

Lady Pamela Hicks had been brought to the hospital by the police and one of the first duties she was asked to perform was the most harrowing task for any daughter, to identify her father's body. 'It was something I really felt I couldn't face but I knew someone had to do it and then, at that very moment, James [the Duke of] Abercorn arrived and offered his help. So he actually identified my father's body and I'll always be grateful to him for that. I was then taken to see my sister and there was no part of her I could recognize apart from one hand, and Timothy was in the bed opposite.

Patricia's injuries were so severe that she was immediately placed on a life support machine, unable to move a single part of her body. She could not even blink.

Pamela, the only senior member of the family uninjured, was moving around the hospital trying to spend a little time with each of her relatives in turn. As she moved to the ward where John Brabourne was being treated she asked one of the doctors what she should say if he asked about his son Nicholas. The doctor replied that Lord Brabourne had to be told and if he asked she should tell him. Fifteen years after the event Lady Pamela's eyes still moisten and her voice breaks as she recalls how she gave the news to her brother-in-law. 'The first thing he asked me when I saw him was "What about Nicky?" and I said, "I'm afraid Nicky is dead."' It was the saddest news she had ever had to tell anyone. In fact, she had to repeat it three times during the day and the one following it, before it sank in.

Lord Brabourne had to cope with the twin griefs of losing his mother and his youngest son on the same day and the way in which he found out that his mother was dead was unintentionally heartless. One of the doctors attending him told him that 'The old lady has gone', and then asked if Lord Brabourne had known her. When he heard that she was his mother, the doctor could have bitten his own tongue out.

The medical staff at Sligo were magnificent. Some of them had been trained in Belfast so they were very experienced in dealing with the sort of injuries the bomb had caused. And a tribute to their skill came when the Duke of Abercorn flew in a specialist team from Belfast so that his close friends should get the very best attention and treatment. The surgeons from Belfast examined Lord and Lady Brabourne and their son Timothy and left immediately, saying they could not improve on the work of their colleagues at Sligo General Hospital.

Patricia remained in intensive care for almost a week during which she was sedated for much of the time but she says she was also much more aware than anyone realized of what was going on around her. She couldn't see anything but could hear at times quite clearly the conversation of the medical staff and she heard someone say that her mother-in-law had died. She guessed that her father had also gone but, knowing how weak she was, she did not allow her thoughts to turn to Nicholas. She said to herself: 'I'm not strong enough to deal with that particular fact right now so, like Scarlett O'Hara in *Gone with the Wind*, I'll think about that tomorrow. I didn't know then that the doctors thought I was going to be blind but I had a vivid vision of that awful First World War picture of the blinded soldiers being led back through the trenches, each man with his hand on the shoulder of the man in front.' Pamela came to see her and told her that Timothy was across the room and he was all right. When she felt strong enough to ask about Nicky she made signs in the air with her finger – she still could not speak. Pamela then brought her some paper and a pencil and she managed to scrawl Nicky's name. Pamela didn't answer straight away but said the light was bad so she'd go outside. In fact she asked the doctor what she should say. He told her the best thing would be to tell the truth. So she went back and said: 'Yes, you're quite right, I'm afraid.' It was confirmation of what Patricia already sensed and what she dreaded to hear. She couldn't even cry.

Several days later she was taken out of intensive care and moved with Timothy to the ward where her husband was, and it was at that point that the grief really came over them all. They were able to cry together, which was a great relief for all of them even though it was very hard for Tim to see his parents in tears. It was the first time any of the children had ever seen them unhappy.

Patricia's recovery was miraculous. Apart from the horrific injuries to her face and eyes, which warranted 120 stitches including some in the eyeballs themselves, and a badly swollen leg, she had also swallowed massive quantities of oil and sea water. For days she was required to undergo painful coughing exercises several times a day to bring up what was inside her lungs. Her eyesight was restored although one eye is affected, and to this day she still has specks of green paint from the boat in her eyes.

When someone of the stature of Mountbatten dies a machine swings into operation to deal with the logistics. The Queen and Prince Philip were among the first to be informed and then various members of the family who were not at Classiebawn had to be told. Mountbatten's eldest grandson. Norton Knatchbull (now Lord Romsey), together with his fiancée Penelope Eastwood, had been staying in Ireland earlier that month but had returned to London some time before the explosion. He was out jogging near his home in Fulham, West London, on that Bank Holiday Monday afternoon. When he returned he switched on his television set which was tuned to BBC1 for the afternoon's sports coverage. The next thing he knew there was an interruption and the announcer, Frank Bough, said, 'We have just had a newsflash. An explosion has occurred in Ireland and Lord Mountbatten has been killed.' It was as sudden as brutal as that. No warning, no indication of what was coming. For a moment he was stunned but within minutes Lord Mountbatten's secretary, John Barratt, telephoned confirming the sad news and, at Norton's request, began making preparations to get him and his fiancée back to Ireland as quickly as possible. John Barratt rarely used the family name to obtain preferential treatment, but this was a matter of the utmost urgency. He contacted British European Airways, who confirmed that seats were available on that afternoon's flight to Belfast and agreed to hold it for a few minutes until the young couple could get to the airport.

At Belfast's Aldergrove Airport Norton and Penny were met by a police and military escort and minutes later an Army Air Corps helicopter arrived to take them to Long Kesh internment camp to collect one of the country's leading heart specialists. He was needed because Lord Brabourne had a history of heart problems and no one knew at that point how serious his injuries were. The helicopter then landed close to the border where Norton and his companion were transferred into an RUC vehicle and driven to a lonely bridge that formed the border between Northern Ireland and Eire. The RUC officers waited on one side as Norton and Penny walked alone across the bridge into Eire where a group of Irish Garda received them and drove them to Sligo. Years later Norton said it was like a dramatic scene from a spy movie about the exchange of agents in the Cold War. However, it worked, for within hours of hearing the news on the television, Norton and Penny, using private cars, military helicopters, scheduled air services and police vehicles from both sides of the border, had reached Classiebawn Castle, and they were able to comfort the surviving members of the family.

Joanna Knatchbull (now Baroness Hubert du Breuil) was working on a film in New York when she was tracked down. 'As soon as I got the phone call I knew that Grandpapa had been killed. It was almost as if we had been expecting it.' She flew back to England that night, arriving at six the following morning, and flew straight on to Ireland. Her father's partner, Richard Goodwin, had told her that her mother's injuries were so bad that she was not expected to live and she should get there immediately.

Her brother Michael-John had been playing golf with a friend in Cornwall. 'We had been away for the whole weekend and we were driving back up the motorway chatting away so we didn't bother to turn the car radio on all the way from Cornwall to Fulham. The police were looking for me but as we were in my friend's car they had no way of knowing where I was. They were looking for my car. Eventually we got back to London and the telephone was ringing in the flat. When I picked it up John Barratt was on the other end. He had been trying to find me all day. He told me the whole thing and I had to ask him to repeat it. I simply couldn't take it all in. And when I heard that my young brother Nicky had been killed it hit me like a sledgehammer. The news of his death was much worse than that of my grandfather's or grandmother's. They were old and had lived their lives, but he was so young.'

Buckingham Palace managed to find David Hicks at home just before he was due to leave for Japan. 'They told me there had been a bomb in Ireland but they could not give me any details so I had no way of knowing at that time whether my wife and three children were involved. They then rang back a little later to say that Pammy and the children had not been on the boat and they were all right. But they added that Lord and Lady Brabourne were badly injured, and that she, at any rate, was not expected to live through the night. I managed to get a flight from London to Dublin and then the Irish Air Force, who were magnificent, put me into one of their fighter aircraft and flew me to an airfield on the west coast, where a helicopter was waiting to take me to Classiebawn. When I got to the hospital Pammy asked me not to see her sister as she was unrecognizable. She said, "She's not even like a human being; it's all wires and tubes. You can't see any part of her." So I went to see Timmy and spoke to him though he was heavily sedated.

'The security services felt it was important to get the children away from Classiebawn and the Abercorns very kindly offered us all accommodation at Barons Court, their home across the border. So I took our three children and Lord Mountbatten's black Labrador, who also had to be cared for as he was already pining for his master, into Northern Ireland. A few days later I attended, with Amanda and Norton, and Penny, Norton's fiancée, the funeral of Paul Maxwell at Enniskillen. Viola, Duchess of Westminster, who was Lord Lieutenant of the County, also attended and the Irish people, once they knew who I was, were terribly kind and sympathetic. Later that same week an Andover aircraft of the Queen's Flight picked us up and brought us back to England.'

Amanda says that one of the things which stick in her mind are the very last words her grandfather spoke to her. That morning before they went out in the boat a very earnest business meeting had taken place in the morning room. Lord Brabourne, Hugh Tunney and several others were there, discussing various things to do with the estate. Whether a new boat should be build – as *Shadow V* was on her last legs – and other items about the letting of the castle. Amanda needed some writing paper from the morning room and walked through the drawing room to get it. Her grandfather, who didn't take part in the meeting, was sitting in the drawing room and when he saw her start to open the door he shouted, 'Don't go in there, you bloody fool' – and those were the last words he ever spoke to her, remembered with affectionate amusement and more than a little sadness.

The family have different views about the murders. Joanna says she is still very bitter that the IRA killed her brother, grandfather and grandmother. She can never forgive them. Michael-John feels guilty that he was out enjoying himself when his family were being butchered. It took him some time before he could accept that there was nothing he could have done to prevent it. Norton says that he felt, and still feels, a deep sadness at the way his grandfather and the Dowager Lady Brabourne met their deaths, but most of all for the two young lives that were ended so tragically, those of his young brother Nicholas and Paul Maxwell.

Ashley, at sixteen, was arguably at the most impressionable age when the tragedy occurred. Looking back on it now after fifteen years he says, 'For Grandpapa, in a way it was the most tremendous of all ends. It stopped him from going gaga; it stopped him from fading into obscurity and it stopped people from being sorry for him. It was the most marvellously dramatic end. For me personally it was especially horrid and for those of us in the family who were even younger because we never became old enough to really talk to him properly and to know him as we would have wished.'

Edwina says she often feels, even today, that she should have been there with her cousins: 'It's a funny sort of guilt that it should have been me and not them. As for my grandpapa, there was no warning. We didn't see him gradually dying; he hadn't been ill. There was no preparation. He just went. But my most vivid memory is of Nicky. We had been playing backgammon before they left to go out in the boat, and the last thing he ever said to me was "We'll finish the game when I get back."'

Amanda is the most compassionate of women and she says, 'I don't think I harbour any great feelings of bitterness, just tremendous sadness, particularly at the loss of my brother.' Lord Brabourne and his wife, who have more cause than anyone to feel bitterness, feel none at all. They have discussed their feelings about the murders and while they both agree that they were unforgivable acts of violence, they feel that bitterness would only ruin their lives and the lives of those around them.

Patricia (now Countess Mountbatten of Burma) says, 'How can anyone press a button that sets off a bomb when they know there are an old man of seventy-nine, an even older lady of eighty-three and three children of fourteen and fifteen on the board? I can't understand any human being acting this way. I don't feel bitter but I do feel total incomprehension and utter revulsion.'

The incident did not sour the feelings Lady Mountbatten and her husband have for Ireland and the Irish people. He says, 'The majority of Irish people are just as warm and charming as they have always been,' while she says, 'There wasn't a doctor or nurse who wouldn't have done absolutely everything to save us and who would have given anything for it not to have happened.'

The Duchess of Abercorn was the woman who, apart from those in his immediate family, was without doubt closest to Mountbatten in the years preceding his death. Their relationship was loving, affectionate and perhaps most important of all, friendly. Sacha Abercorn recalls her reaction to the news of his murder. 'The full magnitude of the disaster seemed to hit me in waves. All those on the boat that day were people I had known all my life. Not only had my godfather been killed but my godson, Nicholas, as well, with Timothy being badly injured. In such circumstances action is the best means of coping. I had just had my third child, however, and was therefore unable to do anything but wait passively for news to come in. As I waited, I recalled conversations of ten days previously when Uncle Dickie had been staying with us [at Barons Court] for his annual visit. He spoke to me then, as on several occasions in the past, about how he did not want to become old and burdensome to those around him. Perhaps I was trying to anaesthetize myself but I could not help thinking that he would have preferred to leave the world in this way, swiftly and suddenly, and at sea where he always felt at home. Though of course he never would have wished for any others to be involved, or for the misery and mayhem that shattered the lives of his family and friends – the world over. People have often asked me whether I felt anger or bitterness about the tragedy. But the feeling that still prevails is one of deep sadness, that human beings can imagine they can ever change a situation through such insane violence. Granted there have been wrongs done in the past on all sides. But to murder an old man because he is a symbol of what one resents, rather than as a human being, defies the laws of intelligence and common sense.'

In the aftermath of the murders many theories were expounded about how it happened and who was to blame. Mountbatten had been warned that the IRA were going to attempt to kill him but, like most people, he believed it could never happen to him.

Sligo is known as a town where a number of IRA activists and many supporters have their homes, and Bundoran, a few miles from Classiebawn, is reputed to be an IRA holiday centre. Some people close to Mountbatten were said to be sympathetic to the movement and one in particular was suspected of being involved, so much so that Lord Brabourne had enquiries made either to prove the allegations or to clear the man's name. The matter was investigated at the highest level and finally it was revealed that the person concerned was in the clear.

Douglas Fairbanks Jr, the American film star, who had been a friend of Mountbatten for most of his life and who had served on his staff during the Second World War, has had high-ranking connections within the United States Government of long standing. Some years after the murder he was told that both his own and the British governments had made contact with the IRA in an effort to find out the names of those responsible. Apparently, they were given two names. They were also warned of the possibility of a backlash, particularly in American, from where much of the funding of the IRA comes. Fairbanks says that there was no official announcement because neither Britain nor the United States wanted publicity, mainly because this might make the murderers into national heroes among the supporters of the IRA.

There is also a further claim that in order to satisfy Britain and America, the IRA offered to punish the murderers themselves and that they were quietly executed. It is, of course, impossible to verify these claims and even if two men were killed, there is no knowing if they were the right ones or if the IRA used the incident as an excuse to get rid of two unwanted members. Following the bomb attack the IRA announced that Mountbatten had been 'executed' to bring 'emotionally home to the English ruling class and its working-class slaves' that the 'war' would continue until they tore out 'their sentimental, imperialist heart'. There was no word about the other victims.

Within hours of the explosion, the Irish police initiated the biggest investigation in its history to find the terrorists responsible for the outrage. Two men were eventually charged: Francis McGirl and Thomas McMahon, an experienced bomb-maker for the Provisional IRA. McGirl was cleared by the three judges because they said there was 'a doubt' in his case. There was no such doubt in the case of McMahon who was convicted of the assassination by two pieces of evidence: green paint from Lord Mountbatten's boat and traces of nitro-glycerine which were found on him. This satisfied the bench that he had planted the bomb, even though it was accepted that at the time of the explosion he was seventy miles away – in police custody. Three months after the explosion that tried, but failed, to tear out the heart of Mountbatten's family, Thomas McMahon was sentenced to life imprisonment.

Twenty-four hours after the bomb the final body was recovered from the sea. It belonged to Twiga (the name is Swahili for giraffe), Patricia Brabourne's much-loved little dachshund who had been sitting on her lap and was blown into the water by the blast and killed instantly. There wasn't a mark on her. At Classiebawn today a stone marks the spot where Twiga is buried. It bears the date 27 August 1979, and is the only memorial in Ireland to that fateful day.

2

A HERO'S FAREWELL

Ronald Allison was the Queen's Press Secretary for five years. He had served as the BBC Court Correspondent and before that as a junior reporter on a local newspaper in Hampshire where his beat just happened to include the town of Romsey and Broadlands. He remembers visiting Mountbatten's home to see which important visitors were expected so that he could write up an account of the comings and goings for his column.

Twenty years later he was appointed to the Royal Household in a position which inevitably brought him into frequent contact with Lord Mountbatten. He says, 'Lord Mountbatten never came to the Palace without popping his head around my office door and coming in for a chat. He loved to see all the cuttings, especially if he was mentioned, and he would also telephone me if a story had appeared about Prince Charles over whom he took a very proprietorial and protective view.' Allison also says that Mountbatten claimed to remember him from those early days as a junior reporter, and as Mountbatten never forgot a face or a name, he probably did.

One of Allison's most bizarre yet amusing encounters with Mountbatten involved the planning for his funeral. Mountbatten took a tremendous personal interest in all the arrangements. There were countless meetings attended by the Lord Chamberlain, as Head of the Queen's Household, Allison, who, as Her Majesty's Press Secretary, was responsible for all media coverage, and representatives of the police and the armed forces, all of whom would have a role to play in what Mountbatten was determined would be a magnificent State occasion. Nothing was left to chance. Mountbatten examined every detail with meticulous attention, even down to the number of velvet cushions – six –

which would be required to carry his decorations, medals and honours.

For every royal occasion an advance party from Buckingham Palace does a 'recce' to check the proposed route, the security aspect of the programme, the press facilities and a million and one other minute details, all of which ensure that royal duties are carried out with maximum efficiency. Mountbatten's funeral was no different. Some years before his death he had laid out his plans with military precision. In order to facilitate matters he prepared an 'informal note' with a few suggestions for the Lord Chamberlain. The note ran to eleven pages.

Not everyone in the Royal Household agreed with all Mountbatten's proposals. At several meetings the Lord Chamberlain, the late Lord 'Chips' Maclean, raised objections to what he thought were rather too grandiose ideas for someone who was, in royal terms, quite far down the list. He lost every battle, as Mountbatten would invariably go over his head and see the Queen; the next time they met, Mountbatten would mention that 'Her Majesty thinks this is a good idea' and that was that. No one, not even the most senior courtier in the Palace, would ever question the Queen, and Mountbatten always got his own way.

During the 'recce' visit to Romsey, the team included Mountbatten himself, Lord Maclean and Ronald Allison, together with their back-up staff. Allison recalls, 'Lord Mountbatten never missed a thing. We all had a copy of the provisional programme that he had devised and he went through everything. We had already worked out the initial part of the day, the service at Westminster Abbey, the seating plan, where all the crowned heads would be placed, the order of precedence and so on. On this journey he wanted to arrange who sat where in the train which would carry his body from London to Broadlands, how long the trip would take and even the menu for the lunch to be served on board.' (Mountbatten's legendary eye for detail was to be fully justified on the day, when the Queen was finishing off her coffee five minutes before the train pulled in to Romsey station.)

Allison continues: 'When we arrived at Romsey, Lord Mountbatten personally checked the stop-watches of the Household who were timing the various segments and measured the number of paces it would take for the bearers to carry the coffin from the train to the carriage outside. Inside Romsey Abbey he knew the exact dimensions of the tablet that was to be placed over his grave, the type of stone that was to be used and he himself decided on the wording to be engraved. It was a most extraordinary performance by a man who was, after all, planning his own funeral – and thoroughly enjoying himself in the process.'

When Lord Brabourne (who died in 2005) discovered that his father-in-law was making the arrangements for his own funeral he said, 'How very macabre. Doesn't it upset you?' To which Mountbatten replied, 'The only thing that upsets me is that I won't be there.'

As far back as 1967 Mountbatten had begun making preparations for his funeral. In a note to Vice Admiral Turner in that year he comments that he agreed with the First and Second Sea Lords that it was a pity that Admirals of the Fleet did not have service funerals 'because naval pageantry was good for morale and public relations'. He also thought, regarding his own funeral, that the Army and Royal Air Force should participate, especially the Life Guards. However, he added, in an uncharacteristically modest tone, that he did not want to make any unpopular demands and would accept a private funeral.

Having said that, he then went on to correspond with everyone who was likely to have a role, writing personally to the British Legion and Burma Star Association, asking them what part they would like to play at the ceremony. The officer commanding the King's Troop Royal Horse Artillery confirmed that it would be in order for a nineteen-gun salute to be fired and in a letter to the Reverend Shearlock at Romsey Abbey, Mountbatten said that he did not want a lead-lined coffin such as that used for Sir Winston Churchill because it was too heavy: 'An ordinary coffin will do.'

In 1971 Mountbatten spoke to the Indian High Commissioner in London, Shri Apa Pant, saying he did not want his involvement with India to be overlooked at his funeral. He pointed out that he commanded the greatest number of Indians ever to serve in a war. In writing to Admiral T. Moorer, Chief of the US Joint Chiefs of Staff, he said how anxious he was that United States forces should be represented. At the same time he was keen that he should not be thought to be trying to increase the size of his funeral for vainglorious reasons. Mountbatten's personal contacts at the highest level were used to good effect; the then Prime Minister of France, M. Pierre Mesmer, wrote to Mountbatten to reassure him of his country's wish to take part, as did General Ne Win, President of Burma, regarding proposed Burmese participation.

Nothing was too much trouble and no detail too small to be considered. Mountbatten wrote personally to the Director of Music of the Life Guards, Captain A.J. Richards, telling him exactly which tune should be used to accompany Rudyard Kipling's 'Recessional' at the service. And in a memorandum for Patricia and Pamela he said that he wanted Vincent Apap's profile of himself to be placed on the family pew facing Edwina's profile and next to his coat of arms.

Mountbatten's private secretary, John Barratt, had possession of the funeral file, several inches thick, which contained all his master's instructions for every aspect of the occasion. There was a list of guests to be invited to Westminster Abbey and a second list, much reduced, of those who were permitted, after the service, to join the family at Broadlands. These lists had been compiled and altered many times over a ten-year-period and the names had to be checked and rechecked as several of them had died in the meantime. Separate sections dealt with the Royal Family, Mountbatten's immediate family, his many relations throughout Europe, his godchildren, close personal friends and a secondary list of friends and acquaintances who should be invited if there was room. There were also the hundreds of organizations, civil and military, with whom Mountbatten had been associated. Each had to be allocated a number of seats according to their importance and, inevitably, some were disappointed to find that they could not be fitted in or if they were, they were seated in positions inferior to those to which they felt they were entitled.

Barratt worked non-stop in conjunction with the Lord Chamberlain's office, who were responsible for the ceremonial side of the funeral services. In addition, tens of thousands of telegrams, telephone calls and letters had to be considered as people from all over the world appeared, claiming close friendship with Mountbatten and demanding places. Barratt said that he had never heard of most of them and they were politely but firmly told there was no chance of an invitation.

At the time of the assassination, John (now Sir John) Titman was Secretary of the Lord Chamberlain's Office in St James's Place. He recalled the flurry of activity when they heard the news: 'Lord Maclean came into the office and found we were rushed off our feet. Telephones were ringing like mad and secretaries were running about all over the place as the funeral arrangements had to be made in a great hurry. There were simply not enough hands to cope with the work. Lord Maclean took one look and said, 'Give me something to do – I don't care what it is, let me help.' So we gave him a list of people who had to be telephoned personally and off he went to his office and worked his way down the list making sure everyone who had to be told was contacted. I cannot imagine any other Lord Chamberlain doing that.'

The logistics of contacting all the Heads of State and other VIPs who had to be informed, plus the mechanics of getting them to London and arranging their accommodation, were formidable to say the least. To add to the problems, the murder had happened in August at the height of the holiday season when most of those who had to be told were away from their homes and offices.

The Queen had decided that the funeral, on Wednesday, 5 September 1979, although not a State occasion, was to be accorded full ceremonial status and, as with all such events, a full-scale dress rehearsal of the procession was held just after dawn two days before the funeral. Ideally there would have been several rehearsals but the suddenness of Mountbatten's death meant that only one could be held. The principal figures, including Prince Charles and Prince Philip, attended a rehearsal of the service, held at dawn, in Westminster Abbey, with further rehearsals taking place at Romsey Abbey. At Broadlands, preparations were made to entertain those friends and relations who would be returning there after the funeral, and as the Queen was one of them, special security arrangements were put in hand.

Many of Mountbatten's European relatives indicated that they would be present including a number of crowned heads, which would have pleased him tremendously. The names read like a *Who's Who* of European royalty: King Olaf of Norway, King Carl Gustaf and Queen Silvia of Sweden, King Constantine and Queen Anne-Marie of The Hellenes, King Simeon of Bulgaria, King Umberto of Italy, King Michael and Queen Anne of Rumania, the Count of Barcelona representing King Juan Carlos of Spain, Crown Princess Beatrix and Prince Claus of The Netherlands, Prince George of Denmark, Prince Ranier and Princess Grace of Monaco, Prince Albert of Belgium, the Grand Duke and Duchess of Luxembourg, Prince Franz Joseph and Princess Gina of Liechtenstein, all were determined to pay their last respects to a much loved cousin, uncle or nephew.

Mountbatten had died on 27 August. Four days later his body and those of Doreen, Lady Brabourne and their grandson Nicholas arrived by air at Eastleigh Airport near Southampton, after being brought from Ireland by Lady Pamela Hicks. The arrival was covered by television cameras and Lord Brabourne, in his hospital bed in Sligo, was asked if he wanted to watch it. He said he did.

Together with several members of the medical staff he watched Lord Mountbatten's coffin being carried out of the aircraft first, followed by that of Doreen, Lady Brabourne and, bringing up the rear, that of his son Nicholas. When he saw the first two coffins he was all right, but when his son's smaller coffin was carried out, he broke down. It was more than he could stand. Waiting on the tarmac to receive the bodies were Prince Philip, Prince Charles and John Barratt, who then accompanied the coffins back to Broadlands where they were laid in the Sculpture Hall.

Two days later, Mountbatten's body was removed to Romsey Abbey to lie in state so that local people, and indeed anyone else who wished to, could pay their respects. They came from all over Britain and further afield and in forty-hours some twenty-five thousand men, women and children filed past as staff from the Broadlands estate stood in silent vigil.

Ashley Hicks remembers one evening just before the funeral when the surviving members of the family were gathered at Broadlands with the Prince of Wales among them. 'We were sitting having coffee after dinner and discussing the moves the following day and how many cars were going to be needed and who was going in which car. We all joined in as one thing our family has always loved is a good argument with everyone having their say. All of a sudden Prince Charles looked up and said, 'Where's Uncle Dickie, he'll be able to . . .' Just for a moment he had forgotten that Grandpapa was dead and that none of us would ever see him again. We were all so used to him settling our arguments. It was a very poignant moment.'

On the evening before the funeral, Mountbatten's body was brought from Romsey to St James's Palace where it lay overnight in the Chapel Royal. This is where the Royal Family, Lord Mountbatten's younger daughter Pamela, her husband David and the surviving grandchildren came to make their personal farewells. As they passed in front of the coffin, Lady Pamela's daughter India, who had been carrying a little posy of violets, broke away from her mother and placed the flowers on her grandfather's coffin. Her parents hadn't asked her to do it, it was a perfectly spontaneous action on her part.

Lord and Lady Brabourne and their son Tim were still in hospital in Sligo and although out of danger, their injuries were so severe that it would be many weeks before they were allowed home.

The distance from St James's Palace to Westminster Abbey is less than a mile. On the day of Mountbatten's funeral it took the procession an hour to cover it. Fifty thousand people lined the route, watching in silent tribute as 131 sailors pulled the gun carriage carrying the coffin alongside which marched its eight pall-bearers of four admirals, three generals and a marshal of the Royal Air Force. Preceding them was Lance Corporal of Horse, Keith Nicklin of the Life Guards, leading Dolly, Mountbatten's black charger, which he used to ride in the Sovereign's Birthday Parade. It was a moving moment as Dolly, with her master's shining black thigh-boots reversed in her stirrups, led the procession out into The Mall. In nearby Hyde Park the King's Troop, Royal Horse Artillery, fired a nineteen-gun salute.

The symbols of Mountbatten's naval and military ranks, the three-cornered cocked hat of an Admiral of the Fleet, his personal sword, and his Gold Stick, which, as Colonel of the Life Guards, entitled him to be the Queen's personal bodyguard, were laid on top of the Union Jack-covered coffin. Walking behind were Mountbatten's grandsons, Ashley Hicks, Michael-John, Norton and Philip Knatchbull, with his son-in-law David Hicks walking beside the Duke of Edinburgh and the Prince of Wales. The Duke of Gloucester, the Duke of Kent, and Prince Michael of Kent completed the family party.

The honour of leading the procession fell to the Central Band of the Royal Air Force. As they began the slow march, detachments of the armed forces of the United States, France and India fell in behind. Then came Princess Patricia's Canadian Light Infantry, the Women's Royal Naval Service, the Women's Royal Army Corps, the Women's Royal Air Force, 1st Bn 2nd King Edward VII's Own Gurkha Rifles (The Sirmoor Rifles). The Massed Bands of the Household Cavalry preceded the Life Guards, the Royal Marines, the Royal Navy and the Massed Bands of the Royal Marines.

Following the coffin were representatives of the Burmese armed forces and senior officers of the Burma Star Association. The Elder Brethren of Trinity House were present, as were detachments of the British Commonwealth ex-Services League, the Royal Naval Association, the Royal Marines Association, the Life Guards Association and Lord Mountbatten's own private ex-service group, the *Kelly* Reunion. Bringing up the rear of this massive display of servicemen and women were the Massed Bands of the Grenadier and Coldstream Guards.

The Lord Chamberlain had worked out the timing of events to the second. The official timetable stated that by 10.18 a.m. the procession would be in position – not at a quarter past or nearly twenty past, but precisely at 10.18. At 10.23 a.m. the Duke of Edinburgh and the Prince of Wales would arrive at the Lower Corridor of St James's Palace, and at 10.32 a.m. prayers would be said by the Sub-dean of Her Majesty's Chapel Royal. The schedule was equally exact for the foreign Heads of State who were told that they would leave the Buckingham Palace Quadrangle at precisely 10.56, exactly two minutes after Lady Pamela Hicks and the younger ladies of the family.

As the coffin was carried into Westminster Abbey, the Lord Chamberlain was seen to step out of line for an instant as he gently and discreetly rearranged a wreath which looked as if it was going to fall off. Mountbatten would have approved.

The Royal Procession formed up with every member of the Royal Family present. The Queen was accompanied by Queen Elizabeth the Queen Mother, Prince Andrew and Prince Edward. Princess Margaret walked alone, behind her Princess Anne and Captain Mark Phillips, in front the Duchess of Gloucester, her mother-in-law Princess Alice, the Dowager Duchess of Gloucester, the Duchess of Kent, Princess Alexandra and her husband the Hon. (now Sir) Angus Ogilvy with their children and Princess Michael of Kent.

The ecclesiastical procession consisted of representatives of all sections of the Christian community: the Archbishop of Canterbury, the Roman Catholic Archbishop of Westminster, the Greek Orthodox Archbishop, the Primate of All Ireland, the Moderator of the General Assembly of the Church of Scotland, the Bishop of London, the Moderator of the Presbyterian Church in Ireland and two priests who would have been specially welcomed by Lord Mountbatten, the Chaplain of the Fleet and the vicar of the tiny parish of Whippingham on the Isle of Wight, where his parents had been buried and, of course, where he had been Governor General himself.

The service went without a hitch; Prince Charles read the lesson in a voice ringing with emotion, the choir and congregation sang the hymns Mountbatten had chosen and afterwards his old friend Barbara Cartland summed it all up when she told John Barratt: 'Wouldn't Dickie have loved all this?'

For Pamela Hicks the funeral was both harrowing and uplifting. She was still in deep shock over the tragedy and did not know how badly injured her sister was, or how permanently she would be affected. She says now, 'I found the service inspiring and it was a wonderful tribute to my father to see all these people from all over the world gathered in the Abbey. There were, of course, moments in the morning when I felt overcome with grief, but I knew for the children's sake I couldn't show it. It was hard for the girls but they managed brilliantly.

As the family waited outside the Abbey after the service, Mountbatten's granddaughter Joanna suddenly felt faint. 'I then took a deep breath and said to myself, "Pull yourself together. Grandpapa would be furious." It worked and the moment passed.' Ashley Hicks did not cry either. 'I suppose it's partly because we as a family have this half-English/half-German blood. We have all had this little bit of training not to break down in tears in public or show emotion of any kind. The main difficulty came when complete strangers would ring up and be unable to speak through their tears. It's not the usual sort of thing that happens when a grandfather dies, is it? One man rang up when we were at our flat in Albany. He was totally distraught and could only give us his serial number, whereas none of us could cry at all. The funeral gave Grandpapa his final, glorious moment. If he had died a slow lingering death through illness, it wouldn't have been nearly so dramatic or touched the public's heart in the same way. But in a peculiar way, the method of his dying and the magnificent occasion of his funeral elevated him back into the limelight in a way he would have relished.'

For little India Hicks it was a particularly emotional occasion. The day of the funeral was also her twelfth birthday. Her sixteen-year-old brother Ashley was the youngest grandson to walk in the procession, which he did proudly with the other male members of Mountbatten's family who were fit enough to walk. The ladies did not take part in the procession but waited inside the Abbey.

When the cortège reached Waterloo Station, where a special train pulled by a locomotive named Broadlands (another of Mountbatten's prearranged ideas) was waiting to transport the funeral party to Romsey, Lord Maclean was seen to step forward and place India's posy of violets on the coffin for its final journey. The flowers had been removed before the procession to make room for the symbols of office; Lord Maclean's thoughtful gesture was seen and greatly appreciated by India's parents.

The family's grief came out the following day when the private funerals of Doreen, Lady Brabourne and Nicholas Knatchbull were held in the tiny parish church at Mersham near the family home in Kent. Pamela Hicks says, 'This was Ashley's undoing. He had been wonderful at Westminster Abbey but to see poor Nicky's coffin being carried in was too much for him. He clutched me crying "Which is Nicky, which is Nicky?" They had been so close and he desperately wanted to concentrate on Nicky at the funeral. It was heartbreaking.'

So at the end of the worst week the family had experienced, they had lost a dearly loved son and nephew, a much missed grandmother and the man who had been the pivot around which their lives had revolved for so long. Mountbatten of Burma was dead and laid to rest – but the legend would remain.

3

THE BATTENBERGS

Mountbatten was born a Battenberg and became a Mountbatten when all along he should have been a Hesse. His grandfather, Prince Alexander of Hesse, was a member of the oldest ruling Protestant family in Europe and, as such, was expected to marry someone of equal rank, in accordance with the stultifyingly formal customs of European royalty in the nineteenth century. The idea of marrying below one's rank was unthinkable; it meant instant ostracism and social death. It could also mean being stripped of one's titles, banned from Court and even banished to live abroad. Such was the fate that in 1851 befell Prince Alexander of Hesse, who was even forced to leave the Russian army and eventually became a general in the Austrian army.

His sister had married the future Tsar Alexander II of Russia and he himself was intended as a husband for the Tsar's niece. Had that marriage taken place, how different would the fate of Lord Mountbatten have been. Indeed, the course of British history in two world wars might well have changed without the participation of the Mountbattens, father and son, and even possibly the present structure of the Royal Family, if Prince Philip had not been guided by his Uncle Dickie.

However, Prince Alexander had ideas of his own about who he should marry and, with his heart ruling his head, he eloped with one of his sister's ladies-in-waiting, a Polish girl named Julie Hauke, and they were married in Breslau in 1851. As a lady-in-waiting at the Russian Court, his wife was not exactly a peasant girl from one of the local villages: in fact, she was not so very far removed in rank from her husband – but far enough to upset the strict social structure of this inbred society. Alexander's brother, Grand Duke Louis II of Hesse, under pressure from the mighty Tsar, showed his anger at the marriage by depriving the newly-weds of the use of the family name. Instead, the defunct, and inferior, title of Battenberg was revived and Alexander was demoted to the rank of Serene Highness from his original style of Royal Highness. His wife was created Countess Julie of Battenberg, at first, without the right even to be called Serene Highness, a courtesy that was withheld for seven years. But the Grand Duke's anger stopped some way short of actually seeing them on the breadline and palaces were made available to them at Darmstadt and Heiligenberg where they had plenty of space in which to bring up their five children, none of whom would ever have a claim to the throne of Hesse. Not that that would be too much of a problem as the throne itself was to disappear long before any of the children.

The Battenberg's eldest son, Prince Louis, was born on 24 May 1854, in Graz, Austria. German was his first language, English a close second which he spoke throughout his life with an accent, described as light by his family and heavy by his enemies. He was eight years old when his parents brought him to England for the first time, to stay at Windsor Castle with Queen Victoria. It was the beginning of a lifetime's love affair with the country whose nationality he would soon adopt and which he would serve with such distinction – and which would, in turn, repay him in such humiliating fashion.

Six years later, in 1868, he left his home in Germany, partly against the wishes of his father, who would have preferred his son to remain and serve in one of the fashionable regiments into which the male members of the House of Hesse had traditionally been recruited. But Louis's cousin, Prince Alfred, already enjoying life as a post-captain in the Royal Navy, had painted a glowing picture of a career afloat to capture the interest of the fourteen-year-old princeling. In this he was aided and abetted by his mother Queen Victoria, who thoroughly approved of the idea of her young kinsman joining the British Navy. There was really no contest. Prince Louis wanted the Navy; his father made only half-hearted attempts to dissuade him and the Queen's stamp of approval decided the issue once and for all.

He was accepted as a cadet little knowing what the next few years would bring. In the nineteenth century the Royal Navy had a reputation for inflicting the most sadistic punishments, employing the cruellest of instructors and offering the worst living conditions in Europe. Every cadet was subject to a regime of vigorous physical abuse, poor food and rigid discipline as a matter of course. Senior officers felt it was 'good for them' and they themselves had been through it all years before so they saw no reason for change.

What Prince Louis hadn't bargained for was the non-stop bullying he had to endure not only from his instructors, but also from his fellow cadets who loved to gang up on this good-looking youngster with the strange-sounding title ('Serene Highness' had a distinctly un-British ring to it) and foreign accent. He was beaten almost every day, especially if he had been given any special privileges on account of his royal connections. He was regarded as being neither fish nor fowl. One day the authorities would invite him to join the senior officers in the wardroom when a member of the Royal Family was expected, much to the annoyance of his comrades who thought he was getting special treatment (which he was); the next he would be back in his own quarters being taught a rough lesson by the 'have nots' who were more than a little jealous of his unique position. It was not only unfair but confusing to a young boy – and at fourteen he was still no more than a boy – whose only previous experience of people of his own age had been with his royal relations whose genteel manners had hardly prepared him for such a brutal baptism in the real world. He eventually managed to overcome his tormentors and stand up for himself but in those early years the temptation to give it all up and return to the security and comfort of Darmstadt was hard to resist.

Prince Louis did not make many close friends in the Navy, though eventually he achieved a degree of popularity among his contemporaries by taking all their bullying without flinching. Because of his background he felt it necessary to be careful in the extreme in his choice of companions and most of those with whom he established any sort of relationship were either royal or at least the holders of ancient family titles. One exception to this rule, in later life, was Winston Churchill, one of the few plain 'misters' who could claim Prince Louis as a good friend, (Churchill would also claim friendship with the younger Louis, though in this case it was something of a love-hate relationship, particularly after Mountbatten's time in India.)

As Prince Louis progressed up the promotion ladder in the Royal Navy he was to suffer continuous sniping from other officers who were envious of his connections, his abilities and the manner in which he was able to combine being a royal prince and a serving officer without too much apparent effort. Nepotism was rife in the Royal Navy at that time and it was fairly common for officers to lobby everyone of influence in order to obtain the best postings. Then, as now, one of the choicest naval duties was a tour on board the Royal Yacht. It was even possible to buy a place until Queen Victoria put a stop to the practice, saying it was unseemly for her officers to be seen bargaining in such a fashion. Prince Louis served on two Royal Yachts, the *Osborne* and *Victoria & Albert*, and it was obvious that the Queen had had a hand in his selection.

Every promotion brought forth charges that Prince Louis was being favoured because of his royal relations and when he accompanied the Prince of Wales (later Edward VII) on a tour of India there were murmurings of discontent yet again. If Louis had one blind spot it was his inability to recognize how his German roots (he was a naturalized British subject) would continue to antagonize his fellow officers. He made no attempt to disguise his accent or dilute his thickened consonants, and most of his leaves were spent in Germany which he still regarded as home. The fact that his brother-in-law was in the fast-expanding German Navy added to the suspicions which many years later were to be used against him and which would eventually force him to resign his position as First Sea Lord.

The Prince of Wales became Louis's closest friend and they shared many pleasures including the favours of Lillie Langry, the Prince of Wales's most famous mistress, by whom Louis had a daughter. In 1978, in a charity speech at a gala in Jersey, Mountbatten acknowledged that his father had had an illegitimate child by Lillie Langry. In turn this lady had a daughter of her own, Mary Malcolm, who became one of BBC Television's first announcers, and when she heard of Mountbatten's public announcement she wrote to thank him. By now she too had married and was Mrs McFadden, living in St John's Wood in London. Mountbatten was delighted to hear from her and invited her to spend a weekend at Broadlands. In his letter of invitation he wrote, 'I am glad you approved of what I said. I think the time has come when it is much better to have the whole thing in the open for there is, after all, a great deal to be said for both sides of the family.' The weekend was apparently a great success and Mrs McFadden was thrilled to be asked to plant a tree in the grounds, writing, 'I was touched and somewhat overcome to be included in such distinguished company.' And in the same letter she goes on, 'While I regret the wasted years I hope we can perhaps make up for them in the years to come.' The date of this letter was 6 February 1979, just six months before Mountbatten was killed. So the belated relationship never was allowed to flourish as both might have wished.

As a single, good-looking and charming young officer, Prince Louis of Battenberg fully enjoyed the attractions of being a paid-up member of the 'Marlborough House Set'. He gambled moderately, drank champagne without showing any after-effects, was a welcome guest at country houses where he paid great attention to the ladies, and could have married many times over if he had so wished. That he waited until he was twenty-nine before becoming engaged meant that he was able to sow all his wild oats as a single man – even if his cousin Bertie, the Prince of Wales, (later Edward VII) continued his extra-marital love life until almost the day he died.

When the time came for him to settle down and marry it was once again to his native Germany that Prince Louis turned to find a wife. The woman who was to become Mountbatten's mother was born Princess Victoria of Hesse in 1863, though her birth had taken place in that most English of locations, Windsor Castle. She was fifteen years old when her mother Princess Alice died of diphtheria and her childhood came to an abrupt end as she assumed responsibility for her brothers and sisters, and even to a larger extent for her father, the Grand Duke, who, in common with most men of his class and generation, knew nothing about bringing up children. He was an affectionate but distant parent who had left all matters concerning his children's welfare to his wife, who in turn supervised the governesses, nannies and nursemaids who did the looking after on a day-to-day basis. Victoria now took over this role. Mountbatten was later to say, 'She was the head of the family in every sense . . . She really acted as Grand Duchess to her father, and ran the household. My mother inherited an extraordinary position. She ran the whole place from top to bottom, and ran her own father completely. He just sat at her feet and did as she said.'

The transition from child to adult with virtually no adolescence in between had instilled in Victoria a self-confidence and assurance that would remain with her for the rest of her life. She was possessed of a formidable intelligence, an enquiring mind and an insatiable curiosity that she would pass on to her children, particularly Lord Louis, who would later claim that 'all the brains in the Royal family came from my side.' The maturity which had been forced on her at such an early age also meant that she was not going to be the usual sort of Victorian wife, acquiescent, placid and always submitting to her husband's wishes. Her natural independence would ensure that her marriage to Prince Louis would be a full partnership in every sense.

Theirs was a relationship built on mutual love and respect but before they could be married the objections of Victoria's father had to be overcome. The Grand Duke did not regard Prince Louis as a good match for his daughter. His inferior title, his lack of a large fortune and, most damning of all, the fact that by marrying Victoria he would take her away from Darmstadt for ever ensured that Louis was not welcomed with open arms by his future father-in-law.

Again it was Queen Victoria, who for four years had assumed the role of surrogate, if long distance, mother to her granddaughter, who used her influence in the couple's favour, and the Grand Duke gave his consent. The wedding took place in Darmstadt in April 1884 with Queen Victoria in attendance and a year later their first child, Princess Alice, was born in Windsor.

Princess Alice, who was severely deaf throughout her life, married Prince Andrew of Greece and the youngest of their five children was Prince Philip, later Duke of Edinburgh. Princess Alice was a delightful and very religious woman and in the latter years of her life she became very close to her daughter-in-law, the Queen, who provided her with a suite of rooms in Buckingham Palace, where she lived until her death in 1969.

In 1889 another daughter, Louise, was born, who was to become Queen of Sweden when she married the future King Gustaf VI Adolf of Sweden, in 1923. Then followed the first boy, Prince George, in 1892, who would eventually become 2nd Marquess of Milford Haven. Eight years later, the family was completed with the arrival of Prince Louis Francis.

At the turn of the century a naval officer and his family led a nomadic existence, and it was no different for the Battenbergs. They had no permanent home of their own, living in a succession of rented houses in England or quarters provided by the Royal Navy abroad, with the occasional use of grace-and-favour homes lent to them by Queen Victoria and later Edward VII. Of course they still had the use of the family properties in German, in particular Heiligenberg Castle, which Prince Louis (the senior) always regarded as his true home.

Lord Mountbatten's mother already had close connections with both the Russian and German Royal Families with three of her sisters marrying into them. On her marriage to Tsar Nicholas II, Alix became Tsarina Alexandra Feodorovna – perishing with him and their five children in 1918 when they were murdered by the Bolsheviks. Princess Elizabeth, also murdered by the Bolsheviks, became the wife of Grand

Duke Serge of Russia, while their youngest sister Irene, who would outlive them all, surviving until 1953, married Prince Henry of Prussia. In two world wars the family would therefore have members fighting on both sides.

This, then, was the extended European family into which the future Earl Mountbatten of Burma was born.

4

EIGHT DECADES

Born on 25 June 1900, Louis Francis Albert Victor Nicholas was the second son of Prince Louis of Battenberg (later the 1st Marquess of Milford Haven) and of Princess Victoria of Hesse. His great-grandmother was Queen Victoria, who attended his christening, and who, at the time of his birth, had been on the British throne since 1837 and Empress of India since 1876. Just a year after Prince Louis Francis (as he was then known) was born, Queen Victoria died and an Empire mourned.

At the time of his death, nearly eighty years later, there was no Empire left to mourn and five more sovereigns had occupied the throne. The young Prince Louis Francis would achieve heights of which his great-grandmother would surely have been proud. After having his royal titles stripped from him when he was seventeen, along with those of all his German relations who were resident in Britain during the First World War, he would go on to amass a multitude of new honours and decorations. He became the first Earl Mountbatten of Burma; Knight of the Garter, Privy Counsellor; holder of the Order of Merit; Knight Grand Cross of the Bath; Knight Grand Commander of the Star of India; Knight Grand Cross of the Royal Victorian Order; Knight Grand Commander of the Indian Empire; Companion of the Distinguished Service Order and Fellow of the Royal Society. In the Second World War he commanded HMS *Kelly*; became Commander of Combined Operations in 1941; Chief of Combined Operations in 1942 and Supreme Allied Commander, South East Asia, in 1943. In 1947 Louis Mountbatten was appointed to be the last Viceroy of India and subsequently its first Governor General. Resuming his interrupted naval career in 1948 he became, successively, Fourth Sea Lord, then Commander-in-Chief, Mediterranean in 1952 and in 1955 he achieved his lifetime ambition when he became First Sea Lord. Four years later he completed a brilliant service record when he was appointed Chief of the Defence Staff. In a career spanning fifty-six years he had risen from being a humble cadet to his final rank as Admiral of the Fleet. His father and older brother, George, would have thoroughly approved.

Even if his father, Prince Louis of Battenberg, had not been chosen as First Sea Lord by Winston Churchill, then First Lord of the Admiralty, the Royal Navy would have been a natural choice of career for his son. In those days of gun-boat diplomacy when Britain's fleet was rightly acknowledged as the mightiest afloat, the Royal Navy was considered to be the finest training ground for young men who would one day help to administer the British Empire. As such, no other career would have been thought suitable for a Prince of the House of Battenberg, with its close connections with the English crown and what was shortly to become the House of Windsor. With the young Louis, as with his elder brother George, there was a natural affinity with their father's adopted country. At the age of twelve His Serene Highness Prince Louis Francis of Battenberg entered the Royal Naval College of Osborne on the Isle of Wight (the island of which he would one day become Governor) and then progressed to the fledgling nautical college at Dartmouth to continue his training.

Before joining the Navy, young Dickie – the name by which he would be known to family and close friends for the rest of his life – grew up near the centre of the gigantic family tree that united Europe's royal houses. He spent much of the year 1908 in Russia, staying with his relations in their palaces in Moscow and St Petersburg. The splendours of the Tsarist Court appealed immediately to the young prince and imbued in him a lifelong love of ceremonial and royal pageantry.

Mountbatten's affection for Britain and all things British stemmed from his parents. His father had been promoted to command the Atlantic fleet in 1907 and, as a naturalized British subject, from the age of fourteen, his loyalty never wavered. Mountbatten's mother, Princess Victoria, was a self-confessed Anglophile who never attempted to disguise her feelings for Great Britain. Mountbatten's elder brother, Prince George, was already in the Royal Navy when young Louis enrolled at Osborne, so there were two figures for him to emulate: father and brother, both of whom were to enjoy distinguished careers in the service of the British Crown.

Throughout his life Mountbatten would claim that he inherited his determination to succeed from both sides of his family. His mother had been tremendously influential, on her own father, on her husband and also on all her children. As far as Mountbatten was concerned the influence would last throughout his mother's long life, until she died at the age of eighty-seven. Even today, the present Countess Mountbatten and her sister Lady Pamela Hicks speak with great fondness of their grandmother and the way in which she guided the whole family. She was also known as the only woman ever to have smoked in Queen Victoria's presence; it happened at Balmoral when the Queen commanded her granddaughter to 'light one of your cigarettes' to keep the summer midges at bay during a walk in the garden.

Mountbatten's father passed on to his son a characteristic that they would both deny at first, but which, at least as far as the younger Louis was concerned, was cheerfully admitted in later life. This quality was a burning desire to be noticed. When Lord Louis's father first entered the Royal Navy he might have had an easier time if only he had kept a lower profile – in the English way. But he was not English. He was German through and through and as such he believed it was important that his presence was felt, even if that involved making himself unpopular with his contemporaries. Similarly, Lord Louis Mountbatten was congenitally unable to hide his light under a bushel. If he achieved something, he wanted the world to know about it and recognize that he was the person who had done it. He used to say, 'If I don't blow my own trumpet, no one else will.'

Mountbatten never denied that much of what he achieved was because of his attitude to his father. He openly confessed that 'I was a great father-worshipper, because I did think he was wonderful.' So it came as one of the earliest and greatest sorrows in his young life when, at the age of fourteen, he learned that his beloved papa had been forced to resign his position as First Sea Lord after forty-six years' distinguished service in the Royal Navy.

Mountbatten, who at that time was still known formally as Prince Louis Francis but Dickie to his family and friends, was a cadet at Osborne on the day his father ordered the British Navy to open fire on all German ships. The date was 4 August 1914, the fourteenth birthday of Lady Elizabeth Bowes-Lyon (later Queen Elizabeth the Queen Mother) and the day on which the First World War, the war to end all wars, was declared. The Admiralty signal said, 'To all Ships. Commence hostilities against Germany.' And it was signed, 'Louis Battenberg, First Sea Lord.'

The man who had served his adopted country for nearly half a century had no hesitation in following the Government's orders, even though it meant he would be fighting against his native land and the place he still thought of as home. Prince Louis's loyalty had never been in doubt, yet within three months of the outbreak of war the wave of anti-German hysteria that swept the country, with mobs wrecking anything that sounded as if it might be German – even dachshund dogs being kicked in British streets – was to cause him to leave the most important post in the Navy.

Twelve weeks was all it took for the scandal-mongers and malicious gossips to destroy a brilliant career. They claimed he could not possibly be loyal to Britain with so many of his closest relations fighting on the other side. A cousin was Admiral of the German Fleet. His German name and title were constantly held against him and newspapers blamed him for the fact that in those first weeks of the war, Britain's naval superiority was being challenged with some success by the Kaiser's fleet.

Finally, Prince Louis could take no more and, in spite of having some private, but not much pubic, support from his political masters, he offered his resignation to the First Lord, the Right Honourable Winston Churchill, MP. His letter was a brief masterpiece in his understanding of the situation and typical of the dignity with which he had always conducted himself. He wrote:

Dear Mr Churchill

I have lately been driven to the painful conclusion that at this juncture my birth and parentage have the effect of impairing in some respects my usefulness on the Board of the Admiralty. In these circumstances I feel it to be my duty, as a loyal subject of His Majesty, to resign the office of First Sea Lord, hoping thereby to facilitate the task of the administration of the great Service to which I have devoted my life, and to ease the burden laid on HM's Ministers.

I am, Yours very truly, Louis Battenberg, Admiral.

Churchill and Battenberg had worked brilliantly together for some years before the war and a close friendship had developed between the two men. But it was not enough to save the sailor from an ignominious departure. Churchill might have been privately saddened at the hand which fate had dealt his old friend but he was first and foremost a politician and a pragmatist, with a politician's inbuilt instinct for self-preservation. He knew that any attempt on his part to try to keep Prince Louis at the Admiralty would be courting political disaster and would make him personally unpopular. He needed the goodwill of the people and if sacrificing an honest man, who also happened to be excellent at his job and a close friend to boot, was the price that had to be paid, then so be it.

Prince Louis's family knew that on the day he left the Admiralty his life was virtually over. His heart was broken and though he lived for seven more years, he never recovered his spirits or his health, and it would be left to his younger son to restore the family's reputation. It would be forty-one years before the final act was to be played out when that same politician, Winston Churchill, would be forced, protesting, to appoint Lord Mountbatten to the post of First Sea Lord.

The young Dickie at Osborne heard the news of his father's dismissal with disbelief. For some weeks he too had been subject to a barrage of abuse from his fellow cadets because of his German name and, as many of his colleagues had fathers and uncles serving at sea, the rumours of the First Sea Lord being a German spy had found their way back to the college where they were repeated to the young Dickie's face. At first he thought the whole thing was a joke. Writing to his mother he said, 'That Papa has turned out to be a German spy and been marched off to the Tower . . . little fools insisted on calling me a German Spy.' But Dickie had learned to stand up for himself and after he had fought a few battles and bloodied a few noses, the other boys called a truce.

When it finally dawned on him that it was, indeed, no joke but a deadly serious matter, he was dumbfounded. The most heart-rending story of his reaction, which he himself confirmed many years later, was of him standing to attention saluting the flag on the parade ground at Osborne, with tears streaming down his face. The romantics among Mountbatten's biographers like to stress that it was at this moment that he determined to avenge the insult to his father and it was then, on that windswept and desolate parade ground, that he set out to become First Sea Lord. It is a nice story and certainly paints a dramatic picture that would have appealed to Mountbatten's sense of theatre. He never denied that he cried when he heard the news of his father's dismissal but he was less emphatic when he discussed his motivation to succeed.

He was asked many times if it was true that it was to right a wrong that he strove so mightily to reach the top. Eventually he would say, 'Too many people say they have heard me say, 'I am going to right a great wrong' . . . for it not to be true.' But he would also claim, probably more accurately, that, as a young man, people would try to put words into his mouth. They wanted him to be portrayed as the avenging son who would nurse his resentment until the family honour was restored. Mountbatten was not, however, a resentful man. It would not have been in his nature to hold a grudge throughout his life, though he did like to pay off old scores when he could. His natural competitiveness was the single most important element in his aim for the top. Ambition was something he could not avoid; it was as natural to him as breathing. Everything he attempted had to be done better than anybody else. The pursuit of excellence was the guidance he followed throughout his life and he saw no point in taking part unless he could win. Not for Mountbatten was the Olympic ideal, 'It's not the winning, it's the taking part that counts'. For him winning was all. He loved to exhort his crews in the Royal Navy, his polo teams, the soldiers under his command, his staff, to better efforts with the words, 'Remember, there are no prizes for coming second.'

Three years after his resignation as First Sea Lord, Prince Louis was to suffer a further humiliation when he was forced to abandon his family name and adopt a new English title. The year 1917 was a difficult one for the British Royal Family, one which might well have been described as an *annus horribilis*. The was was going badly. Casualties were numbered in their millions, zeppelins were raiding London, there was no sign of the promised victory and the people needed someone to blame. Who better than the man who was supposed to be leading them against the enemy – the King. Everyone knew he had German blood in his veins. His grandfather had been pure German, born and bred and, as far as anyone knew, he still retained his German surname of Saxe-Coburg-Gotha – or was it Wettin? Whatever it was, it wasn't English and neither were his relatives the Tecks and Battenbergs. All of them were living off the fat of the land, according to what was then the equivalent of the tabloid press, in grace-and-favour homes, paid for by the British taxpayer. Why should Britain support an alien monarch and his German family?

King George V was outraged; however, he knew that this was not merely the outpourings of a fanatical 'anti-monarchist' press but a real danger which he would have to move quickly and decisively to quash. In outlook and way of life, George V was arguably the most English monarch Britain has ever known. He was a complete xenophobe; he disliked all foreigners and rarely travelled abroad. On one private journey through France he instructed the British Ambassador to arrange his programme in a way that would 'avoid all contact with Frenchmen', such was his distrust of all things non-British.

In 1917, knowing that he had to be seen to be making a gesture, George V decided to proclaim the formation of the House of Windsor. The name was a brilliant choice − suggested by the King's private secretary, Lord Stamfordham − and the news was received by a fickle British public as clear evidence of His Majesty's undoubted patriotism. That was all it took to convince them that George V was indeed an English monarch through and through.

The King also decided that, as he was adopting an English surname, all his close relatives with German titles should relinquish them in favour of names that were unmistakably British. His wife's brothers, the Duke of Teck and Prince Alexander, both serving officers in the British Army, became respectively Marquess of Cambridge and Earl of Athlone.

When the King sent for Prince Louis to inform him of his decision, he encountered no resistance at all to the suggestion that the German title of Prince Louis of Battenberg should be abandoned. Prince Louis said, 'I am absolutely English. I have been educated in England and have been in England all my life. If you wish me to become now Sir Louis Battenberg I will do so.' But the King wanted more than that. He wanted Prince Louis to give up his family name of Battenberg altogether and adopt a new British surname. As it happened, the title chosen was not English at all, but Welsh, and Prince Louis of Battenberg became the first Marquess of Milford Haven, a town on the coast of West Wales. With its distinguished sea-going tradition it was an appropriate choice, even if there is no record of the first Marquess ever having visited his name-sake port. His two sons also assumed non-German names. Prince George of Battenberg became Earl of Medina, while Prince Louis Francis acquired the courtesy title of Lord Louis Mountbatten, this being the anglicized version of Battenberg. He was no longer a Serene Highness. Another member of the Battenberg family, Prince Alexander, who was an officer in that most British of regiments, the Grenadier Guards, was created Marquess of Carisbrook.

It was at Sandringham that Prince Louis was told by the King of the change of name and title. He obviously had no idea of what was to happen when he arrived and signed the visitors' book as Prince Louis of Battenberg. He later confided in his diary, 'I arrived as a Prince and left as a Marquess. It's a queer old world!'

The young Mountbatten, even at seventeen, displayed his obsession with titles and protocol, and was obviously concerned about his place in the order of precedence and that of any children he might have. He asked his mother if he would still need the permission of the sovereign to marry and if his children would be plain Mister, Miss or Honourable?

His mother was far more down to earth about the change in status than the rest of her family. While Prince Louis accepted the demotion with good grace, realizing it was inevitable, he was, nevertheless, not happy about the circumstances which had led to it. His wife, on the other hand, was completely unaffected by having to give up being a princess. She would not have minded being a plain Mrs; in fact she might have preferred it to becoming a marchioness, the sort of title she acquired with the *nouveaux riches*, who were buying such titles by the score from Lloyd George during the First World War.

A more immediate and lasting concern to her was the despicable behaviour, in her opinion, of Winston Churchill in the dismissal of her husband. She considered that Prince Louis had been betrayed by someone he thought of as an old and trusted friend, and she was never to forgive Churchill. Lloyd George also became an implacable enemy of the family when, at the conclusion of the war, he refused to allow Admiral Milford Haven, as he had by then become, back on to the active list, but he was promoted to the rank of Admiral of the Fleet.

The young Mountbatten had had an exciting few years of war, ending as an eighteen-year-old sub-lieutenant on anti-submarine patrols in the North Sea. In 1920 an opportunity arose for him to take part in a venture which was to have far-reaching effects on his future life and he was quick to recognize the chance.

King George V had been persuaded that in order to thank fully those nations in the Empire which had contributed so magnificently to the Allied victory in the First World War, he should send his eldest son, the Prince of Wales, on a personal tour. There was a secondary purpose to the tour: ostensibly to further the heir to the throne's education for his future role as King and Emperor, in reality it was to separate him from the lifestyle he enjoyed; particularly his relationships with various married women.

Dickie Mountbatten was only nineteen when he heard that his cousin David was to set out on an extended visit to Australia, New Zealand and the West Indies, and he determined that he too would go on the trip. Months before the date of departure he started his campaign to be included in the party. He used anyone and everyone he thought might be able to pull a few strings. The Prince of Wales, who had first been approached by Mountbatten, was agreeable, but he didn't do anything about it himself. He always preferred to leave the logistics to others and he thought that Mountbatten could handle that part of the negotiations without his help. Mountbatten then tried to persuade Bertie (later King George VI) and Henry (later Duke of Gloucester) to use their influence, but as time for departure drew nearer and he heard nothing, he decided to take the matter into his own hands.

He could not make a formal application to join the tour; he had to wait to be invited, and the only person who could do that was the Prince of Wales. As anxious as he was, Mountbatten did not feel he could ask for an interview at the Palace, and he knew that the Prince did not like being forced into a corner. Mountbatten then discovered that his cousin was going to attend an important dance in London given by Lady Ribblesdale, to which he, Mountbatten, had not been invited. This mere oversight was not a serious obstacle to the enterprising young officer and he persuaded another friend, who he knew had been invited, to ask the hostess if Dickie might also be included in the invitation list. It was a ploy he would use over and over throughout his life. He was never above asking to be invited somewhere if he felt it was important and useful for him to be there.

He was successful, as usual, and managed to find a quiet moment to remind the Prince of Wales that he had earlier agreed that Dickie should accompany him on the tour. The Prince there and then invited him to go along and, as Mountbatten afterwards wrote in his diary, 'Of course, I nearly jumped out of my skin for joy.'

When the formal invitation arrived it wasn't quite what Mountbatten had expected. Instead of being attached directly to the Prince of Wales's suite, as he had wished, he was appointed Flag Lieutenant to Rear-Admiral Sir Lionel Halsey, His Royal Highnesses' Chief of Staff. In theory this meant that he was supposed to be working as a junior officer looking after the administrative details the Admiral could not be bothered with.

In practice, it meant that for seven months he was 'minder' to the Prince of Wales; keeping him constantly amused, occupied and in a happy frame of mind. It was a role he relished as it gave him access to the Prince at all times, and not for the first or last time in his life, he would use the connection to go over the heads of colleagues who were senior to him both in years and rank.

Mountbatten's natural enthusiasm and self-confidence, coupled with his tender years, ensured that in the early days of the tour he made several enemies among those closest to the Prince of Wales. Most of them had accompanied him on his earlier tour of the United States and Canada, and they had formed themselves into a small clique that resented the interloper who was so familiar with their royal master and even called him by his Christian name. They knew that he had forced himself on to the Prince and, in the first instance, most of them felt he was not going to be of much practical use. However, it didn't take long for Mountbatten to establish himself as an integral and indispensable part of the team, and the others quickly realized that in him they had an ally to whom they could entrust all sorts of delicate tasks which protocol prevented them from carrying out themselves. He was also a useful sounding board about the Prince's moods and, from time to time, a buffer between them and his explosive and unpredictable temper.

It would not have made very much difference if they had tried to isolate Mountbatten from the 'inner circle'. Even at the age of nineteen he had an instinctive feel for power, and he knew that his unique friendship with the man destined to become the next King of England had placed him in an enviable position. It was an instinct that would serve him well throughout his life and for many years the knowledge that he was able – and willing – to go over the heads of the most senior members of the Royal Household, to the sovereign, made a great many people wary of upsetting him.

The tour was an outstanding success on all fronts. The Prince of Wales was the most glamorous young man in the world; the Empire was in the throes of euphoria after four years of war and he was welcomed with open arms wherever he went. Much of the glamour reflected on to his cousin, six years his junior, who was shrewd enough not to compete openly, but clever enough to be seen on every occasion as His Royal Highness's closest companion. They did everything together: riding, shooting, swimming and most of the informal photographs taken on the tour show the Prince of Wales and Mountbatten together, frequently just the two of them. They were almost like brothers and Mountbatten, in one of the many letters home to his mother, wrote, ' – he is my best friend'.

At the end of the seven-month voyage Mountbatten was to say that he had learnt a great deal, mainly through the extended circle of acquaintances he met and also because he had shown, in the public duties he had performed, that he was ready to assume further responsibilities. In other words he had served his apprenticeship; he knew the direction he wanted his career to take and the influential people he had met throughout the Commonwealth would be carefully filed away for future use.

Mountbatten said later that it was in India that he met the three great loves of his life: India itself, Edwina and the game of polo. He was first taught to play the game by his Indian hosts and it became his lifelong recreation and a passion he would pass on to both Prince Philip and Prince Charles. His book *Introduction to Polo*, written under the pseudonym 'Marco', remains the standard guide to the sport and has been reprinted many times.

It was shortly after this tour that the most important event in Mountbatten's life occurred. He married Edwina Ashley. He proposed to Edwina on St Valentine's Day 1922 in India and five months later, on 18 July, they were married at St Margaret's, Westminster, on a day when romance and royalty joined together for what was to be the grandest of weddings. The guest list revealed the widespread structure of the Mountbatten family and its interwoven connections with every royal house in Europe.

At twenty-two, Lord Louis Mountbatten was already a glamorous naval war veteran; his wife, the Hon. Edwina Cynthia Ashley, a year younger, was the daughter of Lord Mount Temple. More importantly she was also the granddaughter of Sir Ernest Cassel, and main beneficiary of his will. On her marriage she inherited a vast fortune which would enable her husband, while not changing the direction in which he had decided his life would go, to pursue it in a style to which he so easily became accustomed.

Even as a young man the extent of Mountbatten's world-wide connections with people from all walks of life became apparent when he and Edwina spent part of their honeymoon in Hollywood, staying at the home of Douglas Fairbanks Sr and Mary Pickford, and even acting in a private film, written and directed by Charlie Chaplin.

In spite of never having to work again if he chose not to, once he had married, Mountbatten decided to continue his naval career, with the full agreement of his wife. His new-found fortune made life as a peacetime officer in the twenties and thirties very pleasant indeed. He was able to indulge in a variety of expensive pastimes without having to rely solely on his service pay. However, in spite of his wealth, social position and royal connections, Mountbatten took his career seriously and worked as hard as he played. He made himself into an expert in radio communications at a time when the subject was highly unfashionable, and with his natural aptitude for languages he qualified easily as an interpreter in both French and German.

On the domestic front the Mountbattens' life appeared harmonious enough in those early years. Two children were born, Patricia in 1924 and her sister Pamela in 1929. But already the cracks in the marriage were beginning to show, with both partners indulging in the extramarital affairs which would litter the remainder of their lives together. A large part of the British Navy was based in the Mediterranean in the inter-war years, and Mountbatten spent a considerable time in this part of the world; years in which he was able to polish his talents as a polo player, scuba diver and water-skier. In 1932 he put his newly acquired technical skills to excellent use when, as Mediterranean Fleet Wireless Officer, he invented a system by which the whole fleet was able to listen to the first of King George V's historic Christmas broadcasts to the Empire.

By 1934 Mountbatten had been promoted to the rank of full Commander and taken over his first ship: the destroyer HMS *Daring*. It was an appropriate name. Some would say Mountbatten was reckless to the point of danger.

At the outbreak of the Second World War in 1939, he commanded a flotilla of destroyers – his own flagship being the ship with which he would for ever be identified: HMS *Kelly*. During the first two years of the war Mountbatten established his reputation as a fearless if at times reckless naval hero. While his men adored him, some of his fellow officers were less complimentary, claiming he lacked basic seamanship and put himself and his ships at risk unnecessarily. It was during the battle of Crete that he lost his ship to a massive dive-bomber attack.

Mountbatten had been given command of the aircraft carrier HMS *Illustrious* but while he was on a public relations tour of the United States, before taking over his new ship, he was recalled to Britain to be informed that he had been appointed Chief of Combined Operations. He was responsible for mounting commando raids on the coasts of German-occupied Europe, one of which, the frontal assault on Dieppe, was to haunt him for the rest of his life. The raid was a gigantic failure, but an invaluable experience for the success of D-Day, and among the casualties the heaviest losses were of Canadian infantry, for which Lord Beaverbrook blamed Mountbatten solely. He would never let him forget the incident – or forgive him.

A vice-admiral at forty-two, Mountbatten was one of Winston Churchill's closest military advisers, and in 1943 he was offered the post of Supreme Allied Commander, South East Asia, directing the war against Japan. His responsibilities included harnessing the skills of various Commonwealth forces with those of the United States and keeping in check the brilliant but volatile talents of commanders such as General Orde Wingate and the American General 'Vinegar Joe' Stillwell. For two years Mountbatten planned the strategy of what had been the 'Forgotten Army' in Burma and his jungle tactics ended in total victory for the Allies. His proudest moment was when he formally accepted the Japanese surrender in Singapore in 1945, and then began the massive task of rebuilding the structure of the former Japanese-occupied countries of the Far East. It was an experience which would stand him in good stead for his next major appointment.

Mountbatten's peacetime public service began in 1947 when the then Prime Minister Clement Attlee persuaded him to become India's last Viceroy, with the specific task of arranging independence for the country. He did so in five months, having reluctantly to agree to the partition of the sub-continent and bringing into existence the countries of India and Pakistan. It also brought about the greatest bloodshed in India's history – part of the blame for which has been laid at Mountbatten's door. The Indians loved him while for most of the Pakistan population he remains a hated and reviled figure. He became India's first Governor General, for less than a year, but Pakistan would not accept him in that role.

Returning to his naval career Mountbatten went back to the Mediterranean as commander of a cruiser squadron, before becoming Fourth Sea Lord and then Commander-in-Chief of the Mediterranean Allied Fleet. It was perhaps the happiest time of his life; he played polo, enjoyed a hectic social life and Malta, where his headquarters and his home were for several years, had always been one of his favourite places.

It was in 1955 that the crowning moment in his career came when Winston Churchill, in one of his final acts as Prime Minister, chose Mountbatten to be First Sea Lord, nearly half a century after offering his father the same post. It was the proudest event in a lifetime of brilliant achievements, surpassing even his appointment four years later as Chief of the Defence Staff.

By the time of Edwina's sudden death in 1960, she and her husband had reached an amicable arrangement. They no longer rowed constantly and were looking forward to a companionable old age together. Her death came as a great shock and he felt the loss deeply.

In 1965 he retired from active duty in the Royal Navy, though as an Admiral of the Fleet he remained on the active list until the day he died.

As an official 'civilian' Mountbatten continued in the public eye. Harold Wilson asked him to conduct an enquiry into prison security after the escape of the Russian spy George Blake, and the Queen appointed him Governor of the Isle of Wight, a post he treated as seriously as he did that of being Viceroy of India. His love of ceremonial and dress uniforms came to the fore when he was invited to become Colonel of the Life Guards – the senior regiment of the British Army – and he enjoyed few things more than riding behind the Queen at the Trooping the Colour Ceremony during the Sovereign's Birthday Parade.

Mountbatten continued to travel throughout the world even when well into his seventies as President of United World Colleges, an office he eventually handed over to his great-nephew, Prince Charles. And at the time of his assassination in 1979, he was preparing for a visit to India with the Prince of Wales later that year.

Mountbatten was seventy-nine when he was killed; standing at the wheel of his own boat. The sea was his first love and if he had to die in such a dramatic fashion, perhaps this was the way he would have chosen.

5

RELATIONSHIPS

'Dickie loved to look at the menu but he rarely ate the main course.' The words are those of Douglas Fairbanks Jr, himself one of the world's great lovers, and the man who arranged many of Mountbatten's introductions to Hollywood's biggest female stars. Mountbatten loved the company of beautiful women and whenever he was in the United States he usually relied on Fairbanks to provide him with the entrée when he wanted to meet someone special in the film world. Rita Hayworth was undoubtedly one of the world's most beautiful women, pursued by princes and potentates. Among her husbands was Prince Aly Khan, the leading playboy of his era, and she enjoyed the attentions of some of the most powerful and influential men on earth. She was a natural target for Mountbatten and there was a mutual attraction between these two superstars. Miss Hayworth had a reputation as a passionate lover and Fairbanks naturally expected that the evening would end in bed but, on this occasion at least, it didn't happen. Their relationship ended at the bedroom door.

Patricia Mountbatten remembers a time when she was at school in America during the war and her father came to visit: 'We were in New York and my parents came out on duty and took me with them to the West Coast where we stayed with Doug Fairbanks Jr. He gave a dance for us and as it was my first grown-up ball I was absolutely petrified. Anyway, Rita Hayworth was there and my father danced with her all evening. He loved dancing and of course she had been a professional so he had a marvellous time.' Mountbatten always had an eye for the girls and he certainly did not lead a blameless life, but many of his so-called lovers were really no more than casual girlfriends with whom he went out to lunch or dinner. He had one or two long-standing serious relationships which his family knew about but nowhere near the number that some people believed.

He liked the chase and enjoyed winning over any woman he fancied, but in real terms he was just an outrageous flirt who rarely carried his conquests to the ultimate end. Sex was something he loved to talk about, and listen to others talking about. Nothing was sacrosanct in his conversations about sex. He was immensely turned on by the idea and enjoyed mild pornography. But he was more a voyeur than a participant, and if others wanted to believe that he was a great lover he was delighted for them to do so. He never corrected the impression that he bedded all the women he knew – neither did he boast of his conquests, and there were quite a number of successful relationships which were complete on all levels.

Promiscuity was something that was foreign to his nature and while he preferred lasting relationships which might or might not be physical, with Edwina the opposite was the case. For her, physical attraction was strongest in the initial stages; the relationship came later and was usually a poor second. Mountbatten had taken an interest in girls since the age of eighteen and in letters to his mother he was always telling her of his latest conquest. Obviously a romantically inclined young man, he went into raptures over practically every girl he met, telling his mother her had fallen in love with 'Marjorie', 'Peggy' and 'Mary' in rapid succession – and out of love just as quickly. He wrote in the most glowing terms of all these young ladies but when he feared that his mother might have heard that he was going to marry 'Peggy' he quickly put her fears at rest: 'Don't worry at all,' he wrote, 'as the idea of marriage has never entered either of our very young brains, but personally (except for the financial point of view) I couldn't look for a better wife anywhere in years to come.' Later on, Mountbatten writes a very lengthy letter extolling 'Peggy's' virtues: 'She is the most ripping girl . . . and I do love her most frightfully. Her father is a retired colonel from the Indian army and therefore, although they live in a very nice house, cannot possess superfluous amounts of money.' He goes on to say that he has now complied with the wishes of Peggy's father to stop seeing her in order to put an end to the gossip, but he adds that he is very miserable and wished he could have married her. The following month he again wrote to his mother claiming to have fallen in love with someone called 'Poppy'.

Three months later, in December 1919, he met the girl who would undoubtedly have become his wife if he had not hesitated and then left her for long periods when he joined the Prince of Wales on a tour of India. Audrey James was the most serious of Mountbatten's early loves and he pursued her at dances, dinner parties and society functions of every variety. In a letter to his mother in December 1919 he admitted his infatuation: 'Mama you simply cannot conceive how lovely she is. Beats anything I have ever seen to a fraggle [*sic*] . . . She gets £4,000 a year from what her father has left her . . . keeps two houses . . . and has a maid and footman of her own, and yet she is unspoilt.' However, in the same letter he lets on that he feels Audrey's mother is trying to match them and he says: 'I am no longer quite a fool, nor am I blind, I am not going to be caught.' Yet he concludes in a masterpiece of contradiction: 'I'd give anything to be married to her.'

Within two weeks of meeting Audrey they were engaged, against the wishes of Mountbatten's mother who did not approve in the least: 'You are far too young and poor, Dickie,' she wrote. The love affair and engagement lasted for nearly a year during most of which Mountbatten was abroad with his cousin Davi, the Prince of Wales. When he arrived back in Britain in October 1920 he found that his fiancée had broken off the engagement, preferring the attentions of someone even wealthier than she, even if he didn't have a title and wasn't related to the Royal Family. The name of Audrey James's new man was Dudley Coats, of the Lancashire cotton family, and it was said that Audrey had chosen the arms of Coats over the coats of arms.

Mountbatten was not used to being dumped by a woman; it was usually the other way round, and he didn't like it at all. But being one of the most eligible bachelors in the country he soon found plenty of comfort elsewhere and within a short time he was to meet the woman who was to share his life for thirty-eight years. Mountbatten's choice of a wife was of vital importance to his future plans. None of the available European princesses was considered suitable: even though the blood was rich enough, the pockets were not.

If he was to concentrate on his naval career, Dickie realized that a man needed to be of independent means. His own modest finances would not be sufficient to see him comfortably off for the rest of his life. And he had already decided that, come what may, the Royal Navy was where his future lay: not only to avenge the humiliations his father had suffered in the First World War – he always denied that this was part of his motivation – but because he had a genuine love of the sea and a burning ambition to reach the top. From an early age Mountbatten had realized that his own limited income was never going to be enough to keep a family, so in nearly all his relationships he made it his business to find out the extent of his girlfriends' wealth – or at least their expectations!

Edwina Ashley fulfilled every requirement as a Mountbatten wife. Even though right up until the time they were married she lived on an allowance of just £300 a year, everyone knew that Edwina's grandfather, Sir Ernest Cassel, was worth millions, but no one, including Dickie Mountbatten, realized just how large that fortune was, or that Edwina's share would be around £3 million.

When he discovered just how large his future wife's fortune was going to be, Mountbatten had some reservations about going through with the marriage. The massive difference in their financial status caused him to reflect that he might be seen by his friends and colleagues as a 'kept man'. Even his mother warned him of the possible consequences of marrying someone so much wealthier than himself.

Apart from her money, Edwina was also perfect in almost every other way. She was beautiful, and Dickie, with the best will in the world, could never have contemplated marrying a plain woman, no matter how large her dowry. He was far too used to the company of some of the most glamorous and elegant women in the country and even the prospect of unlimited wealth would not have been enough to compensate for spending his life with someone who did not have good looks. Throughout his life Mountbatten would be drawn to attractive people, and if they had money, so much the better.

Another of Edwina's positive qualities was her intelligence. She was one of the cleverest women of her generation and a number of people who knew them both, claimed that she was far the brighter of the two. During the Second World War an American general said, 'She is so smart she scares me.'

The third and most important element in the match was that Edwina and Dickie were very much in love; their marriage was in no way an arranged event. But even if it had been, there could not have been a better match.

Mountbatten brought to the Ashley family an entrée to the inner circle of royalty, one that would carry through to the present generation.

She, of course, provided the money which would enable her husband to live the life he had always desired – but had never before been able to afford.

In some ways Dickie got the better bargain. Edwina was never terribly impressed with royalty, as her grandfather had been. Her relations with the Royal Family on a personal level were always cordial, but Dickie could never understand her indifference to titles or her failure to be overawed by his grand relations in the royal houses of Europe. With her this indifference was not assumed; she simply did not think rank was important, though her own servants were never left in any doubt about their respective positions.

Edwina and Dickie's courtship was conducted at lightning speed among the aristocracy of Britain in the twenties. They found themselves on the same guest lists at country house weekends and at parties in some of London's most fashionable houses. When Dickie was invited to spend ten days cruising with the mega-rich Vanderbilts along the coasts of France and Belgium, he managed without too much difficulty, to persuade his hosts to invite Edwina along too.

Their friends were all in favour of the match. As Dickie was regarded as the second most eligible bachelor in the country (his cousin the Prince of Wales occupying first place), and Edwina the most eligible heiress, everyone thought they would make an ideal couple. She gave him finanaical independence, he gave her a status which, while she had never particularly sought it, she nevertheless gladly accepted and enjoyed.

Mountbatten proposed to Edwina in India where she had joined him during his 1921 tour as aide to the Prince of Wales. This was the tour where it was suggested that both the Prince and Mountbatten thought that the British Empire had been invented just for their personal entertainment. It was during this time, however, that Mountbatten first discovered his love for the country; a love that was to be consummated some twenty-five years later when he and Edwina would return as Viceroy and Vicereine.

The young Louis had the tendency to suggest that the British authorities should talk to Ghandi to convince him that 'we should be friends'. It was never to be. The official viewpoint was that Ghandi was nothing but a troublemaker and discussion was dismissed as an outrageous and radical suggestion of the sort only a Socialist would countenance. Some considered Mountbatten's idea to be treasonable. Such was the blinkered opinion that controlled a major part of the British Empire at the time.

Edwina, even at this early stage of their forty-year relationship, fully supported her future husband in his views. Her own political beliefs, then and in the years to come, would find favour much more with the left than with the ultra-conservative right, with which most people of her class identified.

One aspect of his forthcoming marriage that pleased Mountbatten particularly was that the Prince of Wales thoroughly approved of Edwina. His Royal Highness took to her from the moment they first met and she, with her natural grace, exquisite looks and spontaneous and unaffected sense of humour, was a delightful asset at every function she attended with her fiancé.

Dickie proposed at a St Valentine's Day dance on 14 February 1922. He was reasonably sure of a favourable reply as they had both declared their love for each other many times, and it was only because of the death of his father and her grandfather, shortly before Dickie left for India, that he had not proposed earlier.

King George V had given his approval, though strictly speaking Dickie was so far down the line of succession that it was a mere formality. But Dickie liked to think he had to ask the sovereign, and as usual his request was received with due courtesy and replied to with grace. The icing on the wedding cake for Dickie came in the form of the Prince of Wales agreeing to act as best man, thus ensuring that this truly would be the wedding of the year.

As Edwina was still only twenty, and legally a minor, she too had to have permission to marry. But her father was perfectly willing and happily provided her with an affidavit to this effect to show when she applied for the marriage licence. (Dickie was still in India and she undertook most of the arrangements until he returned.)

Twelve hundred guests were invited to the wedding at St Margaret's, Westminster. Sir Ernest Cassel's former secretary, Miss Underhill, had been seconded to Mountbatten for several weeks to help with the mass of administrative details leading up to the ceremony. She dealt with most of the invitations, except those to royalty, 'which, of course, had to be sent by Lord Louis himself personally'.

Mountbatten took charge of all the arrangements, using his recent organizing experience as a member of the Prince of Wales's entourage in India to promote his claims to be the recognized authority on matters of protocol. Actually there was no one to dispute his authority and, in fairness, his claims were fully justified, as his legendary attention to detail was already becoming an integral part of his character. With the attendance of the King and Queen, Queen Alexandra, the Queen Mother, the Princess Royal, the Prince of Wales and his brothers plus many other members of the Royal Family and most of Europe's remaining royalty. Mountbatten was determined that nothing was going to go wrong.

Edwina quickly learned that her future husband's temper could flare up at the slightest provocation, usually when someone, including herself, did not obey his instructions to the letter, or did not react fast enough to his demands, or he felt someone was being obstructive to his wishes. Mountbatten did not tolerate mistakes – in others or himself.

As the day of the wedding approached, the Cassel mansion, Brook House, became the receiving centre for an avalanche of presents that arrived from all over the world. Princes and potentates, millionaires and maharajas, all vied with each other to shower gifts on the couple who apparently had everything. One or two used their imagination in selecting their presents while several evidently thought the couple might encounter stormy weather at some time in the future as no fewer than twenty-four umbrellas found their way on to the display that was arranged in the ballroom at Brook House.

One thing that Mountbatten was not required to provide for his bride was a home. No doubt King George V would have been delighted to grant the couple a grace-and-favour apartment at Kensington Palace if necessary, but the need did not arise. Along with the Cassel millions, Edwina had inherited Brook House, the massive five-storey residence on the corner of Park Lane and Upper Brook Street that her grandfather had bought in 1905 from Lord Tweedmouth – though he did not move in until 1908.

It took three years of non-stop work, using materials brought from all over Europe, to bring the house up to the standard Sir Ernest demanded. This included installing a heavy hydraulic lift for luggage, several passenger lifts, six kitchens, twelve bathrooms and a Turkish bath. The grand entrance in Park Lane was lined with lapis lazuli and marble, as were the main hall, staircase and first floor gallery. Some eight hundred tons of white marble had been imported from Italy for the purpose.

Massive Corinthian pillars rose from the ground-floor to the various levels of gallery and illumination was provided by hundreds of bronze electric lamps, brought specially from Rome. The house also boasted one of the first telephone systems in London – long before Buckingham Palace felt it necessary to do so.

Visitors climbing the grand staircase to one of the vast receptions rooms found themselves facing, on the first landing, a portrait of their host's great friend, King Edward VII. Many years later this same portrait was so admired by King George VI that he asked if he might have it. Edwina, who was never intimidated by royalty, refused but offered to have a copy made for His Majesty, which was accepted. The original now stands in the drawing room of Ashley Hick's house in Chelsea.

Brook House was among the grandest private houses in London and was certainly the finest whose interior had been mainly rebuilt this century (the original house was built in 1850). In spite of the acres of white marble that greeted the eye at the entrance, it still retained the gloomy atmosphere of so many mid-Victorian houses. It was more like a mausoleum than a home. Edwina had never been particularly fond of it, and when the house was demolished in 1936 she shed no tears. But she accepted that, on her marriage, it would become the home that she and her husband would occupy. They shared it with Sir Ernest Cassel's sister, who had been granted permission to live there for the rest of her life. She occupied two floors, with Edwina and Dickie having the rest of the house to themselves.

Edwina, who loved bright colours, was determined to stamp her own personality on Brook House. She ripped out most of the dark panelling in several rooms and replaced it with colour schemes of her own choice, mainly pinks and light blues.

Now that money was no object, Mountbatten was able to alter his own rooms to reflect his tastes, which meant a return to naval austerity. He took over Miss Underhill's office and transformed it into an exact replica of his cabin aboard ship. The walls and ceiling were lined with cork which had been sprayed with white enamel to give it a suitably metallic appearance. The ceiling was lowered and ship's ducting installed, carpets were removed and the bed replaced with a bunk made to the exact dimensions of a regulation officer's bunk, complete with brass handrail to prevent the occupant falling out in rough weather. The windows were replaced with portholes, through which electric fans blew realistic 'sea breezes' into the 'cabin'. One wall was taken out to make room for a view of the Grand Harbour in Malta which, by means of a switch, could be transformed from daylight to moonlight in an instant.

Edwina presented Dickie with a fleet of miniature warships in each of which she had rigged signalling lights which transmitted real Morse-code messages devised by Mountbatten. A tiny generator gave out the gentle hum of turbine engines so that Dickie could feel he really was back at sea, and his desk contained charts and weather reports to make him feel truly at home. There was only one slightly jarring note in what was otherwise a standard naval officer's cabin. Mountbatten had installed a full-size model of an admiral in full-dress uniform in one corner and in another, in a glass case, were displayed his father's decorations, hat and uniform.

The nautical theme was continued in Mountbatten's bathroom which was decorated as if it were under water, with rocks, seaweed, shells and fish painted on every surface.

Mountbatten loved his private suite and proudly showed distinguished visitors such as Mary Pickford, George Gershwin, Noel Coward, Sophie Tucker and Gertrude Lawrence how each of his 'toys' worked. They found nothing strange in his choice of décor. As members of a profession where eccentricity was regarded as the norm, they fully appreciated and approved of any sign of individuality in others. Edwina was amused by her husband's taste but rarely ventured out of her own boudoir to join Dickie 'at sea'.

Very early in their marriage Edwina discovered that Mountbatten had no great interest in sex. He liked the idea of it, but on a sentimental rather than physically passionate level. And, strangely, considering the number of affairs she had with men who were known for their love-making prowess, Edwina was not all that keen either.

She embarked on her career of infidelity within three years of being married, but years later, when Mountbatten knew all about and had, albeit reluctantly, accepted her lapses, her one-time lover, Bunny Phillips, told him that Edwina did not enjoy making love. It must have been an unusual conversation between the two men, one of whom was married to the other's mistress. Not many men would care to discuss their wife's performance in bed with someone who had had more recent and frequent experience with her.

If Mountbatten's straying from the marital path could be said to have been caused by his unhappiness over her infidelity, Edwina's was because of frustration with her husband, and not physical frustration. What infuriated her was his constant demands for attention. He was arguably the most self-centred man who ever lived and wanted Edwina to share all his enthusiasms and ambitions. He saw no reason why she should want a life of her own and anything she did that excluded him made him unhappy. If there was something that fired his imagination or caught his interest, he could not understand why it should not attract her attention in the same way. In his view wives were there to play a supporting role to their husbands and had no need of a separate life.

In Edwina he had obviously picked the wrong woman. She wanted her husband to do well, but she wanted him to do it without involving her. She had her own interests and soon began to feel claustrophobic at his persistent intrusions into what she regarded as the private side of her life.

Mountbatten had always had a wonderful relationship with his mother who supported her son in everything he did, and to whom he confided everything; all his hopes, dreams and ambitions. Now he expected the same unqualified devotion from his wife. She, however, was unable or unwilling to give it. It was a recipe for disaster and the miracle was that they had a marriage that would last until Edwina died in 1960, albeit with varying degrees of stability and mutual affection.

Mountbatten was enchanted by Edwina and never lost his love through all the years of unhappiness she caused him. For her part, even though she recognized his greatness and felt tremendous pride in his achievements, she could easily be irritated by him and for much of their married life her attitude to him was one of resigned tolerance.

If Edwina found comfort in the arms of other men, Mountbatten, who was monogamous by nature, was reluctant to stray from the marital bed, yet when he did so he could never understand why anyone would be shocked. He was almost childlike in his attitude to the opposite sex. He was completely amoral in that he never thought he was doing anything wrong; he rarely even considered the moral aspect of his indiscretions. One of his favourite sayings, regarding his relationships with women, was 'as long as no one gets hurt', by which he really meant 'as long as nobody finds out'.

Patricia Mountbatten knew exactly the sort of woman who attracted her father: 'They had to be youngish, very pretty with long legs and a small waist – rather Victorian figures really. Girls didn't have to be intelligent either. He could be quite attracted to someone who wasn't that bright, if it was going to be just a minor flirtation, but all his real, serious girlfriends were intelligent.'

Among the women with whom Mountbatten had relationships two stood out. One was Yola Letellier, who was certainly the most enduring. Their love affair started in the 1920s, shortly after Mountbatten first discovered his wife's infidelity, and continued for over forty years. The other was Sacha, Duchess of Abercorn. She was his goddaughter, and her father, Lieutenant Colonel Harold (Bunny) Phillips, was Edwina's lover for some years, and the only man Mountbatten ever considered a serious rival for his wife's affections.

Yola Letellier was the woman to whom Mountbatten was devoted for much of his life. She was a glamorous, typically Parisian young woman who was the prototype for Gigi, whose life was portrayed in the film of the same name and played by Leslie Caron. The love affair between Mountbatten and Yola started as a grand passion, developed into a regular liaison and then settled down into a cosy relationship and finally a lifelong friendship.

It began in 1926 at just about the time that Mountbatten first found out that his wife was playing away from home. The discovery came as a tremendous shock and he was devastated, particularly as it soon became apparent that he was the last to know. Edwina moved in a set in which there were few constraints; if someone wanted to go to bed with someone else, married or not, a blind eye was turned. The only rule was that the press should not find out. Even in those days there was an avid interest in the nocturnal affairs of the rich and famous and society formed itself into a self-protective group to preserve to the outside world the impression that all was respectability among the upper classes.

Mountbatten met Yola Letellier, a young woman of great physical beauty, during one of his periodic visits to play polo in Deauville in northern France. In those days it was one of the great playgrounds of the British who could afford it, with its elegant hotels, fashionable restaurants and casinos. Henri Letellier, Yola's husband, one of France's most successful newspaper owners, had been Major of Deauville no fewer than eight times, though when Mountbatten first encountered Yola he mistakenly took her for the wife of a local hotelier. The error probably came about when he asked who she was and confused her name Letellier with 'l'hotelier'. He was a little put out that such a beauty could belong to so lowly a class, not for any snobbish reasons but just because she was so beautiful he had imagined she must be an aristocrat. Even so, he was smitten, and would have been no matter who or what she was.

The relationship developed rapidly. Yola's husband was many years older than she, and Mountbatten found in her a companion who became the most understanding woman in his life. There was an immediate chemistry and they became very close almost at once. Yola made few demands on Mountbatten. She seemed to understand perfectly his frustration and impatience and, like the perfect mistress she was said to be (though she never admitted it), she never once tried to displace Edwina.

Theirs was an affair that lasted for more than forty years during which time the Mountbattens and the Letelliers all became friendly. The acquiescent Henri Letellier knew all about his young wife's affection for Mountbatten, and when Edwina found out about it she acted in a way which some wives might have found difficult to understand. 'She went and made a friend of Yola herself,' recalls Patricia Mountbatten, 'which was nice in a way but also a bit naughty because by doing so she made it very difficult for my father. It was all right for her to have her own boyfriend, but she wasn't so keen on my father having his girlfriend. She suffered from this dreadful jealousy all her life and even when she didn't want him herself she still hated the thought of him with anyone else.'

In 1938, Mountbatten played in a polo tournament in Jamaica. There to watch him were Edwina and Yola together. How he managed to divide his time between them is still a mystery.

Edwina could be mischievous and on more than one occasion Mountbatten would make arrangements to see Yola, only to find when he arrived that Edwina had beaten him to it and had whisked Yola off somewhere else. He actually accused her once of trying to take Yola away from him. She replied, 'Nothing is further from my mind or intentions. Yola and I simply found there was something that both of us wanted to do at the same time.'

It is difficult to overestimate the importance of the part Yola Letellier played in Mountbatten's life. He never tried to hide his feelings for her from anyone in the family and all his colleagues knew about the relationship. Even when he was Chief of the Defence Staff with enormous responsibilities he would find time for her. Whenever he had official business in Paris, he and his valet would stay at her flat, described as 'cosy but not opulent. Typically French with lots of red velvet and crimson silk.' Their evenings would be spent either alone in the flat or at discreet dinner parties arranged by friends. Occasionally they would visit the theatre but Mountbatten's time was limited and usually he would end up working on his papers for the next day's programme before they went to bed.

Yola Letellier became a family friend to all the Mountbatten's. She spent weekends and holidays at Broadlands and Classiebawn and when she visited London she always stayed with Mountbatten. Even the Royal Family were aware of Yola's special position and Mountbatten's valet said that when Christmas presents were being chosen Yola took second place only to the Queen. Mountbatten would design special gifts for Yola and he went to endless trouble to make sure that pieces of jewellery he bought for her had the letter 'Y' engraved on them, based on the drawings he sent to the suppliers.

But Mountbatten never gave any indication that he wanted to marry Yola, even after Edwina's death. His wife had made him promise that he would not marry Yola if he should outlive her, but the promise was not necessary. Mountbatten did not really want to remarry. A comment he made to John Barratt about Sacha Abercorn being a possible bride meant simply that she was the type of person he could have married, not that he was thinking seriously of a proposal. Her pedigree is as impeccable as any aristocrat could ask for. Sacha's grandparents, Sir Harold and Lady Zia Wernher, were among the Queen's and Prince Philip's closest friends, she was always a welcome guest at Broadlands, and eventually became Mountbatten's closest companion.

The Duchess of Abercorn is a woman of outstanding appearance. Tall, slim and stunningly good-looking, she has a figure that belies that fact that she is the mother of three children. Her blond hair, blue eyes and cool elegance, matched by a warm personality, deep intelligence and infectious sense of fun, make her the sort of woman who was bound to attract Mountbatten. What is not so obvious is how the feelings of a godfather for a child he first saw at her christening could develop after twenty years or so into a love on an entirely different level.

Sacha does not remember much about him when she was a child, apart from the fact that he was 'a rather daunting figure'. It was some years later, when she was in her late teens, that she came back into his life. Before that she had been just one of Mountbatten's thirty godchildren. By the time she was twenty-one she had married James, Marquess of Hamilton, heir to the Duke of Abercorn, whose family estate is at

Barons Court in Northern Ireland, not many miles over the border from Classiebawn. Sacha says that Mountbatten welcomed the marriage because 'He thoroughly approved of dukes.' Apart from that obvious advantage, Mountbatten found he also liked James enormously and they became firm friends in the ten years that followed.

Mountbatten and Sacha had become close in the years leading up to her marriage but it was after she became Marchioness of Hamilton (before her husband inherited the dukedom) that the relationship blossomed into the deep and lasting love that caused Mountbatten to reflect to his secretary, John Barratt, that she was the only woman he could ever have contemplated marrying after Edwina. He had professed love for many women but said he had never considered marriage to any of them – except Sacha.

She says he never told her this but that if he had asked her to marry him when she was single, she might well have said yes. The future Duke of Abercorn had known throughout of his wife's special bond with Mountbatten and he, with a rare insight, fully understood the delicate nature of the relationship. He never tried to separate them and with an even rarer sensitivity gave them what she describes as 'the space necessary to cultivate a unique rapport'.

Sacha continued to be a frequent visitor to Broadlands where she and her septuagenarian godfather would spend hours alone together, walking in the grounds and riding in the park. Sacha had learned to ride as a girl but hadn't kept it up and Mountbatten took over her tuition. She says, 'He was a wonderful tutor and liked nothing better than showing someone – anyone – how to do something.' As it happens, he wasn't the best person to teach her, or anyone else, riding. He was a competent horseman, but nothing more. As a young man he had been courageous to a fault but as a technician he had his limitations.

The staff at Broadlands all liked Sacha and they loved having her in the house because Mountbatten always perked up when she was around. If he was feeling down or a bit irritable, a telephone call saying she was on her way was guaranteed to cheer him up and the atmosphere throughout the house improved accordingly. The other members of Mountbatten's family also made her welcome. She had known them for most of her life and even Patricia, who might have been expected to harbour some feelings of resentment towards her because of her own special bond with her father, showed no animosity at all. There was nothing but love and friendship in the feelings of the Mountbatten clan towards this young woman who was obviously bringing Lord Louis such happiness.

Sacha says that when she came back into Mountbatten's life as a young woman there was an immediate chemistry between them. 'It was a huge physical and spiritual attraction on both sides and the fifty-year gap in our ages just melted away.'

Mountbatten at seventy was still a commanding figure; only slightly stooping, firm-jawed and with a full head of hair, even if it was now silver. He invited Sacha to partner him on many occasions when he was invited to functions. The artist Derek Hill says that Mountbatten took Sacha to the opening of one of his exhibitions where they were 'easily the most attractive couple in the room' – though apparently, at first, few would have guessed that they were anything but what they appeared to be, an uncle with his favourite niece.

While Sacha disregarded the generation gap between them, Mountbatten was all too aware of the passage of time. On several occasions when they were alone he spoke about his fears of getting old and senile. 'It was obviously something that worried him a lot and I think the fear of becoming slow and incapacitated gnawed at him as the years went by.'

The complicated entanglements that had plagued both the Mountbattens' love lives continued after Sacha married. His earlier relationship with Yola Letellier had extended to include Edwina in the friendship. Her long-standing love affair with Sacha's father, Bunny Phillips, who assisted Mountbatten in arranging some of Yola's financial affairs, had little effect on the two men's friendship. Mountbatten had always been fond of Bunny, whom he called 'the rabbit' in letters to Edwina, and they remained on the best of terms throughout the affair.

Sacha's mother, Gina (now Lady Kennard), had known both Edwina and Dickie all her life and she was actually told by Edwina that she should marry Bunny. Luckily, Lady Kennard is not a jealous woman so she was not in the least concerned about her husband's past relationship with the woman she had always called Aunt Edwina. After they married she and Bunny became great friends with both Mountbattens and went to stay with them in India. But at the time of their engagement Edwina had been stunned by the news. So was Mountbatten himself. When he heard that Bunny and Gina were engaged he wrote to Edwina saying,

'My darling sweet – what a shock for you all the same.' Mountbatten had at one stage offered to divorce Edwina so that she could marry Bunny. He wrote: 'I had intended . . . to offer to make it easy for you.'

On the subject of her daughter's relationship with Uncle Dickie, Gina Kennard is equally philosophical: 'I am not judgemental about other people, even my own children. All I want is for them to be happy. How they find that happiness is up to them.'

Mountbatten took an extraordinary interest in Sacha's marital affairs and when she and her husband were experiencing difficulties, Mountbatten appointed himself their marriage guidance counsellor. He talked to them both about their problems and advised them that in order to save the marriage they should obey a set of rules that he devised. He saw nothing unusual in his involvement.

Sacha says the fact that she was married made no difference at all to Mountbatten: 'He actually preferred married women as they were safer. He knew it could go only so far and that's what he wanted. No permanent commitment.' In this respect he was exactly like his cousin and one-time best friend, the Duke of Windsor, who was never known to date a single woman in his life.

Sacha says she loved Mountbatten deeply and believes he loved her but she was not 'in love' with him. 'It wasn't the great passion one reads about, but a mutual affection and respect.' Their relationship lasted for more than ten years and survived the birth of Sacha's three children. She says now that Mountbatten gave her a confidence in herself that had previously been missing. 'He was such a powerful figure – with no doubts at all about himself – that some of it must have rubbed off. I know I became a much stronger person through knowing him,' she says.

Theirs was in many ways the perfect understanding. They would go for weeks without seeing each other, but speaking on the telephone practically every day. Then he would demand to see her, and she never refused. There was no permanent commitment on either side, so Mountbatten never threatened the Abercorn marriage, and each was there to fulfil the other's needs as and when required.

They attended many formal occasions including functions at Buckingham Palace, and on one memorable weekend they were together in Paris where they met Mountbatten's oldest flame, Yola Letellier. There was no rancour or jealousy on anyone's part; it was all highly civilized. Sacha says it was also the first time she had experienced what it was like to travel with someone like Mountbatten. 'We drove from the centre of

Paris out to the airport in record time. Our car had police outriders to clear the road ahead and every traffic light was held just for us. Uncle Dickie was used to it of course. It happened all the time. But for me it was quite exhilarating.'

Luckily for Mountbatten he did not have a jealous bone in his body and he could never understand why anyone should show this emotion. He saw nothing unusual in inviting several of his girlfriends to parties at the same time. They were nearly all married anyway, so as far as he was concerned there was no problem.

Occasionally Sacha, together with her husband James, would be invited to one of the Mountbatten houses when other guests included either past or current girlfriends. The thought that this might seem strange didn't even occur to him – or apparently to anyone else either. Their circle employed a curious code of manners whereby liaisons which everyone knew about were completely ignored. It was as if Mountbatten, if not the others, was still living in Victorian times, at least in terms of moral behaviour. This meant that it did not matter what one got up to in private, as long as on the surface nothing was apparent. Relationships came and went – marriages survived.

Everyone knew that Mountbatten loved to show off and enjoyed few things more than dressing up to be admired in one of his many splendid uniforms. Sacha recalled the occasion of Princess Anne's first wedding in 1973. At that time her London home was just around the corner from Buckingham Palace and shortly before the ceremony Mountbatten turned up on the doorstep wearing full ceremonial uniform, bedecked in medals, decorations and sashes. She says he looked magnificent – and knew it! During the Royal Family's obligatory appearance on the balcony of Buckingham Palace, Sacha decided to dash around to the front and see Mountbatten in his finery. She was in the midst of thousands of people all waving frantically to the group on the balcony but she could not see Dickie. Eventually she arrived back home to be told by her housekeeper that he had been telephoning constantly asking if he could come around. So while she had been looking for him at the Palace, he had forgone the opportunity of staying on the balcony, choosing instead to find a back room so that he could ring her.

Sacha Abercorn is also able to dispel the rumour that surrounded much of Mountbatten's love life, but was only mentioned in the press after he was dead – that he was homosexual. 'He never gave the slightest indication of being interested in that kind of activity,' she says, 'although several of his friends were homosexual. He wasn't bothered about other people's sexuality or behaviour. But I really do think he would have found it distasteful himself.'

Mountbatten's former Private Secretary, John Barratt, who died in November 1993, was homosexual and when I met him one of the first items of information he volunteered was that he was gay. He also emphatically refuted the accusation that Mountbatten was of the same sexual persuasion, saying, 'If anyone was in a position to know I was. I told him very early on that I was gay, even though I was married with two daughters, and he said that as long as it never interfered with my job it didn't bother him. Nothing ever bothered him about anyone else's sexual activities. He felt it was their business entirely and nothing to do with him.'

For years rumours had been circulating that Barratt was not merely a secretary but also Mountbatten's lover, and certainly in the latter years of Mountbatten's life John Barratt became his closest companion. He drove Mountbatten everywhere (mainly, he said, because he was terrified whenever his boss got behind the wheel), cooked his supper, helped to choose the clothes he would wear, and generally acted as a combination of secretary, valet and chauffeur. But Barratt insisted they were not lovers and when they discussed the rumours Mountbatten told him to disregard them: 'You and I know they are not true and that's what counts.' Accusations that he was homosexual plagued Mountbatten throughout his life, starting in the 1920s when he and Edwina knew, and were friends with, a number of known homosexual men and several lesbian women.

When he was at Cambridge Mountbatten had become close friends with a charming Irishman named Peter Murphy, a man who did nothing to hide his homosexuality. He and Mountbatten remained close until Murphy's death and throughout his life Mountbatten was aware of Murphy's various flings with men. These never affected their friendship and as far as Mountbatten's family and former staff are concerned, there was never anything more than a lasting but strictly platonic friendship between the two men.

Murphy's role in the Mountbatten household was never clearly defined. An ex-Guards officer with a brilliant mind, his left-wing tendencies found sympathy with Edwina, with whom he became just as friendly as he was with her husband. He acted as an unofficial aide to them both and he was around during all Mountbatten's more important jobs. He travelled with him to India and the Far East and was present when Mountbatten accepted the Japanese surrender in Singapore in 1945. If Mountbatten was undertaking a long journey, Peter Murphy was the man who made sure that suitable reading material was provided. If an extra man was needed at dinner Murphy was always available and guaranteed to sing for his supper. When Edwina was left alone in Britain during Mountbatten's overseas tours, Peter Murphy was on hand as a safe 'walker'.

Apart from his cousins in the Royal Family, Peter Murphy was undoubtedly Mountbatten's closest and oldest friend, who was by his side for fifty years, until he died in 1969, ten years before Mountbatten, who felt his death deeply. For the rest of his life Mountbatten would mourn the loss of his dear friend.

In the early years of the marriage Murphy acted as the go-between when things were not going well with Mountbatten and Edwina, and there were plenty of opportunities for him to use his Irish charm and diplomatic skills to soothe two extremely volatile temperaments. He was able to say things to them both that no one else could get away with and other friends have suggested that it was mainly through his good counsel that their marriage survived several rocky patches.

An intelligent man and a superb linguist who spoke nine languages, Murphy was an asset to any gathering and few Mountbatten social occasions were held without his being invited. His homosexuality meant that he provided no threat to either of the Mountbattens; each felt he was equally loyal and they, in turn, trusted him and respected his opinions, possibly more than any other person outside the family. At one time Murphy had a mild flirtation with another of the Mountbatten's close friends, Noel Coward, but even though Mountbatten was aware of it, it did nothing to impair his relationship with either of them.

Peter Murphy stayed at the various Mountbatten homes for long periods, but he did not live with them and he was not a permanent member of their staff. He received some money from Mountbatten from time to time but the only period when he was salaried was when he accompanied him as an official assistant in the Far East and later, in the same capacity, in India.

Physically he was not an attractive person, balding and heavily built, but his closeness to Mountbatten was obvious to all around them and he enjoyed what was equally noticeable, a special relationship. He was not in the least bit overawed by Mountbatten and, in turn, Mountbatten depended on Peter Murphy for the sort of honest advice that every great man needs.

The most celebrated homosexual in the Mountbatten set was undoubtedly Noel Coward, who delighted in outraging society with his indiscretions. In June 1934 Coward had been staying in Malta with Mountbatten and his thank-you letter was written in the most indiscreet terms which could easily be read as incriminating for both men. It begins:

Dear dainty Darling.

I *couldn't* have enjoyed my holiday more . . . Please ask Peter [Murphy?] not to foul the guest cabin in any beastly way because I do so want to use it again . . . Please be careful of your zippers, Dickie dear, and don't let me hear of any ugly happenings at Flotilla dances,

Love and kisses, Bosun Coward
(I know Bosun should be spelt 'Boatswain' but I *don't* care!)

This is hardly the sort of letter one would expect between two male friends, however close, yet the very fact that Mountbatten allowed it to be consigned to the Broadlands archives, where it could be read by anyone, leads one to believe that in all probability it was innocent enough and simply typical of the sort of flamboyant gesture for which Coward was famous.

Some years later when Mountbatten co-operated with Coward on the making of *In Which We Serve*, one of the most successful films of the Second World War, based on Mountbatten and his time in HMS *Kelly*, Coward encountered tremendous opposition to his playing the Mountbatten part. He wrote to his old friend in September 1941: 'I have discovered that a tremendous whispering campaign has been started by Brendan Bracken and Walter Monckton to the effect that it is most unsuitable for me to play a Naval Officer etc. etc. It has also been officially denied by the Admiralty that the film is based on you and also denied by me in the Press . . . My Captain (D) is quite ordinary with an income of about £800 a year, a small country house near Plymouth, a reasonably nice looking wife (Mrs not Lady), two children and a cocker spaniel. I know you will approve of all this.' Nevertheless, to all intents and purposes

Coward's Captain *was* Mountbatten and Lord Louis never tired of seeing the film.

Perhaps the most convincing argument against Mountbatten being bisexual is that in the fifteen years since his death no one had come forward claiming that he was his lover. It would be perfectly safe for anyone to make such a claim with no possibility of legal action and in an age when tabloid newspapers pay vast sums for such stories about celebrities, particularly those with a royal connection, it would be a miracle for this to remain unpublished.

It is said that no man is a hero to his valet, from whom he can have few secrets. William Evans or, to give him his full naval title, Chief Petty Officer Evans RN was valet to Mountbatten for ten years, during which time he became an unashamed admirer of his late boss. Mountbatten and Edwina taught Evans so many things and involved him in so many wonderful experiences in their travels throughout the world that he finds it hard to criticize anything about them. At the same time he does have one regret about trusting Mountbatten, for which he is still being penalized. In 1965, when Mountbatten retired from the Royal Navy, he asked Evans to do the same and continue working for him as a civilian. At first Evans was reluctant because, having completed sixteen years in the Navy, he did not want to lose his pension rights by leaving before it was due to be paid. Mountbatten told him not to worry as he would 'fix' it. As he had the reputation of being able to fix anything, Evans took him at his word and joined his master in civilian life. The pension never materialized and Evans, who subsequently left Mountbatten's service through ill-health (he said it was 'Mountbattenitis', the disease that struck so many of Mountbatten's staff; they were simply worn out by the speed at which Mountbatten lived and worked), has never been compensated for all those years in the Royal Navy. He is not bitter about it but says that while he was sure Mountbatten was genuine in his offer, nothing was put in writing and that was his (Evans's) biggest mistake.

For ten years Evans probably knew more about the private life of Mountbatten than anyone else. He helped to arrange some of the meetings with film stars such as Shirley MacLaine; 'a wonderful woman who fancied Lord Louis like mad and the feeling was mutual', Audrey Hepburn, 'elegance personified', and Claudia Cardinale, who Evans described as 'one of the most beautiful twenty-year-olds I've ever seen'.

Joining the debate on Mountbatten's sexuality, Evans says that his fascination for beautiful young women, even in his later years, is surely proof enough of his heterosexual preferences. As far as Mountbatten having a relationship with another man: 'Absolute rubbish,' he says. 'I was around him all the time and met all the people, male and female, who came to see him. The opportunities weren't there and he was not a man who did anything discreetly, I would have been bound to know if something was going on. His big 'turn-on' was riding boots and jodhpurs, but only when they were worn by young women with long, slim legs. Men and boys weren't his thing at all. And some of the well-known bisexual men Lord Louis admitted to his house were there mainly because of Edwina. People such as Noel Coward and Malcolm Sargent were her friends really, not his. He put up with them for her sake.'

Like many of Mountbatten's personal servants, Evans became so involved with the family that his job took over. It was more a way of life than just a paid occupation. He had very little free time, and he did not seek any. His entire existence seems to have been bound up, for the years he lived with Mountbatten, with whatever he and the rest of the family were doing. As a valet he knew everything that went on in the Mountbatten household. He witnessed all the comings and goings, night and day, and Mountbatten never tried to hide any dark secrets from him – or anyone else apparently.

The break between the two men occurred in Ireland, at Classiebawn Castle. The family had realized that Evans had not been himself for some time but no one thought it was anything serious. Then, all of a sudden, he packed a bag and just walked away. There was no period of notice and it was some months before they heard of his whereabouts and what he was doing. The relationship between Mountbatten and his valet had been one of genuine friendship without ever becoming familiar and when they parted company it was because Evans could no longer stand 'living with a human dynamo'. He had a complete break-down. But he says he wouldn't have missed knowing Mountbatten for anything and he adds, 'The only way I can describe my feelings for him is to say: I loved the man.'

Alan Warren is a photographer and author who knew Mountbatten for the last ten years of his life. They met when Warren, then an impecunious and impetuous young photographer, simply wrote to Mountbatten asking to take his picture. It was some time before he replied but then, out of the blue, Warren was told to present himself at Mountbatten's house in Kinnerton Street, London, to be inspected. Mountbatten was then already in his sixties, some forty years older than Warren, but they struck up an immediate rapport and remained on good terms until Mountbatten's death.

Alan Warren is today in his forties, a good-looking, elegant man with perfect manners, whose slim figure enables him to wear beautifully tailored clothes to their best advantage. His is refreshingly honest about his own sexuality, saying he loves good-looking and personable people around him 'of whatever gender'. A gregarious man who 'loves a good gossip', he knew Stephen Barry, at one time valet to Prince Charles, who died of Aids in 1989, and who was a source of scores of scandalous stories about his former royal employer, and he was also a friend of the late John Barratt, Lord Mountbatten's former secretary.

Warren says that after that first meeting with Mountbatten he was summoned to Knightsbridge Barracks to take an official photograph before that year's Trooping the Colour Parade. 'I turned up dressed in the photographer's "uniform" of the day: blue jeans, white T-shirt and leather jacket. Being shown into the Officers' Mess I saw a number of Household Cavalry officers, all immaculately clad in their ceremonial dress: scarlet tunics, gleaming breastplates, white buckskin breeches and black thigh boots you could see your face in. They were obviously horrified at my appearance and contrived to act as if I was not there. Then Lord Mountbatten entered the room. He too was dressed as they were – from he waist up – but he hadn't yet put on his breeches and he was wearing a voluminous pair of what today we call boxer shorts, but they were nothing like the sort you see now. He was also wearing black socks held up with calf suspenders. He made no apology for his appearance and wasn't in the least embarrassed at being half undressed. He came over to me, put his arm around my shoulder and drawing me towards the group at the other end of the room said, 'Gentleman, I would like to introduce Mr Warren who is here to take my official photograph.' With that he then left the room to continue dressing and left me with his colleagues. Their attitude changed instantly; they became quite friendly and one of them even asked me if I would take his picture. I said I would and my fee would be £200, a lot of money in those days. At that he hesitated and withdrew to the other side of the room. I never heard from him again.'

Warren took the photographs ordered by Mountbatten. They must have been satisfactory for he received another telephone call telling him to present himself at Buckingham Palace the following morning to take photographs of the Prince of Wales. 'He didn't actually tell me who the subject was going to be until I arrived at the Palace. All he said beforehand was that there were to be some very important pictures taken so I had better dress suitably. I think he was afraid I might turn up in my jeans. The session was very easy. He arranged everything and it was obvious that he adored Prince Charles and the feeling was mutual. They got on so well together and Lord Louis's presence made Charles relax. When they saw the photographs they were very pleased and Lord Mountbatten recommended me to quite a number of his friends who became clients. He was very generous in that way.'

Warren liked Mountbatten and one of his treasured mementoes is a photograph they had taken together – he had earlier had a similar picture taken with Noel Coward. Mountbatten told him: 'If it's good enough for Noel, it's good enough for me.'

Warren has never made the slightest suggest that Mountbatten was homosexual. In fact his view is that Mountbatten probably never even thought about his own sexuality. He certainly didn't care about other people's and if, indeed, he had had any inclinations towards a homosexual relationship, he would not have done anything to hide it. He added: 'I think Lord Louis just liked good-looking people. He surrounded himself with very attractive young men and women, but there was nothing sinister about it. He never asked me about my love life; whether I had a girlfriend – or boyfriend for that matter. I don't think it would have bothered him either way. As far as sex was concerned he seemed very open-minded.'

Returning to Mountbatten's undoubtedly heterosexual love life, one of the common characteristics shared by the women who attracted him was an affinity with horses. It wasn't just the ability to ride and have a good seat, Mountbatten was sexually excited at the thought of women on horseback. In a bedside cabinet he kept a collection of photographs which consisted entirely of women in tight jodhpurs. They might be sitting astride or simply posing alongside an animal, and there was nothing in the slightest bit pornographic about any of the pictures. They were the sort that could be seen in almost any up-market fashion catalogue or equestrian magazine, but they did the trick for

Mountbatten and when his secretary once found him sitting up in bed looking through his collection, Mountbatten had the grace to blush as if he was a naughty schoolboy who had been caught with a dirty book in his possession.

One young woman who became very important to Mountbatten, shortly before his affair with Sacha Abercorn started, was Mary Lou Emery, who later became Mrs David Hyne. Mary Lou was employed at Broadlands as a groom where her duties included riding with Mountbatten at least twice every week. If anything occurred which prevented their riding dates Mountbatten would be furious for days. Physically she fitted the type that had always appealed to him, with a slim, almost boyish figure and a very pretty face, though she is more petite than the usual run of Mountbatten companions. She also managed to bridge the gap beween being a servant and a friend. Although he paid her wages every week and provided her with a house on the estate in which to live, when they rode together she might easily have been the daughter of a duchess. She never forgot her place but an easy friendship developed between them that superseded the normal relationship between master and servant.

In a household like Mountbatten's it was inevitable that gossip would start to circulate and rumours soon abounded about the special relationship. The other servants, both indoor and out, firmly believed that a torrid affair was being conducted during the riding sessions and when John Barratt brought it to the attention of Mountbatten, he was secretly delighted. The idea that others believed he was capable of conducting a clandestine affair with a young woman who was as attractive as Mary Lou appealed to his ego enormously.

Barratt eventually asked him outright if there was anything in the stories. Mountbatten laughed at the thought and suggested that the sheer mechanics required to permit him to make love to anyone in the open air – dismounting, undressing and then dressing again afterwards – precluded such a possibility, lovely as the thought might have been. He told Barratt that he liked Mary Lou as a companion and nothing more. He said there was nothing physical in the relationship and Barratt believed him, but if others thought there was something going on between them Mountbatten was fully prepared to let them. It was flattering to him and did his reputation as a ladies' man no harm at all.

One of Mountbatten's granddaughters said that he was physically affectionate, a man who loved to hug and kiss. It was very important to him. He was a man who wore his heart on his sleeve, though most people would not have thought that of him. She knew all about his women and who they were because he didn't make any secrets of his girlfriends. He loved to talk about them, though when she first found out it came as a bit of a shock because her mother had always thought it was important that the children didn't know that their grandparents were not the ideally happily married couple they had always been led to believe. She thought the most important thing to him was female company and not sex. That's why the marriage didn't work. It was the opposite for her grandmother. She wanted sex; he craved companionship. This need was fulfilled by his daughter, Patricia, who was the one truly great love of his life.

Patricia Mountbatten dismisses all talk about the possibility of her father every remarrying. 'It was something he never seriously considered, no matter how close he might have been to one or two of his girlfriends.'

The main reason was the title. When Mountbatten was created a peer it was known that he had only daughters and was unlikely to have a son as an heir. So, under what is known as a 'special remainder', he received, along with his peerage, the right to pass the title to his heir in the female line, for one generation only. This was not a concession granted only to Mountbatten, and was not given to him because of his royal connections. During the Second World War, Lord Portal received his peerage under the same conditions and for the same reason, and in the First World War, Lord Roberts was also honoured in the same way. Mountbatten had always been determined that nothing would prevent Patricia from inheriting the title of Countess Mountbatten of Burma, and he had told her this on several occasions. So, as far as a second marriage was concerned, any would-be brides were doomed to disappointment.

The Mountbattens' were arguably the most open marriage of their generation. Edwina made no secret of her many love affairs and Dickie, eventually, came clean about his little peccadilloes. Writing to Edwina he said, 'I hope you didn't mind my mentioning about my girlfriends – it was only to show you that they never meant to me what the Rabbit meant to you and so can never come between us, provided you no longer make difficulties about my seeing them as you were apt to do in the old days!' In this, as in so many other things, he completely misjudged his wife's reaction. She never came to terms with his having girlfriends. He thought that as long as he was understanding about her affairs, she would be equally agreeable to his extra-marital relationships. But what Mountbatten failed to grasp was his wife's insane jealousy about everyone – male or female – who might have claims on her husband. She didn't want him, but neither did she want anyone else to have him. And while she felt that her behaviour was her own business and no one else's, not even her husbands', there was no way that she was going to permit him to have a life that exluded her. Which was why, when he started his affair with Yola Letellier, Edwina found ways to become friends with her herself.

There were odd periods when Edwina appeared to accept her husband's need for outside female companionship. In 1945, towards the end of the Second World War, the Mountbattens returned to London from South East Asia for a short visit. Dickie asked Edwina if she minded if he saw some of his girlfriends while he was home. He really could be the most naïve of men at times. To his surprise she readily agreed, or at least made no difficulties, and he wrote to thank her in his usual diplomatic style: 'The sweetest change is the way you have conquered what we all thought was an unreasoning jealousy . . . You can feel easy in your mind that there is real safety in numbers & that I won't do anything silly.' By this time it wasn't a case of Edwina not minding; she simply did not care any more. But the letter probably did nothing to alleviate the problems that existed between them. All it did was to confirm that the rest of the family all thought she was unreasonable. Mountbatten had no idea how patronizing he could sound at times.

One of the most unsavoury episodes in Mountbattens' marriage occurred in 1930 when a naval officer, Commander Tony Simpson, was divorced by his wife, who threatened to cite Edwina as co-respondent. That there had been an affair was not disputed but Mountbatten did not want his wife's name dragged through the courts with all the attendant publicity – and the subsequent disapproval of the King.

Edwina agreed to pay what was in those days a considerable sum of money, £8,000, on condition that her name was never mentioned. It was obvious that the wronged wife wanted only money because she immediately agreed. For the next five years a correspondence was carried on between Mountbatten and Commander Simpson over the financial arrangements with the most surprising aspect being the friendly tone of Mountbatten's letters.

Simpson offered to make restitution of the money paid to his wife by Edwina for what he described as 'what amounts to blackmail'.

Mountbatten replied on behalf of his wife saying she would not hear of him repaying her legal expenses – which were around £5,000 – and saying that Edwina regretted that the affair (unfortunate choice of words) seemed to such a millstone to Simpson. The Commander accepted the release from the obligation but insisted on arranging for his estate, which he detailed in an excruciatingly abject eight-page letter, to go to Edwina on his death. Neither Edwina nor Dickie was much concerned about the financial payments but at the conclusion of the arrangements, Mountbatten scrawled on the back of the final letter from Simpson: 'It is a happy ending to a law case which has lost Edwina £13,000.' There was never the slightest criticism or condemnation of the wife who had committed adultery, or even of the man involved. It was almost as if he was a lawyer dealing with the affairs of a client who was not particularly close.

What made the Mountbattens' marriage so different from others of their class was that, although they had a tacit agreement for what amounted to an 'open' marriage for some years, they never lost their affection for each other. It was not a case of the marriage being merely one of convenience, as with those of so many of their friends.

Throughout Edwina's numerous affairs, serious and frivolous, she may have had fleeting moments when she convinced herself that she should would be better off without her husband, but these never lasted. And while she was unwilling, or unable, to give up her lovers, as long as she and Dickie remained reasonably friendly she saw no reason why they should split up. Similarly, Dickie, once he had come to terms with his wife's infidelity, never seriously contemplated divorce, even though she was, for a time, so openly unfaithful that he would have had no difficulty in obtaining grounds if he had so wished.

Contrary to what many people felt at the time and have since said, they did not stay together for the reasons most commonly given: his need of her money and her desire to retain his title and status. The money was important to Mountbatten and he never denied it, but even if there had been a divorce in the 1930s, he would have received more than enough to keep him in comfort for the rest of his life, so Edwina's fortune was not the rein that held him. He loved his wife and desperately wanted her to love him back in the same way, which is why he put up with the humiliations she heaped on him in the early years of their marriage. Their relationship moved to a much more solid basis once he had faced the problem of her waywardness and confronted her openly.

She was not used to hearing him in such a defiant mood and it cleared the air for them both.

In spite of her apparent indifference, Edwina enjoyed the status that being Mountbatten's wife gave her. If they had divorced she would have been the loser in the society stakes – certainly as far as royalty was concerned. But she was a free spirit and of such an independent mind that if she had intended to go through with a divorce, the loss of a place at Court would hardly have been a consideration.

When Mountbatten first discovered that his wife was being unfaithful he was naturally angry and hurt, but more than this, he was totally confused. He simply could not understand why Edwina needed to look elsewhere when he was available. Affectionate, occasionally passionate and always considerate, he was fully prepared to fulfil her every need – he just didn't know what those needs were. When they had their first showdown and Edwina admitted that at least a couple of her affairs were serious, she added, 'But as they never in any way altered my affection and respect for you I don't myself think of them as such.'

In reply Mountbatten appeared to accept the inevitable; that he could not have her to himself exclusively but that they would remain friends. 'I want you to be as great a friend to me as I am to you,' he wrote. And while, in admitting her affairs, Edwina made no secret of the extent of the involvement, Mountbatten, also trying to make a clean breast of his extra-marital flings, merely showed how inexperienced and naïve he was. 'I have kissed and hugged two or three girls in the past nine years,' he once confessed. Hardly the revelations of an energetic bed-hopping womanizer, even if that is the way a number of people saw him.

By any standards Mountbatten could not be regarded as a sexual athlete. The women to whom this author has spoken, who shared Dickie's bed, all talked of his consideration and tenderness in their relationships; none described him as a passionate or a formidable lover. Where Mountbatten was concerned, it was the idea of sex that excited him – not the act itself. True, he didn't get many complaints about his performance – but neither did he receive all that many compliments!

6

MOUNTBATTEN
AND HIS MONEY

Mountbatten once told his elder daughter, Patricia, that shortly before the outbreak of the Second World War, he and his wife had difficulty in spending their annual income. In 1938 this amounted to some £60,000 after tax, or £1,150 a week; equivalent today to around £115,000 a week.

His personal contribution to the family exchequer was some £300 a year from his own family trust, plus another £300 a year which he earned as an officer in the Royal Navy. The remainder came from the fortune which Edwina had inherited on the death of her grandfather, Sir Ernest Cassel, and over which she assumed full control on her marriage. Cassel left an estate valued at £7,500,000, of which some £2,900,000, plus various houses, came to Edwina on the day she married. The reason for giving these figures is to illustrate the style and grandeur of Mountbatten's life once he had married, and the changes to his lifestyle that access to virtually unlimited money made.

Before that day in 1922 he had enjoyed a rich and elegant life befitting a man who had been born with royal blood flowing freely in his veins. A great-grandson of Queen Victoria, who was also his godmother, his early days as a Prince and Serene Highness were spent in some of the finest palaces and castles in Europe. But there was never a great deal of money available to him, even though his father was more than comfortably off by the standards of the day.

Being related to every European monarch did not automatically mean access to vast fortunes – neither does it today. The junior members of the Royal Family, who do not carry out public duties, are required to earn their own living and those on the fringes even more so. Houses may be made available as grace-and-favour residences in the gift of the Queen, but the days have long gone when the Sovereign accepted financial responsibility for every member of her widespread family.

Once Lord Louis Mountbatten had married Edwina Ashley it became a matter of little consequence that he had no fortune of his own. His wife had more than enough for them both and she was determined that her husband would want for nothing. For the rest of his life he would be able to indulge his expensive habits such as polo, fast cars, elegant clothes from the best tailors in the world, yachts, first class travel and luxury homes in Britain and abroad. Never again would he have to worry about seeing his bank manager and even though he would never lose his reputation for parsimony, and, in later life, would develop a near phobia about being poor, there never was any real shortage – it was all in his mind.

Throughout his life Mountbatten remained anxious about money. When he was single and living on his pay as a naval officer and an allowance from his father, he worried because he could not keep up with the extravagant lifestyle of his cousin David, the Prince of Wales. When he began thinking seriously about Edwina, one of the major obstacles to their marriage, in his mind, was her financial station, which was so far above his own. He wrote to his mother expressing these doubts and she agreed, telling him that it could be a very serious matter for a husband to have a wife wealthier than he, especially if it could give rise to rumours that he was a fortune hunter, planning to live off his wife's income.

Edwina was completely different. She had been brought up surrounded by the most opulent displays of wealth by her grandfather, Sir Ernest Cassel, whose own fortune far outweighed that of even the Royal Family. Nobody in Britain in the early days of this century could match his skills at amassing money – or keeping it – and he revelled in using it to establish a way of living that became the envy of the country, royalty and aristocracy included.

Sir Ernest Cassel had been born into a modest family in Cologne in 1852. There was no fortune for him to inherit and his parents were unable to afford an extended education. Leaving school at fourteen, he became apprenticed as a clerk to one of the major German finance houses where his agile brain and natural aptitude for business soon propelled him into the managerial ranks. He was quickly recognized as a man who was going places and by the time he was twenty-five he had emigrated to England as general manager of Bischoffsheim and Goldsmidt, one of the world's most important financial firms.

Branching out on his own, he displayed a ruthless brilliance rarely seen even among his peers. Within a few years he was a millionaire, investing in overseas railways and other enterprises which sometimes tripled and quadrupled his money within months. He became a legend in financial circles and was said at one time to have made a million pounds in a single day in the late nineteenth century.

Cassel also earned for himself a reputation for scrupulous honesty that was even rarer than business acumen in the world in which he circulated. No one ever had cause to doubt his word and he was never involved in the slightest scandal or shady dealing. he was old-fashioned, upright, a stickler for tradition and family values, and, unlike most of his contemporaries, totally uninterested in gossip or social chitchat.

Once he had made his money, he used the same drive and resolve that had made him into a successful financial figure to forge a new identity. He desperately wanted to become an establishment figure and he set about learning the social graces that would make him acceptable.

He easily adapted to the life of a country gentleman, learning to shoot and ride and also, by judicious investment in bloodstock, became a familiar figure in racing circles, which is how he first became acquainted with the Prince of Wales, later Edward VII. They became much more than mere acquaintances; a deep friendship was formed that lasted until the King's death in 1910. Cassel took over the financial affairs of the Prince, whose gambling debts were, for a time, in danger of becoming a public scandal, and in a comparatively short period set him on an investment course that was to relieve him of all monetary worries. It was rumoured that Cassel not only offered advice to his friend, but also gave hard cash on a number of occasions.

Edward VII never forgot his old friend and adviser, who was included in Court functions at the highest level, in spite of the enmity of many of the old aristocracy who were jealous of the 'upstart Jew who has taken over the monarchy'. Their prejudices were suddenly overcome and their tongues quickly stilled when a number of them also began to reap large profits through following Cassel's advice.

If Cassel had one weakness it was his inability to forgo honours and decorations – a characteristic he shared with his future grandson–in–law, Mountbatten. And the King, using his powers of patronage to the full, made sure his many debts were repaid in kind. Cassel was knighted, being awarded the Grand Cross of the Order of the Bath, was made a Privy Counsellor and reached the highest rank in the sovereign's personal Order of Chivalry when Edward VII conferred on him the Grand Cross of the Royal Victorian Order. Further honours were added when he embarked on a career of philanthropy, giving away more than £2 million to a variety of charities. And when Edward VII agreed to become godfather to Cassel's granddaughter, Edwina Ashley, he knew he had reached the summit of his social ambitions.

Cassel was a magnificent host, a generous contributor to charity and a benevolent supporter of the arts. But he knew the value of every penny he possessed and he did not shower cash on his family. Edwina and her sister Mary were brought up enjoying the finest food, clothes and education that money could buy, but they were not given unlimited expense accounts or vast allowances. Money was something that was usually available when needed, but was rarely mentioned. And Sir Ernest and his granddaughter both preferred it that way.

Even when Edwina wanted to travel to India to join Dickie, shortly before they officially announced their engagement, she had to borrow £100 from a friend to pay the fare because she did not have enough money in her own bank account at the time. And this was after her grandfather had died and left her millions in his will. It had simply not entered her head that her bank would have been delighted to offer her any advance she needed until probate had been granted.

Sir Ernest Cassel left an estate valued at something over seven and a half million pounds, with the largest single portion, twenty-five sixty-fourths, going to Edwina. This meant she inherited close to three million pounds with which she could do exactly as she liked, once she reached the age of twenty-eight, or married, whichever came first. The only proviso in her grandfather's will was that no single investment should exceed one hundred thousand pounds. He believed in spreading the risks and advised his grandchildren, Edwina and her sister Mary, to do the same.

Even if Edwina did nothing with the money, just leaving it on minimum deposit in the bank, she would have an annual income of nearly a hundred thousand pounds – two thousand pounds a week, when the average weekly wage for a working man was only slightly more than two pounds and income tax was barely an inconvenience. Edwina was completely indifferent to money. If she wanted something she usually got it and the bills were sent to her grandfather to be settled. She had been brought up in a world where people did not talk about money and if Dickie tried to discuss their future finances, she always shrugged it off, finding the topic too embarrassing.

He, on the other hand, was never embarrassed to raise the subject. Even though he had been brought up, like so many members of the Royal Family, then and now, to be careful with money, he soon took to the role of multi-millionaire, enjoying every one of the many advantages that unlimited funds brought.

Edwina may have later become an unsatisfactory wife in many ways, unfaithful, jealous to a fault and wildly temperamental, but she was never mean. From the very outset she had decided that when she came into her fortune it would be as much Dickie's as it was hers, and throughout the long years of marriage, no matter how strained their relationship became, they never once rowed over money. It would not have entered Edwina's head that such a subject was worth arguing about. If Dickie wanted to maintain his independence to some extent – and he made valiant efforts to separate his income from hers in the early days of their marriage – she was prepared to let him get on with it, though privately she thought the whole thing was a bore.

Shortly after they became engaged, Edwina told Dickie that she intended to give him a Rolls-Royce as a wedding present. This was not a spontaneous whim by a spoilt young woman who had just come into millions and who wanted to splash out on her future husband, but a thoughtful gesture that had been planned quietly in her mind many months earlier. They had been walking through Berkeley Square one evening when they passed the Rolls-Royce showroom and Dickie had said rather wistfully, 'I'll never be able to afford one of those.' It was not in any way a hint, but at that moment Edwina decided that one day she would get him the best Rolls-Royce that money could buy, and the thought was tucked away in the back of her mind.

Once the question of the wedding present had been agreed, Dickie took up the project with his usual enthusiasm, and without the slightest embarrassment. The Broadlands archives contain files with acres of paper devoted to this single subject. Buying a Rolls-Royce was not simply a question of going into a showroom and handing over several thousand pounds and driving the car away. Each motor was hand-built to its owner's specification and there was a waiting list of many months. Edwina hadn't thought of this when she offered to provide Dickie with the car of his dreams. Even with her millions there was no way that a new Rolls could be built from scratch in time to be handed over as a wedding present, even if she had been able to jump the queue. The Prince of Wales, who was to be best man at his cousin's wedding, came up with a solution. He owned a Rolls-Royce which he was prepared to sell to Edwina and which could be adapted in plenty of time for Dickie's use if enough pressure was brought to bear on Barker's, the coach-builders. Edwina enthusiastically accepted the offer and in the transaction, using his influence with the coach-builders to get everything done on time. The purchase price of the Rolls was £2,000 and by the time had been adapted to Dickie's requirements, almost the same amount again had been spent.

Although Mountbatten was thrilled at the prospect of owning a Rolls-Royce, he told his mother that it would always be regarded as a rich man's car, 'which we both admit, is not always desirable. Similarly the name 'Ford' always moves one to mirth and makes one think of a 'cheap car'. Actually a Ford is not very cheap and certainly far more reliable.' Once the deal had been agreed, Dickie took over the arrangements and, with his usual methodical approach, no detail was spared in making sure this car was perfect. Dickie was eight inches taller than the Prince of Wales, for whom the car had been built originally, so it had to be lengthened to accommodate his six-foot-two-inch frame. He wasn't particularly keen on the colour, and as he wanted the car to be recognized as his and not its previous owner's, the body had to be repainted. Several ample shades were delivered and rejected before he decided on the one he wanted. Edwina raised no objection to any of the demands he made; if Dickie wanted it, that was good enough for her, even though every suggestion involved extra expense.

The question of Dickie's royal ancestry became important in the car's ownership. As a direct descendant of the House of Hanover, Dickie found out that he would be exempt from taxes on any carriages he owned. Did this also apply to cars? The new Road Fund Licence was just being introduced and Dickie instructed Edwina to find out if the exemption applied to this also. He explained in another letter that they would save on petrol tax if the car was registered in his name, as a descendant of George III, so would she object if he became the registered owner? Edwina couldn't have cared less. It might have been important to Dickie, but as far as she was concerned the actual ownership of the car was a matter of complete indifference. She was paying for it, but the moment the present was handed over it became the recipient's. She was never one to give with one hand and take back with the other.

Once Dickie and Edwina were married and she came into her inheritance, he quickly learned how to handle the money as if it were his own. There was nothing unusual in this. Before the Second World War a man automatically took control of his wife's finances once they were married. It was accepted and expected. Dickie, however, used the money not only to provide himself with the luxuries he desired, but to benefit others who were not so fortunate. He was a benevolent employer who rarely refused to help those who had worked for him if they fell on hard times.

Shortly after the marriage Mountbatten employed a German chef named Valentin Schmitt. His wife Ellen was in poor health and they decided to retire and live in Germany. When they left the Mountbattens' employment Dickie paid them a pension of £4 a month. This was in 1925, when a housemaid could be found who would be delighted to be given a job paying £25 a year, so it was extremely generous by the standards of the day. Also in 1925 Frau Schmitt wrote to Mountbatten explaining that her husband, in a low-paid temporary job, could not earn enough to keep them and on 18 October that year Mountbatten sent them a number of cheques to tide them over. He also increased the pension to £5 a month.

Mountbatten was punctilious about replying to the Schmitts' appeals for financial assistance. In a letter written in 1926 Ellen Schmitt asked Mountbatten if he would pay her subscription to the overseas *Daily Mirror* as 'Princess Louis did pay, but arrangements seem to have failed. And Valentin is not eligible for unemployment benefit for a month.' Mountbatten enclosed a cheque (he describes it as 'small') with his reply, and he assumed responsibility for paying for the newspaper subscription, which continued until 1935.

He also arranged for monthly food parcels to be sent from Selfridges to the Schmitts for more than ten years. And if they failed to arrive on the expected day, a letter would immediately be sent from Germany to Miss Underhill, the Mountbatten's secretary in London, complaining of the delay and demanding an explanation. Although the Mountbatten archives do not reveal the exact size of the cheques sent to the Schmitts, it is obvious that he was very generous to these old family servants during their impoverished retirement in pre-war Germany.

In the post-war years Mountbatten became known as a soft touch to anyone who had served with him. But as early as 1924 he acted as a benefactor to a number of former comrades. A man named Bernard Sleep had served under Mountbatten in the Royal Navy and on his discharge on medical grounds he was told by his former commander that he could contact him if ever he needed help. Sleep took Mountbatten up on his offer several times over the next few years, the first occasion being when he wrote saying he did not wish to claim the dole so would Mountbatten find him a job? Some time later Sleep again wrote, this time asking for a loan of £50 (approximately £5,000 by today's reckoning) to help him get started in business. The money was forwarded without question, but a further request, this time for £100 was refused on the grounds that having had one lot of money, he was not now considered to be a priority case.

Many years later, Mountbatten's secretary at his London home, Elizabeth Ward (now Mrs Charles Collins), who used to administer his 'private pension schemes' for former colleagues, recalled an occasion when she made a mistake and overpaid an ex-sailor. She said, 'I thought he would be furious, because he hated mistakes and he would explode with anger whenever anything went wrong. So I was a bit apprehensive about telling him. He snapped at me, 'How much is it and who did you pay it to?' When I told him the name of the man he immediately relaxed and said, "Oh, That's all right, he was on the *Kelly* and lost both his legs. They could do with a little extra." If he felt it was a deserving case he never quibbled.'

On the other hand, he could be extremely parsimonious over tiny amounts. Once when Elizabeth Collins was working for the Mountbattens in Malta, she took it upon herself to order bottled mineral water for her own use as she could not drink the local supply. When Mountbatten found out he stormed into her office shouting, 'Do you realize that this stuff costs 1/6d [7½p] a bottle?' There was no hard and fast rule where money was concerned. He would go to extraordinary lengths to save a few pence and then would be generous to a fault in matters involving hundreds of pounds.

As far back as 1921, Mountbatten recorded in his diary that he was 'furious because I have just found out that certain embroideries I had bought for a Christmas present are to be had from another firm at 70% of the price.'

When he assumed control of Classiebawn Castle on Edwina's death in 1960, he demanded that his agent, Gabrielle Gore-Booth, consult him on practically every item involving money. In a reply to one of her letters in May 1962, he noted that 'you have used three sheets of headed writing paper instead of follow-on sheets. Presumably this is because you have run out of the latter and are therefore using the dearer headed sheets.' But he raised no objections to paying for *The Times* and *Irish Times* for his tenants although this was not included in their lease agreements. He liked to be sure that any prospective tenants were what he regarded as 'reputable' people, going to some lengths to check the background of a certain M. de Glatigny, a Belgian living in the Belgian Congo. Mountbatten took up all his references, writing to banks and diplomats in the former colony before agreeing to let him rent the castle.

A Ford Escort car was provided for the estate but Mountbatten ordered that under no circumstances was it to be used if the milometer was broken.

He became very concerned when a dispute broke out between two of his staff at Classiebawn, mainly because of the amounts he had invested in them. The cook, Miss Fleming, and the steward, Paddy O'Grady, had a flaming row which resulted in the latter resigning, an action he later regretted. Mountbatten told his agent that the dispute must be resolved as he had paid out so much money on both of them. Miss Fleming had been paid in full when the house was empty for two months and O'Grady had been brought to England at Mountbatten's expense for treatment when he broke his arm.

Although, as a landlord, Mountbatten tried hard to accommodate the needs and wishes of his tenants, he remained a protective employer to his staff at Classiebawn. In a letter to his agent in 1962 he told her that tenants would be informed as discreetly but firmly as possible that they were expected to pay between £15 and £20 a week in staff tips. And when Mr and Mrs O'Grady were sent to England for medical treatment Mountbatten insisted that the remaining staff should be given a bonus for 'shouldering the extra burden'.

He also took the part of his steward when a tenant objected to the servant keeping his car in a small additional garage that Mountbatten had had built alongside the castle. Mountbatten ordered his steward to use the garage no matter what the tenant said. He told his agent, 'I would rather lose a bad tenant than a good servant.' And in another minor dispute he paid 50 per cent of the cost of hiring the O'Gradys' television set to protect it from use by the tenants of the day.

Mountbatten also found time to query the amount of rent being paid to the estate by an order of nuns for the tenancy of the White House. He felt it was too low.

He tried very hard to be a businessman and in yet another letter to his agent suggested that the estate's wholesaler should be asked to supply free alcohol equal to the value of a promised discount during the month of August when he and the family would be in residence. Mountbatten was anxious that tenants of Classiebawn should pay for all breakages. On one occasion when a tenant had broken a tray and a radio, he asked them to pay cash rather than supply replacements because he wanted to use the money to buy new items of crockery. On the other hand he was scrupulously fair to his tenants and ordered his staff not to charge them any more than the retail price for any wines and spirits they drank.

For many years the Mountbattens' accounts were dealt with by the established national firm of accountants Spicer and Pegler (now part of Touche Ross & Co). However, in 1946, when Miss Underhill retired as their secretary, the Mountbattens decided to look after the Broadlands accounts themselves, with the annual audit being carried out by a local firm in Romsey, as had been the practice with Edwina's father, Lord Mount Temple. In a letter to Spicer and Pegler on 12 December 1946, Mountbatten wrote: 'Normally I would not quibble at the expense of employing a high class London firm, but you realize that your fees amount to nearly one tenth of our expendable income.' On matters of their own personal taxation, however, they decided it would not be practicable for the local firm to handle their affairs, and Spicer and Pegler retained this valuable segment of their account.

The theme of getting value for money out of servants, suppliers and professional advisers runs through many of the letters housed in the Broadlands archives. When Mountbatten assumed sole control of Classiebawn he was constantly expressing his concern that he would be paying staff for nothing if the property was unlet. He wrote to his agent asking her to arrange that the domestic staff should be persuaded to arrive only a few days before the tenants, when they would be put on full pay. But he agreed to pay a small retainer so that they would all be available when he wanted them. He also tried (unsuccessfully) to get his wine and spirit suppliers to deliver drinks to the castle on a sale or return basis, and for them to pay for the insurance of all wine held at the castle.

In 1962 when the Irish estate was running at a loss of £1,800 a year, Mountbatten threatened to sell it if it continued to lose money on such a scale. And he wrote to his Irish solicitor, Mr C.H. Browne, complaining of the size of his legal bills and telling him he did not expect to receive bills this large in future. He also queried the costs when the same firm (Argue & Phibbs) acted as executors for Edwina's will.

The main reason for Mountbatten's anxiety over financial matters at this time was because of the enormous death duties on his wife's estate. He really did feel there was a distinct possibility that he would have to sell up everything to survive, and while he did perhaps overreact initially, there was some justification for his fears. In a letter to Douglas Fairbanks Jr shortly after Edwina's death he explained that his circumstances were going to be severely reduced. Death duties would account for 80 per cent of the total and of the 20 per cent left out of Edwina's substantial fortune, 7.5 per cent went to each of the girls, Patricia and Pamela, and 5 per cent to himself. He went on to say, 'I shall have 1/- [5p] for every £ she had ... I shall not be able to do things on the scale which Edwina and I could do together in her lifetime, but I am not particularly keen on entertaining or extravagant in my tastes.'

When Edwina died in 1960 Mountbatten wanted to sell Classiebawn, but he was persuaded not to when he learned of the distress it would cause in Mullaghmore and the surrounding area. This is why he decided to rent the castle to holidaymakers instead of selling, a clear indication that his attitude to the estate was not based solely on financial factors.

Mountbatten was always anxious to avoid taxes if possible and, particularly, duty imposed by Customs and Excise. There were several examples of his efforts in this field, ranging from small items of clothing to expensive pieces of jewellery. He showed his shrewdness when he offered his agent at Classiebawn, Miss Gore-Booth, a spare pair of new jodhpur boots for which he had no use. To avoid import duty he proposed getting someone to wear them on gravel so that they would not be classed as new by Irish Customs.

Similarly, he instructed his agent to buy the best quality china (Crown Staffordshire plate) with gold rims and his own cipher, again in gold, embossed on each item, on the basis that the best quality goods are the hardest to break and the easiest to replace. He expressed great concern that the china should be imported into Ireland duty free and told his agent that she should make sure the authorities understood that it could not be obtained in Ireland; a requirement for a duty-free licence to be issued. (He also authorized the installation of electric razor sockets in the bathrooms in order to make Classiebawn more attractive to American would-be tenants.)

During the period when the Mountbattens lived in India, the Viceroy continued his private war against the tax authorities. In 1947, to celebrate their silver wedding, Edwina gave her husband a very special present. It was a ruby-and-diamond-set Star of the Order of the Garter. Once the present had been agreed, Mountbatten put his usual machinery to work to ensure that every detail was exactly as he wanted it.

Collingwood's, the royal jewellers, were commissioned to make the Star, to Mountbatten's own design and specification. He ordered that it should be set in rubies and diamonds and that 'the price should not exceed £1,000 inclusive of any form of British tax or duty.' He noted that purchase tax could be avoided if 'the item is flown to India by aeroplane'. He also instructed Collingwood's to maintain the utmost secrecy about the transaction for 'special reasons'. Commander William (Bill) North, the agent at Broadlands, was used as the intermediary and in a letter to him Mountbatten wrote asking if North could 'personally confirm that no purchase tax would be payable . . . either now or on my return to England and that the cost will not exceed £1,000'. Mountbatten was anxious for North to find out whether, if he had been misled about the price, he would be in a position to refuse delivery. North was requested to seek legal advice. Mountbatten also mentioned in the same letter that the Garter Star was an excellent investment since his GCVO [Grand Cross of the Royal Victorian Order] had increased in value from £350 to £800 in ten years.

The negotiations for the silver wedding gift went on for over a year with Mountbatten insisting that it should be made with rubies and not red enamel, which would have been £65 cheaper and that, in order to avoid purchase tax of £897-10s, the bill must be settled from India. The final outcome was that Collingwood's got the design wrong. The centrepiece of the Star should have featured the heads of King George V and Queen Mary. The jewellers had incorrectly put in a figure of Britannia, which was actually more expensive than the original, but, in Mountbatten's opinion, more attractive and to his taste. He therefore indicated that he was prepared to accept it, subject to consultation with the King [George VI], but if it was not acceptable to His Majesty,

Mountbatten expected a free alteration. The King raised no objections and Mountbatten finally received his silver wedding present.

Pamela Hicks says her father was always anxious to keep his money separate from her mother's, 'so that any presents he bought her or the rest of the family were always bought with his own money. He could never match the money my mother had inherited of course, and he realized this, but was fiercely independent when it came to his personal expenditure.' Pamela added that she felt her father's reasons for building his own rooms in their various houses, such as converting his suite in Brook House to look like his Navy cabin, were a defence mechanism to protect himself from the Ashley millions. 'It was as if he needed his own little nest. And while he and my mother never quarrelled about money, he was always aware that none of their houses belonged to him. My mother was particularly possessive about Broadlands and she wouldn't let him change anything there. She made no bones about the fact that it was her home.'

When he was Supreme Allied Commander, South East Asia, he was given the use of the King's Pavilion in Kandy, Ceylon. Pamela says he loved that house especially because 'he never felt a gust in his own house while he was there and he felt it was his own because my mother was living in England.'

Throughout his life Mountbatten supported many charities, especially those connected with the Royal Navy. Two of his favourites were the Royal Naval Benevolent Fund and the King George Fund for Sailors and whenever these organizations needed extra funds Mountbatten never failed to respond. In 1945 he instructed his naval secretary, Captain (now Rear-Admiral Sir Ronald) Brockman, to make sure that his subscription to his naval charities was twice that of any other individual.

In the closing stages of the Second World War when Mountbatten became Supreme Allied Commander, South East Asia, he was appointed on full pay of £6,000 a year, out of which he paid Indian income tax of £2,400. In addition he was given an entertainments allowance of £1,500 a year which made his net income £5,100. He obviously found it difficult to maintain his standards on such an income and in a letter to the Admiralty shortly after his appointment Mountbatten complained that at his headquarters in Kandy, his official entertainment expenses had only just been met by the allowance even though he had spent three weeks away from base in the United Kingdom and a further ten days in the Middle East. Had he stayed at Kandy without these breaks he would not have been able to cover his official entertaining with his service allowances. There's little doubt that for much of his time in South East Asia, Mountbatten was subsidizing the Government from his private income.

In matters of his personal finances Mountbatten was always scrupulously fair. He never tried to obtain more than he was due but, conversely, no item was considered too small to be included in any claim for reimbursement if he genuinely believed he was entitled to it.

When his ship HMS *Kelly* was sunk at the Battle of Crete in 1941, he had to list all the kit and personal effects he had lost. As his valet had been killed, he had to construct the list from memory, and he thought afterwards that he had probably lost more things than he could remember. But the list included uniforms and other items of naval equipment, plus certain civilian items such as toothbrushes and a gold wrist-watch – and, in keeping with the Mountbatten reputation for throroughness, he records the loss of a pencil!

He also went to what might seem extraordinary lengths over comparatively minor amounts if they involved others. The widow of one of his sailors killed in the *Kelly* had sent him a postal order for ten shillings (50p) so that her late husband's name could be added to a memorial at Chatham Barracks. Mountbatten in turn wrote personally to the Fleet Commodore asking to be informed of any additional cost of including the name and also offering to pay the difference himself, anonymously. He then wrote back to the lady thanking her for her generous gift and telling her how well he remembered her husband as an old friend and shipmate.

Mountbatten's elder daughter Patricia, the present Countess Mountbatten of Burma, says that her father had impressed on her and her sister Pamela from an early age how lucky they were to be well off and not to have to worry about money. 'But he also insisted, even when we were children, that our wealth was not to be abused. For instance, when we lived in Park Lane and we attended a day school, he would never allow us to take a taxi, even in the worst weather. And when we travelled by train, we always went second class, even though he invariably travelled first. He would be up front and we would ride in the rear with our nanny. He used to say, and this was back in the thirties, 'One day we won't have all this and therefore I don't want you to get used to it.''

Lady Mountbatten says the difference in her parents' income created all sorts of difficulties in the marriage: 'Not for my mother, who couldn't have cared less, but for him. He loved all the trappings, the houses, the polo ponies and the Rolls-Royces, but he was always very aware of the fact that it was my mother's money and he was meticulous in keeping his own income to buy presents for her and that sort of thing. It was important to him that he shouldn't be seen to be living off her. Yet at the same time he loved having the use of the money and made no bones about enjoying it. The one thing he hated as far as money was concerned was unnecessary expense. Having been brought up in a family which had very little money, he was always quite careful, even though there was really no need, and if he saw something which he felt was not necessary he would try and remedy it. He wasn't mean with money, but he certainly did not throw it around.'

In the 1930s Edwina Mountbatten had an image as a frivolous, hedonistic young woman who cared about very little except how to enjoy herself. Yet her daughter Pamela says there was another, more thoughtful side to her mother which few knew about. 'She used to spend a fortune on clothes and they were always made with a deep hem and seams, which most people wouldn't have because it spoiled the line of the dress or skirt. She used to explain, "Well, I don't wear my clothes very long and I like to give them to friends who aren't very well off, and if they don't have anything to let down or let out it's no good to them."'

Mountbatten's relationship with Yola Letellier lasted for the best part of fifty years. Theirs was an unusual liaison in that Edwina was fully aware of it and approved. She too became friendly with Madame Letellier and during the early post-Second World War years, when money controls between countries were being rigidly enforced, Edwina's own lover of the moment, Lieutenant Colonel Harold (Bunny) Phillips, also became involved in the financial affairs of Mountbatten's girlfriend.

Just after the war Mountbatten had opened an account for Madame Letellier at Coutts, the royal bankers. The movement of money between France and Britain was very difficult at the time, so Mountbatten provided funds for Madame Letellier to use when she was in the country. On 1 July 1950, he wrote to Lieutenant Colonel Phillips:

My dear Bunnie,

Thank you for your letter of the 27th, enclosing the £35 cheque for Yola. She is probably coming over round about the 20th to spend a few days with us. I will show her the cheque and find out if it would be any use to her for me to cash it and hand her the money in notes. Until I can find out if that would suit her I will not cash the cheque. If it does suit her I will cash it, but if it does not suit her I will tear it up and let you know.

Yours ever, Dickie

The previous year Mountbatten had encountered a certain amount of confusion over Madame Letellier's bank account and he instructed Elizabeth Ward, 'please arrange for the sum of £412-0-0 to be transferred to my No. 2 account at Coutts for her and will you please keep a small private account book in which all details of payments and receipts can be entered to avoid future difficulties . . .'

If there was one thing that Mountbatten really enjoyed in his financial dealings it was the thought that he had secured a bargain. It didn't matter if it was just a few pounds. If he thought he had been clever enough to buy something cheaper than usual he was delighted. In 1951 he wrote to his butler, Charles Smith:

I thought it would amuse you to know that I bought two dozen vests or singlets from the Admiralty supplies which are available to Officers and men on repayment. With purchase tax these 24 singlets cost me £3.2.0d.

I personally cannot see any difference between them and the vests which Hawes and Curtis proposed to supply for £2.7.6d each! I thought that would amuse you as it does show what prices the London shops are now charging.

Apart from the expensive presents which were lavished on him by Edwina during her lifetime, possibly the most extravagant gift that Mountbatten received from an outsider was the one given by Carola Rothschild for his seventieth birthday. Mrs Rothschild was an extremely wealthy American widow who had been a friend of the Mountbattens for many years, and when his birthday was approaching she asked Mountbatten's secretary, John Barratt, for some suggestions.

Barratt knew that his boss was anxious to have a swimming pool at Broadlands, but, understandably at his age, did not feel like spending the thousands installing it would involve. So Mrs Rothschild was delighted to hear that there was something that Mountbatten needed and that he would use constantly. It was hardly the sort of gift that could be bought as a surprise and he had to be let in on the secret at an early stage. He was thrilled at the prospect at being able to swim in his own pool and readily agreed. The pool was built at great expense, with solar heating panels, and a special rail around it so that if one of the dogs fell in it would be able to scramble out. David Hicks reorganized part of the Orangery to provide changing rooms and Mountbatten christened the pool by swimming several lengths, something he liked to do almost every day, according to his secretary, in the nude.

Barbara Cartland was another generous friend whose gifts were appreciated, not only by Mountbatten himself but also by his staff – especially when she visited his secretary's office and found it, by her standards, shabby and ill-equipped. She paid for its refurbishment and provided over £3,000 worth of new furniture. Old friends often found themselves offering gifts to Mountbatten as he approached his eightieth year. He loved to plead poverty and, indeed, he managed to convince himself that he really was in dire financial straits.

Elizabeth Collins remembers one particular day when she had been off work due to illness: 'In the late afternoon I received a telephone call from Lord Mountbatten's bank manager who said he had just had a very strange visit from His Lordship. Apparently, Lord Mountbatten had been into my office in my absence, and, while looking through my papers, had found an account book. Now he was incapable of understanding figures, but somehow he had got it into his head that the books showed that he was overdrawn at the bank. So he marched around to the branch, demanded to see the manager, and asked him how things had got to this stage and what could be done about it. Of course, the manager knew there was no possibility of Lord Mountbatten being overdrawn and showed him his balance to try and convince him, but Lord Mountbatten still wouldn't believe it and it wasn't until I went back to work and explained the real situation that he finally calmed down. He really did think for a time that he had no money left in the bank.'

Of course there were ample funds available to him but he was correct in his belief that there was little cash in his bank accounts. Everything was tied up in trusts and even though he could have borrowed against them if he had wished, he had old-fashioned ideas about borrowing and was convinced that if the money was not in his bank account, it wasn't really his. As a member of the Royal Family, Mountbatten was entitled to keep his affairs private through a 'sealed will', which is what he did. Estimates of his estate run into millions and simply by adding the value of Broadlands and Classiebawn together (in which he held a life interest) it is possible to reach a fairly accurate minimum figure. Three million would seem to be a reasonable estimate but the family prefer not to reveal the actual amount. What is certain is that by most people's standards, Mountbatten was a wealthy man.

Mountbatten loved cars and enjoyed motoring for most of his life. It was a love he inherited from his father who was an early enthusiast, owning a giant Daimler, in which he and his cousin Bertie (later King Edward VII) used to drive from London to Sandringham in the days when horses were more familiar sights on the road than automobiles.

Mountbatten's family said he drove with a carefree abandon 'bordering on recklessness' and with a confidence born of a belief that he was the only person on the road – much to the consternation of other drivers. His last Private Secretary, John Barratt, said, 'Lord Mountbatten took ten years off my life with his driving.' And one of his grandsons said that when Mountbatten drove out of the gates at Classiebawn Castle, he never even paused at the cross-roads – just drove straight across without a moment's hesitation. Strangely, he was rarely involved in accidents on the road and he benefited from a full no-claims bonus on his motor insurance for over fifty years.

His collection of cars was impressive and catholic in its variety. Starting right at the top with the Rolls-Royce which was given to him by Edwina as a wedding present, he went on to own many different types including a Riley, a Standard Vanguard, several Austins, a Peugeot and, in spite of once telling his mother that for some reason Fords were objects of merriment, he bought a number of different models, the last being a Cortina Ghia saloon in 1976. Working on the basis that one should try everything at least once, in 1950 he brought home from South East Asia a huge American Cadillac. It had been a gift from an American general but the cost of maintenance and repairs was prohibitive and he soon disposed of it.

As with all his other purchases, Mountbatten drove a hard bargain when he was buying a car and insisted on his usual standards of perfection being maintained. When he sold his 2½-litre Riley, registration number MLY I (he always tried to get the figure 'I' in his number plates), he said it was 'maddening' to have to accept an offer of £1,250, when a few weeks earlier he could have got £200 more.

During his various periods of duty abroad he made sure that all his cars were exempt from purchase tax. The same applied to those he bought for his family, such as when he paid £810-10s for an Austin A70 for Pamela to use in Malta. And he had enough influence with the Admiralty to have his cars, bought new in Britain, shipped to the Mediterranean free on board ships of the Royal Fleet Auxiliary, thereby saving considerable amounts in transport costs. Considering his reputation as someone who was hopeless with money, Mountbatten was astute enough to check if prices were about to go up when he was planning to buy a car and his suppliers were happy to give him advance notice so that he could get in before any increases were implemented.

When ordering a new vehicle, Mountbatten never accepted the standard factory model as shown in the brochures. He stipulated the exact colour scheme, which had to be exclusive to him, the precise shades of paintwork and the quality and material used in the interior furnishings. For example, his 1951 Riley saloon had to have: (a) Black above the waistline including bonnet top and boot lid; (b) Lower part of body 'Mountbatten blue'; (c) Wings – black; (d) Interior – green leather. Each car he owned had to have his personal cipher emblazoned on the front door panels, and he was equally demanding about the performance he expected from his cars and the standard of workmanship of his suppliers. In 1950 he felt his Riley was not performing as well as it should have. When the garage told him they could find nothing wrong with it, he replied, 'I am amazed at the low standard, for a Riley, with which your people appear to be satisfied.' With Mountbatten there was only one standard – perfection.

Conversely, he was equally generous with his praise for a job well done. He had been persuaded to install one of the first electric radio aerials in one of his cars in 1955. He didn't take a lot of persuading because he was always in the vanguard of innovation and was pleased to be the first to try anything new. After testing the aerial for some weeks he wrote to congratulate the company who had supplied it saying how pleased he was and that it was working very well.

Mountbatten looked after his cars, or at least he made sure that someone else did, and he would no doubt have been delighted to hear that one of his favourites, a 1930 Rolls-Royce in impeccable order, was successfully auctioned at Sotheby's in 1985. It was still carrying its original number plate, LM 3698, which was his old Mayfair telephone number combined with his initials. His first Rolls – a 1922 Silver Ghost Cabriolet with a body by Barker, which had been designed in part by Mountbatten – is now on permanent exhibition in the Mews at Broadlands. It was given to the family after being bought for Mountbatten by Sirdar Aly Aziz, some years after Edwina's death, when he himself felt he could not afford to buy it back. There was no reason why he could not have bought it; but like so many wealthy people, particularly those of royal blood, he was always convinced he was poor.

7

UNCLE EUROPE

Throughout his life Mountbatten cherished and nurtured his relationship with not only the British Royal Family, but also those of other European countries. As a young man he frequently visited his many relations in Germany, Russia, Sweden, Spain, Norway and Greece and, in the latter years of his life, he assumed the role of 'Uncle Europe' – becoming the elder statesman or father figure to many of them, much as his great-grandmother, Queen Victoria, had become 'Grannie Europe' a hundred years earlier. Though Mountbatten's influence could in no way be compared with that of Victoria, he liked to think of himself as the patriarch of European royalty, and his eldest grandson, Norton, Lord Romsey, said, 'He loved to collect crowns.'

While it is true that in return they regarded him with affection, Lord Romsey says that the advice he offered, usually unasked for, was often ignored. 'He loved to think of himself as being pivotal in the affairs of the royal families of Europe. I think he fondly imagined he had huge influence over them all, which I somehow doubt. His attitude to royalty was the only side of his character that I didn't care for. I didn't really mind the fact that he liked to surround himself with glittering company, that was his own choice.' Mountbatten's son-in-law, Lord Brabourne, says that while Mountbatten was not pompous himself, 'He loved the pomposity of royalty. He adored it and he was thrilled to bits being still on the printed royal list. It meant so much to him.'

King Constantine of The Hellenes, living in exile in London, remembers Mountbatten with love, admiration and respect, but he also recognized some of the minor flaws in this otherwise great man. 'I remember as a child Dickie coming over to Corfu, where we had a summer palace, from his naval base in Malta. My mother, [Queen

Frederika] who was a great practical joker, went on board his ship and found his cabin where she proceeded to make an 'apple pie' bed. His naval valet was so frightened of Dickie's reaction that, after she had left, he returned the bed to its original condition. He knew that Dickie hated being the victim of practical jokes even if he liked doing them himself and he had a fearful temper if he thought he was the butt of any jokes.'

On another occasion when Mountbatten had risen to fairly senior rank in the Royal Navy he again visited Greece. This was shortly after King Constantine's father, King Paul, had been promoted to the rank of Admiral in the Greek Navy on his accession to the throne. Apparently, before he became King, he and Mountbatten were often leapfrogging each other in the promotion stakes and there was a certain amount of competition between them (as some people would claim there was later between Mountbatten and his nephew Prince Philip, once Philip had become a member of the Royal Family, though Philip himself was to say that he was completely unaware of any rivalry).

King Paul took a great interest in the welfare of his men, and one of his innovations was to introduce the bush shirt into the Greek Navy's uniform as a lightweight summer dress. It was ideal for the climate and during Mountbatten's visit, the King showed him one of the shirts and gave him several for himself. He even suggested that Mountbatten should get the Royal Navy to issue the garments, but warned him, 'On no account do I want to hear that you have called it the Mountbatten Shirt.' His Majesty knew that Mountbatten loved to lift ideas from other people and then introduce them as his own original thoughts. Of course, what happened was precisely what King Paul had forecast. Mountbatten enthused about the bush shirts to such an extent that they became standard issue in the tropics and were known as the 'Mountbatten Shirt'.

On a more serious note King Constantine says, 'No one could have been more helpful or constructive than Dickie when I came to the throne and even more so when the military dictatorship took over in Greece in 1967 and I came to live in London. He was instrumental in arranging meetings with Harold Wilson, the Prime Minister, on a private basis, when he would invite Mr Wilson (as he then was) to his house in Wilton Crescent and then leave us completely alone. He just provided the premises and never became involved in the discussions. He never once tried to be present at those meetings nor did he ever try to influence me or the Prime Minister or ask what went on between us. It was a wonderful example of Dickie using his connections for my benefit and displaying a sense of diplomacy that some people might have thought at odds with his usual methods.'

King Constantine also remembers Mountbatten as a quite magnificent, if slightly formal, host at Broadlands. 'He went to endless pains to make sure everyone was comfortable, visiting their rooms to check that everything was as it should be. But he was hopeless at balancing house parties. He never considered whether the group would get on with each other. If he wanted them there he just invited them even if, on occasions, one or two of the guests plainly hated the sight of each other.'

Mountbatten's obsession with protocol and the order of precedence was another characteristic that King Constantine witnessed. 'He came to see me in Greece several times when I was on the throne. On one occasion he arrived when he was Chief of the Defence Staff, an enormously important and prestigious position, and one which warranted full service ceremonial when he arrived. The trouble was that he had also been invited to a State Banquet at the Palace and he was very concerned about his place at table. Should he remain in the position dictated as a service chief or demand to be moved higher up as a member of the royal family? It was the sort of problem Dickie would puzzle over for hours. I still can't remember how he resolved that particular one but you can be sure it was the way Dickie would have wanted it. He usually got his own way. There was another occasion when he was holding discussions with my Chief of the Defence Staff, General Pipilis, and I was waiting at the Palace to see the General myself. Eventually I got fed up with waiting so I telephoned Dickie and told him that he would have to let my general go as I needed him urgently myself. He replied, 'All right, but can I come too?' Dickie didn't like being left out of anything he thought he should be included in.'

King Constantine recalls that at Broadlands Mountbatten was just as punctilious about protocol and tradition. For example, when the Queen visited she would always sit at the head of the table, following the old custom that whichever house the sovereign graced with her presence became her house, with the host sitting at her right hand. This practice has been continued by the present Countess Mountbatten and her husband.

King Constantine also recalls some of the tiny rules that Mountbatten felt were important: 'Dickie insisted that everyone's name and title in full should be printed on the name cards fastened to their bedroom doors. He would not tolerate abbreviations, which made it difficult for his staff when it came to some of the more highly decorated guests.' He was also not above arranging things so that his most important guests received the best attention. King Constantine remembers his first visit after he became King. 'His attitude to me changed overnight. Before that I had been just a junior relative, always welcome, but receiving no special attention. Once I was a King, however, my status as a guest improved immediately. Dickie fiddled the draw for positions when we went shooting so that I found myself in the number one position and my place at table also improved dramatically. Everyone knew what was going on, but no one minded. That was just Dickie; one of his harmless but slightly snobbish eccentricities. You would never get that sort of reaction from his grandson, Norton [Lord Romsey], the present mast of Broadlands, who is much more relaxed and laid-back as a host, no matter who the guests are.'

King Constantine gives one further example of Mountbatten's love affair with honours. On the Broadlands estate there is a special tweed which is worn only by immediate members of the family (and estate staff). King Constantine liked the look of it and on one of his visits asked Mountbatten if he might have some to have made up into a suit for himself. 'Dickie refused, saying that no one outside his closest relatives was permitted to wear the tweed and he could not break the rules for anyone, even a king. I then told him, jokingly, that if he would let me wear it I would make him an honorary colonel in the Greek Royal Guard. A few days later, when I had returned to London, a parcel arrived containing a bolt of the cloth with the message 'From the future Colonel of the Royal Guard' – Dickie simply could not resist the opportunity of having yet another title. If he liked to think of himself as Uncle Europe, well, what harm was there in that? He was welcome at every royal house in Europe and if he took himself slightly more seriously than the rest of us did, it was all done with great affection.'

In spite of these idiosyncrasies, King Constantine remembers Mountbatten as a great influence and someone to whom he could always turn for advice. 'He was never too busy to listen and when it came to helping me and others nothing was too much trouble. I miss him greatly and I know many other people, royal and otherwise, who do too.'

That Mountbatten did take himself seriously in the royal context was illustrated time and time again. Lord Wilson of Rievaulx, the former

Prime Minister, recalled one of the Garter services at Windsor Castle at which Mountbatten was present. The twenty-four Knights of the Garter would gather in the robing room at Windsor prior to the service in St George's Chapel. It was an occasion never missed by Mountbatten who loved the pomp and ceremony and enjoyed parading in his magnificent Garter robes. On this particular day he was not seen as the other Knights got ready. Then he suddenly appeared, fully robed, through the entrance reserved for the sovereign and other members of the Royal Family. When he was installed as a Knight of the Garter he was not included as a Royal Knight, who are outside the normal complement of twenty-four, but as a standard KG, in precisely the same way as all the other recipients of the honour. By using the royal entrance, he alienated some of his colleagues unnecessarily and sought to elevate himself beyond the rank and file members of that august body.

Another example of Mountbatten's insecurity as a minor member of the Royal Family was his refusal to speak in the House of Lords. As someone who rarely refused a public platform to air his views, one would have expected him to make great use of the Upper House. But he never did, even though he indicated that he might do so on at least one occasion during a debate on defence cuts. The reason put forward as to why he declined the opportunity was that it was a custom that royal members of the House of Lords did not speak, and if he did, he would be admitting that he was just the same as all the other non-royal peers. Apparently he felt he was constrained by the same rule as the royal dukes – which did not apply to him. Anyway, in recent years the rule has been broken by both the Prince of Wales and the Duke of Gloucester. Members of Mountbatten's family say that the real reason he did not take part in debates in the House of Lords was that he had a lifelong dislike of becoming involved in politics; also, as a serving officer for much of the time when he might have spoken – for example, during the Suez crisis of 1956, when he disagreed violently with government policy – he was barred from speaking.

Mountbatten would go to endless pains over the smallest detail, to make sure that everything was exactly as it should be, whether it was the correct order in which decorations should be worn, a seating plan for even the most informal meal or a massive ceremonial in which he was to play a part. And if there was one occasion when he really came into his own, it was when there was to be a royal visit to one of his homes. Such was the case in 1951, when King George VI, Queen Elizabeth and their younger daughter, Princess Margaret, came to stay for a few days at Broadlands.

Mountbatten corresponded with his agent, Commander North, on the many arrangements that had to be made, and nothing was too small or insignificant for his personal attention. On the subject of the number of servants and police officers who were to accompany the royal party, there was no need for any debate. Protocol demanded that the Master of the Household would have responsibility for this aspect of the visit, and Mountbatten merely needed to know the numbers in order to allocate accommodation. The arrangements for shooting were, however, matters for which he personally assumed responsibility, and he wrote to North ordering that 'The King, of course, must have the best position each time.'

North was also instructed to make sure that there were no leaks to the press about the visit although, privately, Mountbatten would have been delighted for the world to know that he was acting as host to the sovereign and his family. The King had indicated that he wished to keep the visit informal, which in royal terms meant that he did not want any strangers included on the guest list, so Mountbatten was required to submit the names of those he proposed to invite many months in advance. There was nothing untoward in this at the time, though today it would be most unusual for a royal host to be asked to supply such information.

The security precautions when royalty is expected are necessarily stringent, though in the 1950s they were not nearly as strict as they have to be today. Mountbatten told his staff that four firemen should remain on duty during the night with a fire engine parked behind the stables. One Special Branch officer was to be stationed inside the house at all times. During daylight ours a plain–clothes officer was to be on duty in the park with another inside the house. A uniformed police constable was to be posted at each lodge gate and a motorcycle patrolman was to be in a permanent state of readiness on the Bournemouth road. The correspondence dealing with these arrangements ran over several months before the date of the visit and each query was answered by Mountbatten by return of post. Not surprisingly, the royal visit was an outstanding success; anything less would have been thought by Mountbatten to have amounted to failure.

As a host Mountbatten was as demanding of his guests as he was of himself. At Adsdean, the house he and Edwina rented near Portsmouth in the 1920s, he issued each guest with a set of forms he had devised himself and which had to be completed in triplicate: one for the guest, one for the staff and the third for Mountbatten himself. On the forms, the guest was required to state what time they wished to be called in the morning (there was not a lot of leeway as breakfast was served at eight o'clock prompt). They also had to tick off the food and drink they wanted for breakfast and indicate if they were going to be in or out for lunch, afternoon tea and dinner the following day. There were further questions to be answered on other requirements, such as, did they intend to play golf? If so, were clubs to be provided or had they brought their own? How many needed horses? If sailing was preferred please indicate so that the correct number of boats could be hired. If they planned to use the tennis court, the time should be indicated, and if guests were expecting further friends to join them for the day, who were they and at what time would they be arriving and departing?

The forms were intended to make life easier for the staff and Mountbatten thoroughly enjoyed collating the information. He failed to understand why some guests found it tiresome. The only visitors who were not required to obey these rules were the royals, who could do whatever they liked, whenever they chose. In the Mountbatten lexicon there was always one set of rules for royalty (which was their own), and another for everyone else.

David Hicks says that his father-in-law was unpopular with nearly every member of the Royal Household, 'Because he was able to bypass them and go straight to the Queen, which they hated. If he rang the Palace he would say: "It's Lord Mountbatten, put me through to the Queen."' (This is precisely what the present Lady Mountbatten and Lady Pamela Hicks would do today.) 'He took great pleasure in going around the private secretaries, which, of course, annoyed them immensely. They loved to isolate the Queen and they wanted everyone to go through them rather than directly to them. His relationship with the Queen was very special and he used his personal charm on her to great effect. She had a very soft spot for Dickie as he'd been very close since she was a girl. It was a very long-standing avuncular position that he held in the Royal Family. Her Majesty loved to tease Dickie and she was just about the only one who could really get away with it. The trouble with Dickie was that in spite of his brilliant achievements he never really knew who he was. He wasn't a member of the aristocracy; he had royal blood but he wasn't fully accepted in the Royal Family, so he held a peculiar position that somehow left him very insecure.'

Sir Martin Charteris (now Lord Charteris of Amisfield) was a member of the Royal Household for twenty-seven years, five of them as Private Secretary to the Queen. During his time at Buckingham Palace he came into frequent contact with Mountbatten and was one of the few courtiers with whom he became friends. Lord Charteris has a tremendous sense of fun and got to like Mountbatten. He remembers him with affection tinged with some scepticism. 'Dickie liked to give the impression that he was just a simple sailor, when in fact he was anything but. Far from being simple, he was as cunning as a barrel-load of monkeys and one of his favourite ploys, which I soon saw through, was to pretend he didn't fully understand if something was happening that he didn't like. By appearing to be confused he gave himself extra thinking time.' Charteris says that everyone in the Household knew that they had to be wary around Mountbatten, 'because he had the ear of the Queen. In point of fact,' he adds, 'he didn't have it nearly as much as he thought. But the very fact that others believed it to be so was enough.'

There was one subject that Mountbatten brought up time after time while Charteris was at the Palace and that was the return of the Duke of Windsor's property to Britain. 'Every time he went to the Windsor's house in Paris, in the Bois de Boulogne, they used to say they hid the snuff-boxes in case he put one in his pocket. It wasn't because he wanted anything for himself, he just felt, particularly after 1972 when the Duke died, that England was the rightful home for most of His Royal Highness's personal possessions. But the Duchess was having none of it. She was just as obstinate as he was.'

Mountbatten also tried to persuade the Duchess to leave her jewels to the Prince of Wales but in this he was again unsuccessful. When he asked the Duchess why she did not want to comply with his request she replied, 'Why should I? He's never been a favourite of mine.' The Duchess knew that when she had arrived in London in 1972 to attend the funeral of her husband, it had been intended that Prince Charles would be at the airport to welcome her. When she discovered that Mountbatten had been drafted in as a replacement because 'royal personages are not sent to airports' – except to greet heads of state – she sensed the hand of the Establishment once again working against her. Apparently Mountbatten had convinced himself that he was acting on the Queen's orders when he lobbied the Duchess, which was not the case. Her Majesty was not in the least concerned about such matters as the Windsor jewels, but she allowed Mountbatten to carry on if it pleased him to do so.

Charteris recalls how Mountbatten would love to go on board the Royal Yacht *Britannia*, and how he would always check beforehand to make sure he had his favourite cabin. 'He was great fun on board and always organized the shipboard entertainment. On one trip to the South Seas he taught us all, including the Queen and Prince Philip, to do the New Zealand "Haka" or war dance.' On another voyage Mountbatten sent for Charteris 'on a matter of extreme urgency'. 'When I arrived he had an enormous chart before him on which were laid out the plans for his own funeral procession. The "urgent matter" he wanted to discuss was in which order his decorations should be carried in the state procession. He saw nothing strange or macabre in discussing such details. He enjoyed it tremendously.'

Charteris says that Mountbatten's influence with the Queen was nowhere near as great as he liked to give the impression it was. The Queen liked Dickie a lot and obviously he occupied a very special place within the family, but although he liked to think he was involved in all the great issues of the day, I cannot recall a single instance when his advice was asked for on any matter of importance. Dickie had his own method of persuading the Queen to do his bidding, which was to go on and on until, just to get rid of him, she would agree. But only on subjects which might be important to him, but not to anyone else. Her Majesty is far too astute to be swayed by anyone in this way where vital issues are concerned.'

A number of people who worked with Mountbatten said that he was rude and overbearing. Lord Charteris found him to be exact opposite. 'He was the most courteous of men in my presence. He was unfailingly polite and kind and as far as I know, he never behaved towards any of the Household in any other manner, and certainly he never treated me like a servant.'

On one of the Queen's overseas tours in the 1970s, the itinerary included Jesselton, Borneo, the town in which Edwina Mountbatten had died in 1960. When they arrived, Mountbatten asked the Queen and Martin Charteris if they would care to see the room where she had died. 'It was a very moving moment,' recalls Lord Charteris. 'Dickie was still deeply distressed and being there obviously meant a great deal to him. In fact in all the years I knew him, his love and affection for Edwina was the one thing that never seemed to change. I know he had many weaknesses and could be very devious, but where his wife was concerned he was one hundred per cent genuine. He never wavered for an instant.'

Charteris believes that towards the end of his life Mountbatten became something of a figure of gentle fun to some members of the Royal Family. 'They used to pull his leg a lot. Especially when they wanted to get him started on one of his wartime tales. They would deliberately say something controversial, knowing he would take the opposite view, as he had many times before. Most of his stories had been heard over and over again. There was nothing malicious in what they did, they were all far too fond of him for that. It was just their idea of fun. But they wouldn't have done it twenty years earlier, and what some of them failed to understand was that he was usually in on the joke all along. Dickie always knew what was going on and often played along just to amuse them. It was very good-humoured on all sides and I know practically every member of the Royal Family still misses him greatly – and what's more they are very proud of his achievements.

Mountbatten's relationship with the Queen was unique. He saw her more often than almost any other member of the family and she knew she could rely absolutely on his support in everything she did. In his eyes she could do no wrong.

Some of Mountbatten's critics claim he used his royal connections to further his own ends but Her Majesty also used his vast experience for her benefit. She knew that he had contacts at all levels all over the world and she would ask his advice when it would have been difficult, if not impossible, for her to ask an outsider.

The Queen does not normally enjoy gossip but she always found her Uncle Dickie amusing and she liked his company, particularly as he met so many people outside her own circle and could bring her news of what was going on beyond the confines of the Court. Her Majesty liked Mountbatten and enjoyed their chats but she knew that when he called to see her there could occasionally be an ulterior motive, even if what he was after wasn't for himself. He could be very persuasive but in most cases the Queen had already decided what action she would take before she saw Muontbatten and it wasn't always his words that affected her decision – she just let him think it was.

This was not to say that she did not value his advice. She did. He had achieved many great things in his life and she was not slow in calling on him if she felt he could help. However, like her father King George

VI, the Queen recognized that Mountbatten, even in later life, had a burning ambition, and any opportunity to advance himself was seized with determination.

On the other hand, Her Majesty liked to discuss certain sensitive issues with Mountbatten, knowing that if she wanted him to keep their conversation confidential, nothing on earth would persuade him to open his lips – not even to his wife or daughters. When they met, the relationship was so informal that they could talk about any subject under the sun. The Queen also used Uncle Dickie as her private envoy on delicate family matters, one of which she had to keep secret even from her own mother. This was when she wanted to contact the Duke of Windsor, the man who, as a young girl, she had adored as her favourite uncle. Elizabeth II never harboured the ill-feelings towards him that her mother felt, but it took much of Mountbatten's tact and discretion to maintain a difficult relationship. Like her, Mountbatten remained fond of the Duke after the Abdication, but unlike the Queen he did not have to disguise his feelings because of the Queen Mother's obvious resentment of her brother-in-law's behaviour.

In the early days of her reign, the Queen occasionally had a query about constitutional matters. When this happened she would ask Mountbatten to draft her questions – in his own name – which he would then show to the ex-King for his comments. This strictly unofficial correspondence has never been revealed, but it proved invaluable to the Queen at a time when she was still feeling her way as sovereign. One of the reasons why senior members of the Queen's Household believed that Mountbatten was never asked to advise on important matters was that they were the ones who were excluded from the discussions. When the Queen wanted to talk over a delicate matter with Mountbatten she made sure no one from her staff, of whatever status, was present. The talks were completely confidential.

On a number of occasions Mountbatten acted as go-between for the Duke of Windsor and the Queen and it was a two-way traffic, particularly over the question of the Duchess of Windsor being granted the right to be called Her Royal Highness. The Duke naturally wanted his wife to receive the same courtesy as he did and never stopped trying to get it for her. He enlisted the aid of Mountbatten who, while he was sympathetic, was also a realist and knew that such a possibility was highly unlikely. There was a time, just before the Coronation in 1953, when it was thought that the Queen might confer the title on the Duchess; the

Household felt it was going to happen and it was thought that sufficient time had elapsed since the Abdication for the matter to be brought to a satisfactory conclusion. But it never occurred. The stumbling block was said once again to be the Queen Mother, who never forgave the Duke and Duchess for forcing her husband to accept the throne.

Mountbatten himself frequently discussed the Windsors with other members of the Royal Family, and on one occasion it was rumoured that he had told the Queen that a statue should be erected to Wallis Simpson in a prominent place in London. When he was asked, with some acerbity, why, he replied: 'Because without her, we would not have you.'

He also acted as an intermediary between Princess Margaret and the Duke of Windsor when Her Royal Highness wanted the Duke to give her away at her wedding to Antony Armstrong-Jones. As her own father, King George VI, had died, the Princess felt it would be appropriate for her uncle to act in his place. But once again pressure was brought to bear and Prince Philip was drafted in to perform as surrogate father for the day.

Mountbatten was delighted to help the Princess, even though he was saddened and angered by the timing of the announcement of her engagement. Edwina had only recently died and he was still in mourning and he felt that, as a mark of respect, the engagement should have been postponed. In fact, the Court was in joint mourning for a week as Alexander, the Marquess of Carisbrooke, had also died a few days earlier. The reason given as to why the announcement of the engagement could not be postponed was that the press had got wind of the story and the Palace was afraid they might break it before an official announcement could be made. Privately, it was said that Princess Margaret had made up her mind to get engaged, and nothing was going to stop her.

Practically all the members of the Royal Family were recruited by Mountbatten to support his many causes and one they were delighted to endorse was United World Colleges, of which he was President. On one occasion he organized an all-star concert at the Festival Hall, at which his old favourite Grace Kelly acted as Commère and Frank Sinatra topped the bill. The entire Royal Family attended but when Sinatra sang 'The Lady is a Tramp', while facing the Royal Box, Mountbatten was not amused. Later he told Sinatra not to bring his music with him when he joined the rest of the party for an after-show reception at St James's Palace: 'You will not be required to sing for you supper.' And when

Sinatra duly turned up at St James's Palace accompanied by a number of bodyguards, he alone was admitted, being told by Mountbatten, 'This is England not America.'

One of the most senior members of the Royal Family with whom Lord Mountbatten's name was always associated was his nephew, Prince Philip, Duke of Edinburgh. Ever since 1922 when the young Philip had been taken on board a British warship, together with his parents, Prince Andrew and Princess Alice, Mountbatten's sister, as they were brought to safety following revolution in Greece, Mountbatten and his elder brother George assumed responsibility for their young kinsman. Mountbatten liked to claim that he was a surrogate father to Prince Philip, arranging his eduation, providing him with a home when his parents' marriage broke up and, later, persuading him to join the Royal Navy.

There is a certain amount of truth in these claims but they are not entirely accurate. I put several of these points directly to Prince Philip who agreed that Mountbatten did indeed provide him with a 'father figure' but this was during and immediately after the war and not in those early pre-war days. Prince Philip says that Mountbatten was extremely generous with his hospitality to a nephew who had no home of his own in Britain, but that when he first arrived in Britain as a schoolboy, Mountbatten was away most of the time in the Royal Navy. It was his mother, the Dowager Marchioness of Milford Haven, with his wife Nada who acted *in loco parentis* until George died of cancer in 1938.

Mountbatten used to say that he was the one who decided that Prince Philip should attend Gordonstoun. Prince Philip said Mountbatten had no part in that decision but he did have a considerable influence on his decision to join the Royal Navy in 1939. After the war, when they were both serving in Malta, Mountbatten introduced his nephew to the game of polo, and it was at Broadlands that Prince Philip learned to shoot under the guidance of his Uncle Dickie.

Patricia Mountbatten has known Prince Philip all her life and they have remained the closest of friends. He has his own name for her, which only he uses. He calls her 'Kipper' for some reason which no one seems able to remember. When Prince Philip and Princess Elizabeth were starting to get to know each other seriously, just after the Brabournes had married, the Princess went to stay at the cottage in Kent where they were living at the time. As Lord Brabourne recalls: 'It was an absolutely foreign way of life for her. She had never lived that sort of existence and she was enchanted, though her maid could not believe it when she saw where we lived. However, I then became great friends with Prince Philip also and as a family we have remained on the closest terms. Prince Charles is Patricia's godson.' He, in turn, is godfather to the Brabournes' twin sons Timothy and the late Nicholas.

There is no doubt that one of the proudest days in Mountbatten's life was when Prince Philip married King George VI's elder daughter, Princess Elizabeth. John Brabourne says, 'It was the most wonderful day for him. To see someone bearing his own name marrying the future Queen, who he had always placed on a pinnacle, high above everybody else.' As a seasoned Court campaigner, Mountbatten was able to help Prince Philip, who had by now been created Duke of Edinburgh, through some of the sticky patches in the early days of his involvement with the Royal Household, never hesitating to do battle on his behalf with senior Court officials and anyone else if he saw the need.

Prince Philip, who has inherited certain of the Mountbatten characteristics, particularly an unwillingness to suffer fools gladly, always knew that in Mountbatten he had a champion who had his nephew's best interests at heart. His Royal Highness did, however, find Mountbatten's tendency to try to organize other people's lives rather irritating, even if his advice was offered with the best possible intentions. And there is no doubt in Prince Philip's mind that the Queen's decision to adopt Mountbatten-Windsor as the family name for her children would not have happened without Mountbatten's persuasion.

Other members of the Royal Family and old hands in the various Royal Households have often suggested that Mountbatten was a 'user', who liked nothing better than to flaunt his royal connections in order to push through a plan of his own. Prince Philip is more diplomatic in his description. He prefers to call Mountbatten a 'manipulator' but does not deny his extraordinary ability to get his own way.

As two naval officers, Mountbatten and Prince Philip enjoyed many of the same jokes and shared an earthy sense of fun. Mountbatten was an accomplished raconteur who loved to dominate a dinner table with his immense repertoire of jokes and entertaining reminiscences about his widespread family, his thousands of friends and acquaintances, his time in India and, most of all, his service career. These were usually triggered by association and consequently, as Prince Philip recalled, some of them became 'rather familiar' over the years. One of the Queen's most senior ladies-in-waiting, with more than a quarter of a century's service and countless dinners and banquets to her name, was more direct.

'I told the Master of the Household, who arranges the seating plan, if I had to sit through one more account of how Dickie won the war, I'd scream.'

The only occasion when Lord Romsey could ever remember his grandfather being out-talked was at a dinner party at Broadlands when one of the guests was the man who had founded the Avis car hire company. Lord Romsey said, 'Mr Avis talked non-stop for two hours. He didn't draw breath and no one, not even my grandfather, could get a word in. Finally, after several attempts to open up the conversation my grandfather had to give in. He had been beaten by this American and he surrendered with very bad grace. He was not a good loser and he hated the idea of someone else taking over at his dinner table.'

In his younger days Mountbatten formed close friendships with his royal cousins, David (later the Duke of Windsor), Bertie (later King George VI), Harry (Duke of Gloucester) and George (Duke of Kent), who was the person in the Royal Family to whom he was closest for many years. When the Duke of Kent was killed in a flying accident in the Second World War, Mountbatten acted as a friend and adviser to his widow, Princess Marina, and assumed certain responsibilities for her three children, Prince Edward, the present Duke of Kent, Princess Alexandra and Prince Michael.

Prince Michael says that as he did not have a father to turn to it became natural to ask Lord Mountbatten if you needed advice. 'The one thing I remember above all others about him is that whenever you went to see him, no matter how busy he was or occupied with important affairs, he always made you believe that your problem was the only thing that concerned him. And once he had taken it on his commitment was total. He would go to endless trouble on your behalf. Funnily enough I didn't know him all that well until much later in my life and I kick myself that I didn't make the point of seeking his help earlier.'

The most celebrated cause for which Prince Michael enlisted the help of Mountbatten was his proposed marriage to Baroness Marie-Christine von Reibnitz and he explained why he needed all the help he could get. 'We had no end of difficulties with the marriage itself. My wife had been married before, although this marriage was annulled in Rome. She was foreign and, the biggest obstacle of all, she was Catholic, which was hardly the most helpful combination. But Lord Mountbatten shared my convinction that she was the right wife for me and so we sat down and discussed how best we could get the marriage accepted from the religious point of view. I am quite sure that without his help things would not have gone so smoothly. He was an elder figure in the family and so everyone tended to listen to him and he could say things that no one else could have got away with.'

He was also able to use his wide range of contacts to assist the young couple. 'He spoke to politicians and representatives of the Church, people I might have been able to see eventually but when he telephoned they always answered immediately. He took an immense amount of trouble over us. He was a superb diplomat, using his skills in the most delicate manner on our behalf. He would say, "No problem is insurmountable. There's always a way." He then proceeded to break the thing into small parts and tackle each one as it came along. He approached it all as he would have a military or naval problem, devising a plan of action, identifying targets and proceedings to achieve them one by one. That was how he dealt with matters of Church and State as they affected us. The Queen gave her permission for the marriage, but as my wife was Catholic the ceremony was held abroad to conform with the Act of Settlement in 1701.'

Prince Michael believed that Mountbatten was always careful about the contacts he made because he felt that you never knew when they were going to be useful. 'He said that nothing is for nothing. It may not be tomorrow or the next day, or even next year. But the time will come when you might need a favour, and throughout his life he worked on the principle that nothing succeeded like a successful network of personal contracts.'

Prince Michael also says that Mountbatten had an extraordinary sense of historical perspective and this has been exemplified many times by the items he had stored in the archives at Broadlands. Mountbatten told Prince Michael that what was commonplace today would turn out to be of interest to future generations – which is presumably why he kept such mundane items as laundry lists, receipts for shirts and ties and seating plans for meals held seventy years earlier.

Like almost everyone else in the Royal Family, Prince Michael became used to hearing the same stories over and over, most of them featuring Mountbatten in a favourable light. His Royal Highness said, 'I remember in 1964 when we were both guests at the marriage of King Constantine in Athens. We had been to a party held in an hotel just outside Athens and Lord Mountbatten gave me a lift back into town in the early hours of the morning. We sat in the back of an enormous American car; he put his feet up on the back of the front seat, lit a large cigar and spent the entire journey telling stories about his service career in which he increased in importance with each one.' Prince Michael concluded, 'He was a man of enormous charm, panache and good humour and we were devoted to him.'

Mountbatten was an integral part of the Royal Family and he was included in every private party and family occasion. The only member who kept him at a certain distance was Queen Elizabeth the Queen Mother. Whereas the others were affectionate and even loving towards him, she always seemed slightly wary and though she greeted him cordially there was never the spontaneous warmth between them that existed between him and Prince Charles or even the Queen.

The reason was that the Queen Mother remembered that Mountbatten had been the closest friend of her brother-in-law David, when he was Prince of Wales and later King Edward VIII. She recognized early on that Mountbatten always wanted to be on the winning side and when, after the Abdication in 1936, he suddenly transferred his allegiance and affection to her husband, the new King, she was suspicious of his motives. Prior to this, she and the then Duke of York had lived comparatively quietly and they were never part of the fast and glamorous 'Prince of Wales Set' of which Mountbatten was an enthusiastic and active member for many years. Although Mountbatten had been friendly enough with Bertie, it was more of a casual acquaintanceship than a real friendship, because the Duke of York was not then considered to be of great significance in royal circles. His domestic arrangements as a happily married man with a young family were totally different from those of his older brother, who was single, glamorous and regarded as the most eligible bachelor in the world. They had little in common and Mountbatten was, in some ways, more of a brother to his cousin David than were his own natural brothers. In Mountbatten's eyes, David could do no wrong. Since their first overseas tour together in 1921, Mountbatten had made himself virtually indispensable to the Prince of Wales and, inevitably, part of the glamour attached to His Royal Highness rubbed off on Mountbatten.

Their close relationship continued for fourteen years and, to be fair to Mountbatten, even after the Abdication, he remained on good terms with the Duke of Windsor, trying to act as a conduit between him and the rest of the family. But Mountbatten was a realist who knew that if his own position within the Royal Family was to be maintained he needed the goodwill of the King. Accordingly he became the most loyal of the new sovereign's subjects and very quickly found himself back in favour at Court. But while the King himself had always enjoyed Mountbatten's company, and secretly envied his glamorous image, Queen Elizabeth did not care for him with the same warmth.

Not only had she disliked the lifestyle of her brother-in-law, with his string of affairs with married women, his gambling, nightclubbing and generally frivolous attitude, she also did not particularly want her husband to be King. She had never expected to become Queen Consort and the consequent upheaval to her own life, when the Abdication was announced, aroused feelings of resentment towards Edward VIII and all those associated with him – which of course, included Dickie Mountbatten.

Mountbatten himself recognized that he might become a target because of his apparent defection and in later life he told his private secretary, John Barratt, that he had had great difficulty in deciding what to do for the best as it was not only an awkward time for the individuals concerned, but that they had to decide what was right for the country. This explanation smacks somewhat of self-justification as it could hardly have mattered to anyone but himself if he had decided not to throw in his lot with the new King. George VI was particularly fond of the Mountbatten girls and even had a pet name for Patricia; he called her 'Plucky Pat'. Queen Elizabeth, who was widowed in 1952, never got over her feelings of distrust for Mountbatten in spite of the many efforts he made. So nothing could have been more ludicrous than the suggestion made shortly after Edwina Mountbatten died, that Her Majesty might become Mountbatten's second wife.

If Her Majesty ever heard the rumour she might have been amused, but she was more likely to have been horrified at the idea. And she was certainly not above making a joke at the expense of the Mountbattens, even on the occasion of Edwina's burial at sea. As she watched on television the coffin being despatched into the ocean, the Queen Mother, in her sitting room at Clarence House, remarked, 'Well, Edwina always did like making a splash.' When this was repeated to Mountbatten some time later, to his credit, he laughed uproariously, not in the least offended by what some people might have thought a rather tasteless remark.

The Queen Mother remained on the friendliest terms with Countess Mountbatten and her husband, and they loved to visit her at Clarence House.

Mountbatten remained friends with the Duke and Duchess of Windsor throughout their years of exile and even though he did not find the Duchess the easiest person to like, he said she had been good for the Duke and a loyal wife. They, in turn, engaged Mountbatten to lobby the Queen on their behalf to try to get the Duchess accorded the right to be known as Her Royal Highness.

After his first efforts at the time of the Coronation, Mountbatten made several further attempts but gave up in the end, telling his secretary that the Queen Mother was the stumbling block. She was adamant that no such recognition should be forthcoming and nothing could persuade her to change her mind. And, as Mountbatten said, the Queen would never do anything to offend her mother, so for the rest of her life the Duchess of Windsor was denied the style that has been given to the wife of every other royal duke.

The Windsors stayed at Broadlands when they visited England for the first time since the Abdication, for the unveiling of a statue of Queen Mary. Mountbatten told his staff that the Duchess was to be treated with the same courtesy they would extend to any other member of the Royal Family. However, he did not bow to her as he did to her husband, neither did he order his staff to do so, leaving it to them, but saying he thought it would be polite if they 'accorded her the same niceties they did to the Duke'. This led to some confusion among the domestic staff who did not know whether to address the Duchess as Your Royal Highness as Your Grace. On at least one occasion the Mountbatten butler became completely mixed up, using both forms of address in the same sentence. Perhaps it would have been easier if Mountbatten had laid down hard and fast rules instead of leaving it to the discretion of his servants.

On the occasion of the Duke of Windsor's funeral, Mountbatten was slightly put out when he offered to escort the Duchess back to the aircraft that was to take her home to Paris, only to be informed that the Lord Chamberlain, Lord Maclean, had been detailed to perform the duty. Mountbatten felt that as an old friend and a senior, in years if not in status, royal, it would have been courteous to have allowed him to see her off, but protocol demanded that a Court official and not a member of the family should attend. On this occasion he did not risk taking the matter up with the Queen herself, as he did in numerous other instances.

All the younger members of the Royal Family knew that if they needed an emissary to plead their cause with the Queen, there was no better advocate than Mountbatten. He could get away with saying things to Her Majesty that some of the others found impossible to contemplate, and he was one of the few people who could drop in to see her practically at will. If he thought that too long a period had passed since he last had seen her – and he never allowed a great length of time to elapse between visits to the Palace – he would instruct his secretary to telephone the Queen's Page to enquire if she was free and then announce that he would like to pop in for tea and a chat, and he was rarely turned away.

Of course, Mountbatten's relationship with the Queen went back to the days when she was a young girl. The present Countess Mountbatten remembers the formation of the Buckingham Palace Girl Guide company and how she became a member. 'The King and Queen decided that they wanted the Princesses [Elizabeth and Margaret] to join a Guide company. It obviously wasn't practical for them to go out and join an ordinary group, so they invited some of the daughters of their friends to form their own company at the Palace. It was known as the 1st Buckingham Palace Company and I became one of its first Patrol Leaders, with Princess Elizabeth as my Second. We had about twenty girls and as I was one of the only ones who had been a Guide before I was appointed a Patrol Leader. I thought Princess Elizabeth was very efficient though she told me later that she had been rather frightened of me. I suppose one was aware, even then, that it wasn't everyone who could belong to the Buckingham Palace Company and I knew that it was something out of the ordinary. But I certainly didn't treat the Princesses any differently from the other girls.'

Mountbatten's love of honours and decorations as well known in the Royal Family and if at times it became a little wearing, the Queen and her family normally accepted his near obsession with resigned good humour. Some of his detractors say that he yearned to be created a duke, like his royal cousins, and when he heard that Winston Churchill had declined the honour, he had said, 'I wish it had been me.' Obviously, if he had been offered a dukedom he would have accepted; he never refused a promotion in his life but, in fairness, no member of the Royal Family whom the author spoke to remembers him lobbying for such a title.

Prince Philip believes his uncle would have risen to great rank even without his royal connections. In fact, his birth may have militated against him as there were certainly politicians and others of influence

1. The two-year-old Prince Louis Francis on his mother's knee at Darmstadt in 1902, with Papa, sister Louise (sitting) and Alice, and elder brother Georgie. (Reproduced by permission of the Trustees of the Broadlands Archives)

2. Peterhof 1908, with Dickie surrounded by female relatives – Aunt Ella, sister Louise (wearing the hat) and the girls Olga, Marie and Tatiana. Anastasia is supported by Dickie's Mama. (Reproduced by permission of the Trustees of Broadlands Archives)

32. The family at play – Mountbatten with sons-in-law, David Hicks and Lord Brabourne, Pamela and several Mountbatten grandchildren on the beach at Classiebawn, Ireland. (Reproduced by permission of Lady Pamela Hicks)

33. One of the last photographs taken of Lord Mountbatten, at Classiebawn, on the Saturday before the August Bank Holiday Monday, 1979. This is perhaps how he would wish to be remembered – surrounded by grandchildren (India, Edwina and Ashley Hicks) and some of their young friends. (Photograph by Derek Hill)

who used his relationship with the Royal Family as a good reason for not promoting him.

The late Duke of Gloucester, Mountbatten's cousin Harry (Prince Henry), was the last royal Governor General of Australia, serving from 1945–47. When the time came for him to hand over his position he desperately wanted Mountbatten to succeed him. He felt that Mountbatten's experiences in the Far East during the war and his respect and friendship for Australian troops, coupled with the fact that Mountbatten had shown a great affection for the country, equipped him perfectly for the role. The Duke had discussed the matter with the Australian Prime Minister Mr Chifley, who was responsible for submitting suitable names to the King, and the reaction had been favourable, as Mountbatten was seen to be totally outside politics, a prerequisite for any successful candidate.

However, having held the post of Supreme Allied Commander during the war, Mountbatten now wished to resume his naval career as a rear-admiral so the idea was still-born. When Mountbatten did not take up his former career in the Navy but instead was appointed Viceroy of India later that same year, it placed the Duke of Gloucester in a delicate position. He did not want the Australians to feel slighted by Mountbatten's apparent preferment of India to their country so he explained personally to the Prime Minister the reasons for Mountbatten's withdrawal and these were accepted.

When Mountbatten was appointed Viceroy it fell to the Duke of Gloucester once again to carry out a royal duty involving his cousin. The King was abroad in South Africa and not due to return until after Mountbatten had left for India, so in order that he could be invested as Knight Grand Commander of the Indian Empire and Knight Grand Commander of the Star of India, the Duke was asked to perform the ceremony in the King's name. He did so in a somewhat casual fashion, arriving at Mountbatten's small London house in a taxi, not an official limousine, carrying the regalia with him in a shopping bag. Before he could hand it over, there was a moment of panic when it was discovered that the Duke had left the bag containing the insignia in the taxi. Luckily they managed to recover it just in time.

The simplicity of the ceremony was not to Mountbatten's taste, neither did it appeal to his sense of theatre. He would have preferred a full-scale investiture at Buckingham Palace, with the Gentlemen of the Household in Waiting attending in full dress uniform, a band of the

Brigade of Guards playing in the State Ballroom and his family there to witness the occasion, but he did appreciate that Prince Henry had taken the trouble to come himself; it is highly unlikely that he would have done so for anybody else. Lord Brabourne says that at the lunch that followed, Prince Henry kept shouting at Mountbatten, 'Why you to be Viceroy of India, Dickie, why you?' all the while roaring with laughter. Of course, Mountbatten and the Duke had known each other all their lives. They had been at Cambridge together, where Mountbatten had tried to widen Prince Henry's social life and introduce him to several undergraduates with whom he would not normally have come into contact.

Mountbatten marvelled at the Prince's lack of concern for protocol; just as, a few years earlier, he had been amazed at his reaction to the reception which Lord and Lady Mountbatten received when they arrived as his guests in Australia. As the sovereign's representative, the Governor General was used to attracting tremendous attention wherever he went and expected the limelight to be focused on him at all times. When the Mountbattens visited Australia the crowds went wild with excitement and everywhere they went they were greeted with cheering crowds and flag-waving enthusiasm. Mountbatten was, after all, the hero of the Second World War, the man who had defeated the Japanese and he was without doubt the most popular figure in Australia at the time. The Governor General did not mind in the least having the public's attention diverted from himself. He joined in the welcome wholeheartedly and wrote to his mother Queen Mary that Mountbatten was 'a great hit'. Prince Henry had never been a competitive person; he had never felt the need to be. He was totally secure in himself and never sought to be the centre of attention.

Mountbatten, on the other hand, hated being overshadowed in any way and found it difficult to understand how someone else could stand aside and allow centre stage to be occupied by another without feeling jealous. It was one of the characteristics that set him apart from the more senior members of the Royal Family – except, perhaps the Queen Mother, who, although she had been thrust into the position of Queen Consort, thoroughly enjoyed the attention she attracted thereafter and never lost the opportunity to exploit her undoubted talent for publicity. This was one of the qualities she and Mountbatten shared.

Mountbatten had a particular affection for the Swedish Royal Family which started when his sister Louise became Crown Princess (later Queen) of Sweden on her marriage to the Crown Prince (later King

Gustaf VI Adolf) in 1923, and continued when Gustaf's grandson, the present King of Sweden, succeeded to the throne. The old King lived to be over ninety and he strongly resented what he regarded as Mountbatten's interference in his country's affairs, when his brother-in-law had the temerity to suggest that perhaps the time had come for him to abdicate in favour of a younger man.

King Gustaf was said (by those who never knew him) to be the most boring monarch Europe had known and he is best remembered (somewhat unfairly) as the first 'bicycling sovereign'. He and his family took to riding around on bicycles in an effort to introduce a more democratic form of monarchy in their country (a custom followed shortly afterwards by the Danish Royal Family). His wife also broke with tradition by doing her own shopping and paying with her own money; something no member of European royalty had ever done before. Nevertheless, King Gustaf was fully aware of his own position and status and he was not going to allow someone like Mountbatten to dictate to him in the matter of when and how he should rule. It took a number of frank and at times icy discussions between the two men before Mountbatten finally got the message that his involvement was not required.

When the young Carl Gustaf was looking for a wife Mountbatten again took it upon himself to find a suitable young woman. He loved to act as a royal marriage broker, even if the people concerned did not always welcome his involvement. He suggested several names to Carl Gustaf, all of which were politely but firmly rejected as the King had ideas of his own about the sort of woman he wanted to marry. However, when he finally met the person who was to become his Queen he did come to Broadlands to talk the matter over with his great-uncle.

Silvia Sommerlath had no connections with European royalty; she was a commoner and a German. The former did not matter to the Swedish people; they preferred a love match with a commoner to an arranged marriage with some minor princess (unlike previous generations when princes of the royal house had been forced to relinquish their royal titles and accept inferior ones on marrying commoners). But the question of Miss Sommerlath's nationality was a problem. The King was not sure if his people would be prepared to accept a German on their throne.

Thinking he knew what was Mountbatten's usual attitude to royal marriages, he expected opposition to the match. What he had not realized was that his great-uncle was above all else a realist who knew that if the monarchy in Sweden was to be saved, this marriage to a commoner could well be an influential factor. Many people in the country had ambivalent feelings about their Royal Family and there was a strong movement for the abolition of the monarchy altogether. Mountbatten told Carl Gustaf that he was fully in favour of the marriage and that his people would see the new Queen as someone with whom they could identify much more easily than any of those who had reigned in the past. Carl Gustaf was delighted to have such an endorsement from someone whose opinion he respected so highly and Mountbatten's approval increased when he met the bride-to-be at a family wedding. He liked her on sight and felt that Carl Gustaf could not have made a better choice.

Patricia Mountbatten says her father was the last member of their family to figure in the printed list of British royalty, 'So he was a minor royal if you like, who was there by birth, but we, his children, were not included in the list so we are certainly not royal. It ended with him and in a funny sort of way he actually earned his royalty. By the end of his life he had done a tremendous amount of good for the Royal Family so he fully deserved to be included.'

Mountbatten himself could never forget his royal connections. Neither would he ever allow anyone else to forget. His children, though, had and have a more relaxed attitude to royalty, without in any way feeling less respect than he did. It's just that they were brought up in an environment where it was not unusual that kings and queens were relations and likely to drop in at any time. Lady Mountbatten explained her feelings about European royalty when she was a child. 'We might say, "Oh yes, the King of Spain's coming to stay again. Which one is he? I think I remember him . . . or is that the King of Greece?" It was more a matter of identifying them correctly rather than the fact that it was a King coming. There was no great excitement in our house at the prospect. It was no big deal.' She also remembers as a very young girl seeing Charlie Chaplin at Brook House: 'I was much more impressed by Charlie Chaplin arriving than the King of Spain.'

It was in the latter years of his life that Mountbatten came to have a closer and more honoured place in the Royal Family. He had always been included in traditional family gatherings like christenings, weddings and funerals, but during the last twenty years or so of his life he reached a unique position with his royal relatives. It may have something to do with his age, but it was more likely because of his unfailing good humour, his unending patience and his wide experience outside the usual royal circle.

Nobody, not even the Queen herself who is the most experienced monarch in the world, could match his network of contacts – not just with statesmen, politicians and leaders of society, but with a wide variety of people of all classes, from all walks of life. He represented a vast range of experience quite beyond that of anyone else in the Royal Family and he was able to act as an extra pair of eyes and ears whenever the Queen needed information she was unable to receive from official sources.

As a royal 'Ombudsman' Mountbatten turned his analytical and logical mind to family problems and attacked them in precisely the same way he had in other spheres throughout his career. He could recall names and dates from half a century earlier without hesitation and whenever anyone in any of Europe's royal families needed to know something about one of the others – and not just a birthday or significant anniversary – it was to Uncle Dickie that they turned. He had an encyclopaedic knowledge of his far-flung European relations, and a prodigious memory that rarely let him down.

He had been a key figure in the most momentous constitutional event of the century – the Abdication of his cousin King Edward VIII in 1936. Even though he had been against the Abdication, urging the King not to give up his throne, he kept the friendship of the former sovereign, who had been his closest companion and best man at his wedding, for the remainder of his life. Mountbatten even offered to stand as best man at the Duke of Windsor's wedding and was slightly hurt when this was declined. The Duke felt that if his own brothers would not support him, he would prefer to go completely outside the family. He also mistakenly believed that as an ex-King he did not need a best man but supporters, as is the custom with royal weddings. When it was pointed out that this was not the case he reluctantly asked an equerry to be his best man.

Mountbatten did not attend the Duke of Windsor's wedding; he felt his presence would only serve to underline the absence of the bridegroom's brothers. But the Duke harboured deep feelings of hurt and resentment towards Mountbatten for many years, and it was only when he raised the subject and asked why Dickie had not accepted his invitation, and was then told the reason, that he forgave him for what he thought had been a deliberate slight.

The special relationship between Mountbatten and Prince Charles has been well documented and the Prince himself remarked, 'I admire him more than almost anybody I know.' Mountbatten's eldest grandson, Lord Romsey, said, 'If there was a special relationship, it wasn't between my grandfather and any of his own children. It was between him and Prince Charles. That's who was really special to him.

Mountbatten's attachment to Prince Charles was well known and goes back as far as Charles's childhood. Mountbatten encouraged his own grandchildren to read all sorts of publications and took out subscriptions for them, such as *Motor Sport* and *Flight* for Norton, and *Animals* and *Eagle* for Michael-John. He included Prince Charles in his reading group and paid for him to have *Eagle* for many years. When the Prince reached fifteen it was suggested to Mountbatten that the subscription should be cancelled as this was a somewhat juvenile magazine. Prince Philip however, thought the subscription should be renewed and Mountbatten continued to pay for this light relief for his 'honorary grandson.'

There is no doubt that Mountbatten became a close companion and confidant of the future King and they shared a love of royal ceremonial and State occasions. There is also little doubt among other members of the family to whom I have spoken that, had Mountbatten been alive in 1992, the domestic situation between the Prince and Princess of Wales might have been somewhat different. Mountbatten had a fanatical belief in duty. It was the principle that governed his life and his every activity and he would have spared no efforts in his attempts to keep the couple together.

Mountbatten's granddaughter Joanna, now Baroness du Breuil, says she and her mother have many times discussed the situation of the younger royals and what he would have done. 'I think that Grandpapa would have "courted" the Princess of Wales to get her on his side. He was a great charmer and the ultimate public relations man who loved good-looking women of all ages. He would have put himself to immense trouble to win her confidence and then he would have used emotional blackmail to prevent the break-up, using every trick in the book. She is an emotional woman and he would have played on that aspect of her character. There's no doubt that he would have been heartbroken and horrified at the way things have turned out.' Whether he would have succeeded we shall never know but everybody seems to agree that the Royal Family today needs a Mountbatten more than ever.

Within the Royal Household there are many stories told about Mountbatten, most of them showing how he nearly always got his own way. One story which they tell with relish ended the other way. It concerned the arrangements for the Coronation in 1953. The programme came under the direct supervision of the Earl Marshal, the Duke of Norfolk, who personally chaired all the major meetings dealing with every aspect of the ceremonial.

At the final committee meeting in St James's Palace, barely a week before the Coronation was to take place, when every last detail had been agreed and all that needed to be done was a last-minute check of the arrangements, the Earl Marshal asked if there were any final points. A senior Royal Navy officer, representing the First Sea Lord, offered the suggestion that, as the Royal Navy was the senior service, it should provide the Queen's Guard at Buckingham Palce on Coronation Day. The Duke, who had listened without raising his eyes from his agenda, asked, 'Pray, who made that stupid suggestion?' On being told, 'Earl Mountbatten of Burma, Your Grace,' he muttered in an audible voice, 'Bloody King-maker.'

It was the former Prime Minister, Harold Wilson (now Lord Wilson of Rievaulx) who described Mountbatten as the 'shop steward of royalty' and he fully lived up to the title, which he knew about, and relished.

In 1951 when a new Royal Yacht was being planned, Mountbatten acted as the link between King George VI and the Government. He held long discussions with both the King and Queen about the accommodation the yacht should have and told the Admiralty that Their Majesties were anxious to restrict the size of the yacht and control the cost. He was also instrumental in making sure that the original specification included the possibility of converting *Britannia* to a hospital ship in time of war. Mountbatten was also involved in negotiations with a number of wealthy Americans who had offered to subscribe to the cost. In a letter to Sir Alan Lascelles, the King's Private Secretary, he said that this offer might divert some of the criticism from the British public, but he would prefer to see money coming from the Dominions rather than from citizens of the United States, who, he felt, should not contribute to the cost of the British monarchy.

He was also involved in the design of the yacht, using his lifelong interest in the cinema to get modern projection equipment installed on board. He anticipated the row which broke out thirty years later when one of the excuses given for not using *Britannia* in the Falklands campaign was that she used the wrong type of fuel. As far back as 1956 Mountbatten wrote to Admiral Sir Ralph Edwards, then Controller of the Navy, saying he was astounded at the fact that *Britannia* used diesel oil instead of furnace oil. 'You will remember we gave up diesel in favour of furnace oil at Broadlands last year for economy and reliability of action, so the Navy still seem to be lagging behind Broadlands.'

One piece of equipment that was invented by Mountbatten and is still in use in the Royal Yacht is the full-length electrified table mat in the State Dining Room. It consists of a pad running the entire length of the table into which an electric lamp can be connected at any point without the need for the usual two or three-point plugs. It is extremely useful and enables the electric candelabra to be used anywhere on the table, depending on how many guests are seated.

He openly delighted in all things royal and never tried to hide his pleasure. In 1950, his cousin King George VI granted him the honour of displaying a crown on his motor car when he had to attend official functions. It was a small gesture and one that was fully deserved as Mountbatten carried out many functions in his various capacities, several of which were of a royal nature. But he took immense satisfaction in being able to fly a standard with a crown on it; the more so because, once it had been spotted, all traffic lights metaphorically turned green at his approach.

8

MATCHMAKER

If there was one aspect of Mountbatten's character that tended to irritate the other members of his family it was his insistence on meddling in their personal affairs. Whether it was their education, how they spent their holidays, the clothes they wore or especially their romantic entanglements, he was incapable of minding his own business and letting them get on with their lives in their own way.

It happened with practically all of them, occasionally with near disastrous results. When his grandson Norton first introduced his wife Penelope to Mounbatten, long before they had even begun to think of marriage, the older man immediately started planning the wedding. Norton Romsey is a man of great independence and even as a young man he fought against what he regarded as his grandfather's interference. 'At fifteen he tried to persuade me to go into the Royal Navy. He even got me an unofficial trip for three weeks in a ship, where I wore a midshipman's uniform and lived and worked as a junior officer. I wasn't in the Navy and nobody but he could have arranged for his grandson to have such an opportunity. But I thought then that it wasn't for me and I rebelled against being pressurized by him. As it happens, I've since found out that I was wrong and he was right. A few years in the Royal Navy would have taught me how to work with people and learn to manage men; all things I have had to learn the hard way outside, and which are invaluable now in running Broadlands.'

Before her marriage, Lady Romsey was Penelope Eastwood, the daughter of a wealthy businessman who had retired to live in Switzerland. His daughter had been educated abroad and when Norton invited her to Broadlands for the first time she had no idea that she was going to move into a world in which royalty was commonplace, and one which revolved around her boyfriend's grandfather. In fact she had no idea who that grandfather was and even when she was told the name it meant nothing to her.

Lord Romsey said, 'When I invited Penny to Broadlands for the weekend I told her that one or two other people would be here, including Prince Charles, and I added, "And of course, my grandfather will also be there." She didn't react and when I said that Grandpapa was Lord Mountbatten it obviously still didn't mean anything to her. Of course she had been abroad for some years but she must have been one of the few people in England to whom the name Mountbatten meant absolutely nothing.' Lady Romsey says that from the first moment she met her future grandfather-in-law he charmed her. 'It was something he couldn't resist. He loved all young women and could turn on the charm like a tap – and it worked.'

Once he had decided that Norton had made a good choice he did everything in his power to push things along, much to the annoyance of both parties. 'We were feeling our way gently at our own speed,' says Norton. 'Neither of us was in a hurry to commit ourselves, but sometimes he would try to force us together and make plans for the future. In fact it was counter-productive because Penny felt she was being pressured and she reacted accordingly.' Lady Romsey agrees: 'I felt I was being forced into a corner and much as I enjoyed Lord Mountbatten's company, his attentions were occasionally a trifle overpowering.'

Both Lord and Lady Romsey feel, even now, that if Mountbatten had left them alone they might have married earlier than they did. He took so much for granted that they both decided to step back a little and take stock. All they wanted was for the relationship to be allowed to develop at its own pace; with Mountbatten, everything had to be done at top speed – 'Full-ahead' was his favourite command.

Lord Romsey was angry at the time at his grandfather's interference, which he felt could have damaged his prospects with Penny, and he told him so. 'He was astounded and genuinely surprised to think that I believed he was interfering. To him nothing was more natural than that he should encourage us to marry. It never crossed his mind that he should have left us alone, but when I pointed it out he took it with good grace; he always did. You could have a row with him and he never sulked. Of course the great shame was that he was killed a few weeks before we were married, so he never saw his great plan come to fruition.'

Mountbatten's granddaughter Amanda is acknowledged by the rest of the family to have been one of his great favourites. Their birthdays were close together and she feels that perhaps it was this that brought them into what the others describe as a 'special relationship'.

When Amanda was in her teens Mountbatten took her with him to Kenya where he tried, unsuccessfully, to involve himself in the way she dressed and her general appearance when they were invited to formal functions. She said later that he hadn't done it in an arrogant way. He was simply concerned that she should make the best of herself and, as she was not in the least interested in clothes, perhaps it was as well he took such trouble. But her parents were not at all keen that he should become involved in this aspect of her life. They resented his efforts to change her appearance and told him so.

Amanda says that if her grandfather did interfere in her life he did it in the nicest possible way. 'He took me to my first grown-up party and he was the perfect escort. He didn't leave my side all evening and danced nearly every dance with me which must have been very boring for him but it made my evening.' On another occasion Amanda accompanied Mountbatten to a formal function at Buckingham Palace and to make sure she knew the correct form they had a special code which they used when she was being presented to various celebrities. 'Before we went,' Amanda recalls, 'he showed me the difference between a short curtsy and a full, deep one. Then he said he would hold on to the edge of my skirt and if he gave a quick tug it meant a short curtsy and if he gave a long tug this meant a deep curtsy, "Because that means you're meeting a crowned head." He was very particular about such things. He adored the protocol and regarded it as terribly important. It wasn't a question of snobbery at all, it was just good manners.'

Mountbatten did exactly the same thing with Amanda's elder sister Joanna, and she was rather irritated: 'I felt like saying to him, "You don't have to bother, I know what to do." But you couldn't say that to him. He wouldn't have taken the slightest bit of notice anyway.'

The most celebrated of Mountbatten's efforts as a family matchmaker came when he tried to pair Amanda up with Prince Charles. The heir to the throne was the world's most eligible bachelor and both the Queen and Prince Philip were anxious that their eldest son should find a suitable bride. It was a perfect situation for the patriarch of the Royal Family who loved nothing better than solving personal problems of this kind. It also provided him with an ideal opportunity to consolidate his own position within the Royal Family by marrying his favourite granddaughter to the future King.

He had actually thought of trying to match Amanda's sister Joanna with Prince Charles at one time, but that was short-lived idea as they had very little in common, so all Mountbatten's efforts were concentrated on the younger sister.

Prince Philip was all for it, saying, 'At least we won't be getting a stranger in the family.' Mountbatten set about arranging the match with his usual enthusiasm and methodical approach. Prince Charles was invited to Broadlands at every opportunity and often found that Amanda would be there also. Mountbatten never missed a trick.

Amanda has never spoken publicly about her relationship with the Prince of Wales, believing this is a private matter about which the least said the better.

Her grandfather may have been devious but to everyone in the family he was absolutely transparent. The antics he got up to in his efforts to throw the young couple together were patently obvious to all who saw him in action – except Amanda, who didn't catch on for some time.

John Barratt was around on nearly every occasion and remembered that most of the pressure was on Prince Charles who, at the time, was completing a radio course during his Royal Navy service. Mountbatten arranged for His Royal Highness to live temporarily at Broadlands and then he would invite Amanda down and manoeuvre them into situations where they were alone. Amanda still does not believe this was the case; she thinks that the main reason her grandfather opened his home to Prince Charles was because of their extremely close relationship and that they wanted to spend time together.

Whatever the reason, Mountbatten's matchmaking very nearly worked. Barratt said that Amanda and Prince Charles would not have noticed each other if her grandfather had not been around and if he hadn't tried to throw them together. It was not difficult to see how he could have thought they might have been an ideal couple. They had a lot in common. Both loved the outdoor life, sailing, riding and hunting, and they shared a deep concern for the environment. However, Mountbatten's attitude to relationships was based on what he knew about European royalty and the way they accepted arranged marriages, or at least the way they had in his younger days. But this was one area where he was completely out of touch with modern thinking.

Barratt felt that Mountbatten's attempts to marry Amanda into the Royal Family were not just ambitions for her or even himself, but a genuine desire to help the Prince of Wales find the right wife. 'He absolutely adored Prince Charles and would do anything for him.' The relationship between Prince Charles and Amanda eventually settled down into a good, lasting friendship but Mountbatten never really gave up. Until the day he died he was hoping that somehow they would still get together. That there was affection on both sides has never been denied but Amanda, in her own words, 'was more interested in student politics than the State Opening of Parliament'. So she went abroad and the romantic interlude was over.

Not everybody in the Mountbatten family agreed with his actions as a matchmaker. When Lord and Lady Brabourne found out about his intentions they were less than pleased. They had married for love when they were both young and theirs has been one of the great, romantic love stories of the past forty-seven years. They are a living example to their children of what a truly successful marriage, based on mutual love and respect, can be. They wanted all their children to marry only for love, whether it was to an artisan or an archbishop, and Mountbatten's attempts to arrange a marriage between their daughter and Prince Charles caused one of the few serious disagreements between him and the Brabournes.

When John Brabourne asked Mountbatten's elder daughter Patricia to marry him, back in 1946, she had some doubts about her answer. She talked it over with her father, as she always did with matters of importance, and asked his advice. She told him that she cared deeply for John but that she was not swept off her feet and asked what would happen if she did marry him and then a couple of years later someone else came along whom she could not resist. Mountbatten replied that he knew she had a great sense of duty and loyalty and that, no matter what her private emotions might be, she would always take the honourable course. He also said that love often follows, even if there is not a deep passion at first. And in their case he was right. They have been married for nearly half a century, had seven children and wherever John Brabourne is in the world he has never passed a day without telephoning his wife. They have what many people would regard as an enviable marriage – a perfect partnership.

Their daughter is now happily married and, as Lady Amanda Ellingworth, is the mother of two small sons. One thing of which her grandfather would have been sure to approve is that her husband's name is Charles — at least she complied with his wishes in that respect.

9

IN COMMAND

On New Year's Eve 1932, Mountbatten was appointed captain of HMS *Daring* – his first sea-going naval command. *Daring* was a destroyer of 1,400 tons with a top speed of 34 knots, and for a young lieutenant commander, just about the most glamorous ship in the fleet.

Mountbatten fully realized his good fortune and wrote: 'A captain is God Almighty – he can do exactly what he wants to do with his ship ...You can make yourself hated or loved. And for all this they pay you – pay you for doing the most wonderful job in the world.' His euphoria was short-lived, however, as within weeks of his new command he was ordered to take the ship to Singapore where he had to hand over his brand new destroyer in exchange for an old and much battered First World War craft.

The replacement was named HMS *Wishart* and Mountbatten, displaying his genius for making things appear better than they were, told his assembled crew on the day they took over that she was actually a very special ship indeed whose name was revered every day in the Lord's Prayer: 'Our Father "wishart" in Heaven.' It was not a very good joke but ordinary seamen of the pre-war years were not used to hearing their officers make jokes, even ones as feeble as this, and it went down very well. Neither were the men accustomed to having their morale lifted. The relationship between seaman and officer was distant, distrustful and, as far as the men went, one of unquestioning and instant obedience. Discipline was harsh; the men expected nothing less and Mountbatten's attitude was a complete revelation to most of them and showed that their new skipper might not be as bad as they had feared.

Just about everyone in the Royal Navy had heard the name Mountbatten. His wealth, his royal relations and his glamorous wife, who was rarely out of the gossip columns, ensured that Mountbatten became famous in the Navy long before any of his later achievements made him front page news.

The sailors were naturally suspicious of all their officers, and rightly so. The officers came from a different class (few rose from the ranks in those far-off days), they spoke with a different accent that marked them out as superior beings, and there was very little genuine concern about the welfare of those men of the 'lower deck' in the Royal Navy of the twenties and thirties. The men expected to be treated like dirt and in most cases they were not disappointed.

In Mountbatten they found someone different. He not only demanded the respect due his rank, he also desperately wanted to be liked – by everyone, fellow officers and ordinary seamen. As it later turned out, he was more successful with the seamen than he was with the officers, many of whom felt he was brash, conceited and insufferable in his attempts to reach the top. Mountbatten was determined that his ship would be the best in the fleet and his crew would be seen as the most efficient. If this meant raising their morale so that they would share his ambitions, that was the way he would do it.

It has long been a golden rule in the services that one never volunteers for anything. Mountbatten managed to change this attitude among all his crews by taking them into his confidence and making them feel they were almost as important as he was himself, as part of the team. But just as every team has to have a captain, nobody was ever left in any doubt who was the captain of this team. His enthusiastic approach to gunnery, seamanship and even sports activities did not find favour with everyone. Some of the old 'China Station' hands, with years of service behind them, were not prepared to enter into the spirit of things in the way Mountbatten wanted. They were reluctant 'volunteers' for his various schemes, but they were careful to hide their cynicism from their young commander.

Part of Mountbatten's success throughout his life was because he fervently believed that if he thought something was worth doing, everyone else would think so too. He never quite came to understand that not everyone was all that interested in being the best at everything. Most of them just wanted a quiet life – which was something no one got when Mountbatten was around. As HMS *Wishart* sailed back to Malta from Singapore, Mountbatten organized all sorts of activities to keep his crew alert. He started a ship's newspaper (though what he found to put in it day after day when there was no ship's radio or any other means of finding out the latest news is something of a puzzle). He also formed a ship's band, a concert party and organized matches between the stokers and deck-hands in an effort to keep them all in a competitive frame of mind. Some of Mountbatten's officers were less than pleased at the frenetic pace of life on board – especially when they were sailing through the Indian Ocean in temperatures of a hundred degrees or higher. But Mountbatten's efforts paid off. By the time they were back on station in the Mediterranean, he had turned *Wishart*'s crew into a happy and efficient ship's company – even if his personal popularity was not at its highest with all of them.

If there was one aspect of Mountbatten's character that really annoyed many of his fellow officers in Malta when he first arrived on the island, it was his extravagance. Three-quarters of his colleagues were living on their service pay and the fact that Mountbatten had money to burn – and showed it – rankled with them. In those early days, shortly after his marriage, Mountbatten took great pleasure in showing off his 'toys', whether it was the latest model sports car or a flashy speedboat, and his reputation as a wealthy playboy sailor made him unpopular for a time. The description of him as nothing more than a playboy was undeserved because he certainly worked as hard as he played, and as for his money, he never deliberately flaunted it; he was just so keen on enjoying every moment that he never gave a second thought to other people's feelings.

His determination that his ship's crew would win everything in sight also made him a number of enemies – and made his crew equally unpopular with their shipmates in the rest of the fleet. As far as Mountbatten was concerned there was no sharing out of prizes; he had to win the lot. His men were used unsparingly and events which, in previous years, had been highly entertaining as rival crews competed with each other now became matters of the utmost seriousness. One former colleague of Mountbatten said, 'He took all the fun out of Fleet Regattas because he never left anything for the other chap. He had to have every trophy and then crowed about it.'

That he was tremendously successful is evident. The manner of his achieving this success, though, was not attractive. There was none of the traditional modesty the British demanded from their winners. He appeared to by trying just a little bit too hard. This was to be one of Mountbatten's blind spots throughout his life; an inability to accept success gracefully. For a man who prided himself on being able to get along with anyone and who believed that he was, at heart, a sensitive soul, it was a curious weakness. But Mountbatten was a mass of contradictions. He loved royalty and being included in their ranks, yet he could enjoy hours of conversation with the plumber working on the heating system at Broadlands. When he married, his pay as a junior naval officer was just £300 a year, but he saw nothing incongruous in turning up for work in Portsmouth in a Rolls-Royce. In his career he worked hard and all his promotions were obtained through merit, but he also used his relationship with first King George V, and, later, his son King George VI, if he felt he could bypass the normal channels to get what he wanted. He would have been hurt and mystified if anyone had suggested that he was being sycophantic in inviting senior officers to his large country house, Adsdean, in Hampshire, where they met some of society's leading personalities. He didn't seem to realize that these same officers would not have dreamed of socializing with someone of his junior rank if he had not been who he was.

The Second World War was the making of Mountbatten. In six years he rose from commander in the Royal Navy to become an admiral, in addition to holding the ranks of lieutenant general in the Army and air marshal in the Royal Air Force. He leaped from holding a modest sea-going command to the dizzy heights of Chief of Combined Operations, adviser to Winston Churchill and finally Supreme Allied Commander, South East Asia. Like so many heroes before him, it took a good war for Mountbatten to realize his full potential, and he seized the opportunities with both hands.

Just a week before the outbreak of the Second World War in 1939, Mountbatten, by now promoted to the rank of Captain, assumed command of the ship with which his name will be forever identified: HMS *Kelly*. She was the flagship of the eight-strong Fifth Destroyer Flotilla of which he had also taken command.

By one of those happy coincidences which seemed to occur frequently to Mountbatten, the ship contained the most luxurious captain's quarters in the Royal Navy. And this was one instance when it had nothing to do with his status or private wealth. It was simply that HMS *Kelly* had been chosen to transport King George VI and Queen Elizabeth across the English Channel on a proposed State visit to Belgium in the summer of 1939. Although the voyage was to be a comparatively short one of only several hours, the Admiralty had insisted on spending money to convert the captain's cabin into suitable royal accommodation. A private bathroom had been built adjoining the cabin (the only ship in the service to have this facility), new carpets had been laid and special insulation installed to make the cabin as quiet as possible. The galley was equipped with the latest ovens, capable of cooking meals for up to twenty people at a time, which Mountbatten's personal Maltese steward would prepare when his skipper entertained on board. The declaration of war forced the cancellation of the visit but, happily for Mountbatten, not the removal of the extras which were to make his life on board very comfortable indeed, until the *Kelly* was sunk during the battle of Crete.

The ship was called on for royal duty on only one occasion; in fact it was the first wartime task she performed and one which brought particular pleasure to her skipper. Mountbatten was ordered to France in the early days of the war to bring to safety the exiled Duke and Duchess of Windsor. He docked in Cherbourg on 12 September 1939, just nine days after the war had started, and the Duke and Duchess and their entourage, including four corgis and a chauffeur, embarked. Winston Churchill, as First Lord of the Admiralty, had issued the order to rescue the former King and his wife, and had also, as a courtesy to the Duke who was an old friend, sent his own son Randolph to accompany the couple back to England. The return voyage to Portsmouth was uneventful, carried out mostly under cover of darkness, and Mountbatten recalled later that the Duke of Windsor congratulated him on the splendour of his quarters, saying, 'You're doing yourself very nice, Dickie.' The only thing that displeased the Duke was the manner in which his arrival back on British soil for the first time since the Abdication was marked. He had asked for no formal reception but the Admiralty, disregarding his request, had installed floodlights on the harbour wall and a full Royal Marines Band was on duty to play His Royal Highness ashore.

The *Kelly* was involved in action almost from the beginning of the war, but evidently not quickly enough for Mountbatten who claimed a 'probable' when he depthcharged what turned out to be a shoal of fish. Two months later he was involved in the first of his mishaps when he found he had inadvertently wandered into the middle of a minefield in the Tyne Estuary. There was a massive explosion as the *Kelly* hit a mine and she had to be towed back to Hebburn for repairs. Years later, at a *Kelly* reunion, Mountbatten told his men that he had known all along that they were in a minefield, and that he had been ordered to take that route against his own advice, but that he had decided to keep the fact from his crew in order not to alarm them.

Nevertheless, Mountbatten was held responsible for taking his ship into the minefield without due care but he managed to divert attention away from himself by focusing on a single incident that had occurred during the action. One of the stokers had panicked and deserted his post, an offence punishable by death in wartime. Mountbatten assembled the 240 men under his command and told them, in suitably dramatic fashion, that he did not blame the man but himself for not being able to impress his own personality and doctrine on the unfortunate sailor. He then proceeded to let him off with a caution, a decision that sent Mountbatten's popularity soaring. The incident was highlighted in the film based on the exploits of the *Kelly: In Which We Serve* with the part of the cowardly sailor being played by Richard Attenborough. The disgraced stoker later distinguished himself by winning an award for gallantry, but he never once attended any of the *Kelly* reunion dinners or contacted any of his shipmates.

When the *Kelly* had been repaired and Mountbatten had got her back she had scarcely been at sea a few days when she was involved in another incident, this time with one of our own ships. On convoy escort duty in the North Sea, the *Kelly* went too close to another destroyer, damaging both ships extensively. *Kelly* was ripped down her entire length requiring emergency repairs at Scapa Flow, the giant naval base off the north coast of Scotland, before limping back to London where the major damage was repaired. There was no doubt where the fault lay this time; it was *Kelly*'s. Mountbatten had not been on the bridge at the time of the incident and the officer of the watch could have taken evasive action to avoid the crash, but as captain he carried the can. His ship became a laughing stock and so, to the delight of several of his colleagues, some of whom were very senior officers, did Mountbatten. Admiral Ewing obviously took some pleasure in recording that 'The ever efficient Mountbatten had given orders to his radio operators that should they ever hear an explosion they should immediately send out a signal "Have struck a mine." On hearing the noise of the impact between the two ships, the signal was automatically transmitted. The other destroyer, HMS *Gurkha*, received the signal and replied: "That was not mine but me."' It took some time to live down, and was hardly an auspicious start to a war that would eventually make Mountbatten's reputation as a great leader.

In May 1940 the *Kelly* was involved in an action which would bring its captain bouquets and brickbats in equal measure. Leading a flotilla of destroyers, escorting the cruiser *Birmingham* on a hunt for mine-laying ships off the Dutch coast, Mountbatten, impatient for action, signalled the mother ship using a bright Aldis lamp, thereby advertising his presence to any enemy craft. One of his more flippant signals read: 'How are the muskets? Let battle commence.' Within minutes a German torpedo had struck *Kelly* killing twenty-seven of her crew and wounding dozens more. The ship had to be towed back across the North Sea where they reached the Tyne to the sympathetic cheers of hundreds of dock workers.

When the official report of the incident was written it recorded that the *Kelly* had contributed to her own downfall. She should not have been in the area where she was struck, Mountbatten should not have sent unnecessary and conspicuous signals and the conclusion was that he had fallen into a carefully prepared trap. For any other captain it could have proved fatal to his career. But Mountbatten, who was blessed with being able to turn disaster into triumph, emerged with glory. His mistakes during the action were erased by the dramatic impact of his arrival back in Britain.

As the *Kelly* limped home, its commander and crew were greeted like heroes. The public warmed to this gallant officer and his men who had refused to lie down and die in the North Sea and Churchill himself, who could always recognize a good public relations opportunity, wanted Mountbatten to be awarded the Distinguished Service Order for his conduct in bringing the ship back. But Mountbatten had powerful enemies in the Admiralty and he had to be content with being Mentioned in Despatches, much to his own annoyance. When both Churchill and the Duke of Kent were unsuccessful in getting him the decoration he felt he deserved, he wrote: 'If the King's brother cannot get his cousin the same decoration as every other Captain (D) has been given, then the powers working against me must be very powerful indeed.'

He didn't have to wait too long for the coveted DSO; at the end of that year he learned that the Lords of the Admiralty had, in fact, recommended him for the medal, which made a pleasant start to 1941, a year which would see him losing his beloved *Kelly* in another disastrous naval action.

In May Mountbatten was ordered to take his destroyer flotilla to assist in the defence of Crete from a land assault. His superiors, and Mountbatten himself, knew that their task was impossible and that there was little chance of them surviving. There was to be little air cover and when they were attacked by twenty-four Junkers dive-bombers, first the *Kashmir*, *Kelly*'s sister ship, was sunk within two minutes and then *Kelly* herself swiftly followed after receiving direct hits from three enemy aircraft. She sank so quickly that as she went down her propellers were still turning and her guns still firing. Nine officers and 127 ratings were killed: Mountbatten and the survivors were fortunate indeed in being picked up by HMS *Kipling*, another of his flotilla, and taken to Alexandria. There the first person to greet him was his nephew, Prince Philip, who told him, 'You look like a nigger minstrel,' a reference to the fact that Mounbatten was still covered in oil. It was the end of Mountbatten's sea-going wartime career, but the beginning of his climb to the top.

In assessing Mountbatten's qualities of seamanship, his official biographer, Philip Ziegler, wrote

> Mountbatten was not a good flotilla leader, or wartime commander of destroyers . . . Mountbatten was impetuous. He pushed the ship fast for little reason except his love of speed and imposed unnecessary strain on his own officers and other ships in the flotilla. Above all he lacked that mysterious quality of 'sea-sense', the ability to ensure that one's ship is in the right place at the right time . . . among all his peers who have expressed an opinion the unanimous feeling is that, by the highest standards, he was no better than second rate.

No one, not even his worst enemies, ever questioned his courage. He was brave to the point of being a danger to himself and those around him. He also led something of a charmed life in those first two years of the war. By the law of averages he should have been killed at least three times and he took no precautions to protect himself when he was in action. Others have claimed that it was because he lacked imagination that he was so brave; he simply could not picture what it would be like to be blinded or horribly burned as so many of his shipmates were. If he had been able to imagine the consequences he might not have been so reckless. Whatever it was that caused him to disregard personal danger, he always led from the front. His men had a magnificent example to follow – and he must have been doing something right, because many of them were willing to join him in whatever enterprise he was next going to undertake.

Rocky Wilkins is the man responsible for keeping the memory of the *Kelly* alive to this day. He founded and ran the *Kelly* Reunion Association and, at the age of eighty, still had total recall of everything that happened on board. Rocky joined the Royal Navy in 1934. He had served in the Royal Scots Regiment before that but walked out because 'I couldn't understand a word they were saying' (Rocky was a true Londoner), and joined the Navy the next day, without bothering to tell the Army he was leaving. Rocky said that 'Lord Louis was impossible to argue with. He just wore you down until you ended up agreeing with everything he said.' He also said that Mountbatten was a good 'lower deck officer' – meaning the ordinary seamen got on with him much better than they usually did with officers. And it was this popularity with the lower deck that caused him not to be universally liked by the other members of the ward room.

Rocky Wilkins said that Mountbatten was fair but he could be a strict disciplinarian and he liked to find punishments that fitted the crime. When Rocky failed to attend church parade and was asked the reason by Mountbatten he replied, 'I'm excused on account of my religion, sir.' Mountbatten then said, 'You're not a Roman Catholic, are you?' 'No, sir, I'm a Jewish atheist.' The following day Rocky was ordered to report to the dockside where an escort was waiting to take him to the nearest synagogue, which he had to attend for lessons for the next three weeks. Mountbatten had taken the trouble to telephone the Rabbi, who agreed to take part in the punishment, and thereafter Rocky Wilkins never missed a church parade.

The postscript to the incident was that for years after they had both left the Navy, whenever they met, Mountbatten would greet Rocky with the Hebrew word 'Shalom.'

One of the ratings on board the *Kelly* was named Harry Lord. One day he was working on the bridge being watched by Mountbatten sitting in his captain's chair. Lord was wearing his regulation steel helmet on which his surname had been painted. Seeing this, Mountbatten ordered him to remove the name or add his initial, saying, 'Remember, there's only one lord on board this ship and it's me.' Actually, Mountbatten was not correct for his First Lieutenant was another genuine lord: Lord Hugh Beresford, but nobody was about to remind him of his error.

Among senior officers Mountbatten made significant enemies, particularly over the ease with which he was able to move in the highest society. An admiral said that one of Mountbatten's problems was that he never knew his place. He always thought he was as good as any officer, no matter how senior he might be. In point of fact, Mountbatten usually thought he was better than any officer and it was this unshakeable belief in himself that allowed him to make the decisions he made, sometimes involving thousands of lives, without losing a moment's sleep. Another of his critics, Admiral Cunningham, told a dinner guest in Malta, after Mountbatten had departed, that 'The trouble with your flotilla, boy, is that it was thoroughly badly led.'

If his sea-going war had ended, the most exciting and far-reaching episode was just beginning. Mountbatten did not know that he would not be seeing action from the bridge of a warship; he had been told to expect command of HMS *Illustrious*, an aircraft carrier, which he was to collect in the USA. But in the meantime he had been involved in discussions with Churchill and other leaders on many occasions, and while Mountbatten's superiors in the Admiralty were not entirely in favour of their royal colleague, Churchill found in him a kindred spirit.

Mountbatten had never been one to hold his tongue and his opinions found great favour with Churchill, who ordered him back to Britain from America to take on a special job. Mountbatten had no idea what it was and at first he was dismayed at losing the command of one of the largest ships in the Navy. When he returned to Britain it was to discover that, at the age of forty-one and still only a junior captain, he was to be given command of Combined Operations, leapfrogging scores of other talented officers in a promotion that would cause others to hate him for the rest of their lives. Nobody appeared to approve of the appointment, except the most important figure of all, Winston Churchill – and there was one other ally, Mountbatten's cousin, King George VI, who was thoroughly in favour.

It was on 4 March 1942 that Mountbatten was told by Churchill that he had decided to make him Chief of Combined Operations with the acting ranks of vice admiral, lieutenant general in the Army and air marshal in the Royal Air Force. In making the appointment Churchill overruled the First Sea Lord, Admiral Dudley Pound, who told him that the Navy could not approve it and that 'the Service will not understand a junior in a shore appointment being given three steps in rank'. The opposition made no difference to Churchill; he had decided and that was enough.

Within Combined Operations itself news of Mountbatten's appointment was received with acclaim. Since their information they had been regarded as relatively unimportant by the three services but now, with a leader with such a reputation, they knew they stood a good chance of being taken seriously at last. Everyone knew that Mountbatten had a private line to the top and that he would not hesitate to use it, and so his new colleagues were hoping that his connections would enable them to do the job they so desperately wanted to do.

Once Mountbatten found his feet, which did not take long, he was ecstatic about his new job, particularly as he became the youngest vice admiral since Nelson (Lord Beatty had been forty-four when he reached the same rank). Writing to Patricia he said, 'Although the Army and Air Force are pressing me to get Lieutenant General's and Air Marshal's uniforms, I am, at present, too shy and plead insufficient coupons' – an unusually modest remark from someone who, even at the stage in his career, was known for his vanity.

The job he took on was an important one as he was in charge of all amphibious training and development for the eventual 'Second Front' – the invasion of Europe. As part of the preparation and to test both men and equipment, Mountbatten staged a number of small but daring raids on the coast of Nazi-held Europe, some of which brought him great praise from the Prime Minister. Mountbatten's successes as Chief of Combined Operations far outweighed his failures, yet he is remembered in this role mainly for one gigantic failure, the blame for which was laid firmly at his door.

On 19 August 1942 Allied Forces made a frontal attack on the heavily fortified port of Dieppe. The raid had been planned for months but unfortunately there was no one man in overall control of the operations. Officers of equal rank were given command of various parts of the invasion, but although it was seen as a Combined Operations project, Mountbatten was not given the ultimate control. Nevertheless, when the post mortems were held in the months – and years – following the disaster (which is what it turned out to be) he was blamed as the man responsible for the deaths of over a thousand men, with two thousand being captured. The Dieppe raid was doomed not to succeed even before it began. No one could agree on the form the attack should take, the strength of the German opposition was seriously underestimated, and the tough, battle-hardened British commandos were replaced by equally brave but inexperienced Canadian troops, who would make up the bulk of the casualties.

Lord Beaverbrook believed that Mountbatten had sent his countrymen to their deaths and never forgave his former friend. His group of newspapers maintained a continuous attack on Mountbatten, in whatever he did, for many years afterwards and he forbade his editors from reporting anything favourable. Whoever was at fault, Mountbatten always took a defensive attitude when discussing the affair and even if he was not solely to blame, he was only once more in his life (in India) to attract such harsh criticism.

During his period as CCO his old friend Douglas Fairbanks Jr, who was already serving as an officer in the United States Navy, wrote to him hinting very strongly that he would like to join his elite group. Mountbatten was in a position to get almost anything he wanted and within a short time Fairbanks was transferred to his staff to learn how mixed amphibious operations worked. Fairbanks was not in on the Dieppe raid and when it was over, but before the extent of the failure was known, he sent a telegram of congratulations to Mountbatten. It was well meant but misplaced. Some time later Fairbanks was summoned to Mountbatten's office and told that his 'celebrity status' was endangering the effectiveness of Combined Operations. Not only was it an embarrassment to the command but a serious threat to security as so many people recognized him coming and going. He would have to go.

Fairbanks had worked well away from the sharp end of Combined Operations and Mountbatten, believing that his friend felt the same way as he did about missing the action, arrange for him to be transferred to an operational station to take part in a number of dangerous actions. Fairbanks has always readily admitted his reluctance to be a hero, but to his credit he fought with distinction on several hazardous missions. Another of Mountbatten's characteristics was that he not only had exaggerated confidence in himself, but in his friends also.

Away from the rigours of war for a long weekend at Broadlands, Douglas Fairbanks remembers one incident that showed how vulnerable Mountbatten could be. The two men were walking in the grounds when they were joined by Edwina. Mountbatten, in civilian clothes, was wearing a favourite old Tyrolean hat with feather attached. Edwina told him to take it off because 'it makes you look so frightfully German'. Mountbatten was tight-lipped with anger at being so humiliated.

After Dieppe, the remainder of Mountbatten's time as CCO passed comparatively uneventfully and at the end of his tour of duty the opinion was that he had been successful, if flamboyant, and a brilliant organizer. His part in preparing for the invasion of Europe was later fully recognized by his peers and although he was by then some 6,000 miles away, the acknowledgement gave him great satisfaction.

Plainly his powers of leadership were greater than his abilities as a ship's captain, and his next appointment was to confirm this feeling. He wanted to return to sea; Churchill would have none of it. Mountbatten was a great personal favourite with many of the attributes Churchill felt he had himself.

In 1943, the Prime Minister proposed Mountbatten as the new Supreme Allied Commander, South East Asia, with orders to retake Burma from the Japanese. President Roosevelt had the right of veto over this appointment and a large number of names was suggested before Mountbatten was mentioned. Some were rejected out of hand because the Americans couldn't stand them, others proposed by the Americans were not acceptable to Churchill – two of them because they were naval officers and he did not believe sailors were sufficiently well versed in land warfare to be able to conduct battles in the jungle. Eventually Mountbatten was suggested and Churchill, conveniently forgetting that he too was a career naval officer, enthusiastically endorsed his appointment.

Most of the opposition to the new supreme came from other senior British officers such as Admiral Cunningham who said, 'It rather defeats me how he can imagine he is the man for the job . . . I think most people in the Service have just laughed.' And one of the great names in military circles, General Claude Auchinleck, expressed his surprise, mainly because of his own disappointment at being passed over as commander of the Army in Burma. Ironically, after the war Mountbatten was forced to dismiss Auchinleck from his command in India, when he (Mountbatten) was Governor General.

American newspapers carried dozens of stories condemning the appointment. Their antagonism was because they believed Mountbatten had been preferred to their own General MacArthur simply because of his royal connections. The anti-Mountbatten campaign lasted for eight months after his appointment had been confirmed and only died down when events of greater importance demanded recognition.

Considering the size of the task and the thousands of lives that he would be responsible for, it was surprising that Mountbatten – and his colleagues, the Chiefs of Staff – had the time or inclination to devote their energies to what seems in retrospect a very minor matter: his rank in the services. As Chief of Combined Opeations he had held honorary ranks as Lieutenant General in the Army and Air Marshal in the RAF. In his new post he had been promoted to full Admiral in the Navy, but when the question of his possible promotion to similar ranks in the other two services was proposed, the Chiefs were adamant that it should not be. They gave some half-baked reasons that he would be setting a precedent, but in reality it was pure jealousy. They were successful in preventing him from getting the promotion but he did retain his honorary ranks, of which he was very proud. All this took up valuable time when Allied soldiers were living and fighting in appalling conditions, and even if Mountbatten himself spent far too much effort on his own behalf, he was realistic enough to know that the main job was to win the war in the Far East, and that is what he set out to do.

Determined to raise the spirits of the largely demoralized units fighting in the Far East, Mountbatten used the tactics he had proved so successful on the *Kelly*. One of the biggest complaints among the ordinary soldiers was the lack of information. They had no idea how the war was progressing, what they were supposed to be doing and what was happening elsewhere. Mountbatten changed all this. No one knew better how to get the men on his side. He was expert in public relations and before he met the men under his command he ordered his staff to find out details of their personal lives: where they came from, if they were married, how many children. Then he would visit the various units and have the officers paraded before him, but with enough distance between each one so that the others could not overhear what was being said. Then he would put the same two questions to each one: Where do you come from and how long in the Army? He would then bring out his recently acquired information about the man, who would immediately think he was being singled out for special attention. It was a routine that never varied and it always worked. Mountbatten became known as the soldier's friend and he was just as effective with a small outpost of twenty men as he was when confronted by a thousand.

He never neglected the smallest detail and at his headquarters there were files on practically every man under him. When commendations were required a ready typed letter to the recipient would be prepared for his signature with a personal message included, and when letters of condolence had to be sent to families of men killed the letters would invariably contain another personal memory. Mountbatten, of course, never wrote any of them himself. They were prepared by clerks and he merely signed them.

One of the main criticisms levelled against Mountbatten as Supreme Commander was that he was always empire building, expanding his staff continually and finding jobs for all his old cronies from Combined Operations. His own Chief of Staff asked him not to make the same mistakes he had made as CCO and more than a few people had a field day when it was revealed that, in the midst of all the preparations for an attack on the Japanese, he had appointed a former banqueting manager as his ADC. Mountbatten was mystified and deeply hurt by the accusations, saying, 'In spite of an undeserved reputation to the contrary, I dislike large staffs and have done everything in my power to keep my own staff down.'

One of the supremo's sternest critics was the American General 'Vinegar Joe' Stillwell, who admitted an undying hatred for all things British. At first Stillwell thought Mountbatten was going to be easy to deal with and would take his side against his imagined enemies among the Allies, especially the Chinese, but when he discovered that Mountbatten liked to be boss, he quickly revised his opinion. When they first met, Stillwell told Mountbatten that 'You are the only Britisher I have met who wants to fight.' Shortly afterwards he described him as a 'fatuous ass, childish Louis, publicity crazy'.

It is not my purpose to detail Mountbatten's career as Supreme Allied Commander, South East Asia. That episode of his life has been well documented elsewhere. That he was successful has never been disputed. The campaign in the Far East was well organized, brilliantly planned and superbly executed. Mountbatten had magnificent officers and men under his command to whom most of the credit must go. But if it had failed he would have been blamed as the Supreme Commander, so he must, by the same token, be allotted the same degree of congratulation in its success.

In 1944, one of his most respected commanders, General Pownall, writing about Mountbatten after leaving South East Asia, said, 'His manner was always so admirable when one found fault with him . . . He would apologize, promise to mend his ways . . . and then, so soon afterwards, go and do the same thing again. He hates a row and wishes to be popular and well thought of, and indeed is almost pathetically surprised when he learns that there are people who do not care for him or his way.'

Mountbatten prided himself that he understood how the minds of those under him worked. He encouraged his men to speak out but, for the most part, they told him what he wanted to hear. So he was rather taken aback when on one of his tours of inspection he asked a Wren how she liked the Navy, to hear her reply: 'It's a load of bloody rubbish.' What happened when her immediate superiors, who were standing within earshot, heard this heresy has not been recorded.

The end of the Second World War in 1945 brought the offer of an honour that for once Mountbatten considered an insult. In December of that year he was told by telegram that he was to be offered a barony. When he learned that two of his fellow wartime leaders, Alexander and Montgomery, were to be created viscounts, he was furious. The reason he gave was that it was an insult to offer him, as Supreme Allied Commander, South East Asia, a lesser honour than those given to commanders in other theatres of war. 'I shall definitely refuse in the interests of SEAC,' he said. In the end a compromise was reached and he accepted a viscountcy, but even in this there was some controversy. By becoming Mountbatten of Burma he had assumed proprietorial rights over a placename that had been associated closely with one of his own generals, Bill Slim, whom many people regarded as the true liberator of Burma. Slim himself did not contribute to the argument and there is no evidence that Mountbatten was seeking to immortalize his own name in this romantic fashion to do down his old comrade. He identified with the men of the 14th Army, the 'Forgotten Army', completely and it was to preserve the memory of those who had fought and died that he adopted the name of the country as his own.

10

VICEROY OF INDIA

When the Second World War ended, Mountbatten found himself as the victorious Supreme Allied Commander in the Far East, responsible for the welfare of nearly 130 million men, women and children. Having accepted the unconditional surrender of the Japanese forces in Singapore, Mountbatten then became the most powerful figure in the liberated countries; the single authority, charged with making decisions affecting the lives of every person living in those countries which had been occupied by the Japanese. It was not a task from which he shrank. His old boast that he could do everything better than anyone else stood him in good stead as he set about providing food, transport, a free press, telecommunications, and, most important of all, restoring law and order. His immense self-confidence was a major factor in the success he achieved in those early post-war months. Any other man might have found the job too daunting. Not Mountbatten. He relished the challenge and ruled his new 'Empire' as a benevolent dictator. His word was law and the speed at which he worked meant there was no time for argument. Right or wrong, he made the decisions.

His mother had warned him not to court popularity or to be concerned with public opinion. 'Do what you believe to be right and be prepared to be judged by history . . . All you've got to think about is whether your children and grandchildren will think you've done well.' She could not have offered sounder advice to a man who, even then, wanted nothing more than to be admired by his family. She struck exactly the right note – as she knew she would.

Although he did not know it at the time, the months Mountbatten spent setting up new administrations in the immediate post-war period were to prove invaluable to him in his next job. He could not have had better training for the task ahead.

As he prepared to resume his naval career and continue his climb to his ultimate goal, to be First Sea Lord, Mountbatten was once again interrupted – this time by Prime Minister Clement Attlee, who summoned him to an urgent meeting. He was informed that the then Viceroy of India, Lord Wavell, a distinguished and honourable soldier, had failed in his efforts to obtain a settlement between the various political parties and the main Hindu and Muslim leaders, in the run-up to the granting of independence to the sub-continent.

Attlee wanted Mountbatten to take on the job. At first Mountbatten refused on the grounds that if Wavell had failed no one could succeed, but his excuses were half-hearted. The fact that someone else had failed to accomplish something never deterred him from attempting it. In reality, this was probably the only time he genuinely did not want to be offered such a post. The reason was that he was determined to become an Admiral of the Fleet, and any further interruptions in his career structure could, he felt, destroy his hopes for good. Edwina Mountbatten did not try to influence her husband in his decision, but secretly she was pleased at the prospect of becoming Vicereine and hoped he would accept. Clement Attlee, in choosing Mountbatten, had not overlooked the part Edwina would play, saying that one of the qualities that Mountbatten would bring to the position was that he had 'an unusual wife'. Mountbatten was of course very flattered to be offered the post – any man would have been, and he knew that this was the chance of a lifetime. This was an opportunity to carve his place in history as the last Viceroy of a country that had for a hundred and fifty years been the jewel in the crown of the British Empire.

Mountbatten voiced his reservations about taking the job to his cousin, King George VI, even suggesting that should he fail – and failure was a word foreign to his nature – it would reflect badly on the Royal Family. The King countered his arguments by telling him how brilliant it would be for the family if he should succeed. He knew then that he had to accept.

In typical Mountbatten fashion, though, he made a number of extraordinary demands before agreeing to the Prime Minister's proposition, the most important of which was his right of freedom to act without first having to refer every decision back to the

British Government. Under the old system each minor policy decision could take weeks to be resolved and he knew that unless he could act on his own authority there was no chance of getting agreement from all those involved in the time allowed. Another of his demands was that he alone should have control of the honours list at the end of his term of office. Even at this early stage, before he had been formally appointed, he was determined that any patronage that was going to be used when it was all over would be in his gift and not that of the Government.

He also insisted on having the use of his old York aircraft, MW102, that he had travelled in as Supreme Allied Commander, South East Asia. The aircraft was fitted out as a VIP transport with a refrigerator, constant hot water, money-changing facilities, fully equipped kitchen, a cocktail cabinet with wines and spirits, cigarettes, playing cards, intelligence cameras, typewriters and two Thompson sub-machine guns. Mountbatten told his daughter Patricia that he did not believe they would be able to find his old aircraft and that this would give him a reason for declining: it was 'No York − no job'. But there was no easy way out for him and, in truth, he did not want one.

Mountbatten also demanded the right to employ his own staff, the most important appointment being that of General 'Pug' Ismay, Churchill's former Chief of Staff, as Chief of the Viceroy's Staff. In addition he had no intention of going to India without his own inner cabinet of Admiral Ronnie Brockman as personal secretary, Alan Campbell-Johnson as press attaché and Peter Murphy as his private confidant and sounding board.

He knew he was in a strong position. He was the only candidate for the job and time was of the essence so the Government were only too willing to meet his conditions, which, in any case, were hardly likely to prove obstacles. It was just Mountbatten's way of showing his independence and underlining that he was a reluctant recruit.

Every demand was met by Attlee, who did not want to be bothered by mere details as long as the result was a peaceful end to this massive burden of what had become a troublesome Empire. Independence had been promised in 1942 as a reward for the support of Indian troops against the Japanese, and even earlier, in the 1920s, moves towards granting independence had started. In any case, the cost of maintaining a government in India was proving a drain on the finances of a Britain whose own funds were sorely depleted after six years of the most expensive war in history. So in monetary terms alone, Britain wanted out of India.

The transfer of power was the main stumbling block. Mountbatten's task was to find a solution that would be satisfactory to all sides and not result in too much bloodshed.

Attlee could not have made a better choice. The name Mountbatten was still fresh in the minds of millions of people in India and what was to become Pakistan. His style of leadership in the war had appealed to the hero-worshipping indigenous population of this vast contry. And with his royal connections and a wife whose own wartime reputation had caused her to become revered in Asia, plus a personal charisma that charmed most of the people who met him, Mountbatten was exactly the right man in the right place at the right time.

He was given fifteen months to achieve a solution to a problem that for the previous twenty years had made no noticeable progress, and he was determined that no one and nothing was going to stand in his way. By June 1948, the handover of power was to be complete. Mountbatten knew that if he was going to get the job done in the time allotted he would inevitably make some enemies. He could not please everyone and he did not even try. There was only one way – his way, and come what may, fifteen months from the time he stepped on to Indian soil, nearly two centuries of British rule was going to end.

As it happened, when Mountbatten arrived in India he realized that fifteen months was far too long for the period of transition. The Indian Civil Service was breaking down and he knew that the longer the negotiations went on the more bloodshed there was likely to be. So he insisted on a shorter period, which was immediately reduced to five months, so that instead of June 1948 as the deadline, he now had August 1947 as the date by which he had to complete the handover of power.

The question of the timescale alters depending on whose version of the events one believes. Mountbatten claimed that he was the one who insisted on setting a definite date for independence and that Attlee demurred, in case of embarrassment to the British Government should the date not be met. Papers which the author consulted in the Mountbatten archives appear to confirm that Attlee did not have a firm withdrawal date in mind and that it was Mountbatten's idea. Mountbatten felt that to go to India without the Hindu and Muslim leaders knowing there was a definite date for withdrawal would weaken his own position immeasurably. They would be suspicious that he was not there to end colonial rule, merely to delay the decision.

Attlee in turn claimed that he had told Mountbatten how long he had to complete the job and, some time later, it was revealed that the Cabinet's India Committee had discussed a deadline long before Mountbatten was approached. Whichever is correct, there is no doubt that Mountbatten was right in insisting on the date being set before he left Britain. As a serviceman who had operated thousands of miles from the base of power, he knew from experience how little value to place on the vague promises of politicians.

Once Mountbatten had been confirmed in the post, Attlee left him to get on with the job. In fact he was glad to do so. If things did go wrong, the blame could always be laid at the Viceroy's door. The means were not all that important – it was the end that counted. Britain wanted to be rid of its Empire and Mountbatten was the man do do it. The task needed someone with a ruthless single-mindedness – and that is exactly what it got.

Winston Churchill, the man who had forsaken Mountbatten's father during the First World War (though he had tried to persuade him not to resign), now had the son to blame for 'giving away India'. It was many years before the two men spoke to each other, and while Churchill professed affection for Mountbatten, he never really forgave him for the enthusiasm with which he oversaw the break-up of the most significant part of the British Empire. In November 1947, eight months after the Viceroy had taken over, Churchill grudgingly admitted to Mountbatten that he had done well. 'You know I have a high regard for you, as I had for your father . . . I am too much grieved by what is happening in India to write more. But you always have my good wishes and admiration for your achievements.'

To blame Mountbatten was completely illogical as he played no part in the political decision to grant India its independence, but Churchill wanted someone to blame and who better than this great war hero, whom he considered to be one of his protégés? It was Churchill, of course, who had made Mountbatten Chief of Combined Operations at the age of forty-one, and then, in full agreement with President Roosevelt, who most certainly would not have allowed such an appointment if he had not been convinced of Mountbatten's ability, promoted him to be Supreme Allied Commander, South East Asia, some two years later.

When Mountbatten accepted the position as Viceroy, Churchill took it as a personal insult and considered it an act of betrayal. There was little he could to to prevent Mountbatten taking on the job as he was now out of office, having been swept aside by the landslide victory that brought Labour into power in the first post-war election. As Leader of the Opposition, Churchill retained some vestiges of influence, but his views were never going to sway the Government, just as those of the Opposition failed to persuade him to change his mind during the war. In Attlee's opinion, Churchill was an anachronism, whose views on the Empire were at least fifty years out of date.

The only guidance which Mountbatten had from the British Government when he took over as Viceroy was that they fully recognized that India fell naturally into two parts, Muslim and Hindu, and that it was possible that these parts could be separated geographically.

Mountbatten's task was made all the more difficult in that the three men with whom he had to negotiate to resolve what were, in effect, irreconcilable differences were each as determined as he was to get his own way. They were Pandit Nehru, leader of the ruling Congress Party, which was dominated by Hindus, Mohammed Ali Jinnah, leader of the Muslim League, and Mahatma Gandhi, the 'father' of modern India, whose pacifist views conceal an iron stubbornness.

Jinnah was demanding a separate state of Pakistan to be formed out of the six Muslim majority provinces: the Punjab, the North-West Frontier Province, Baluchistan, Sind, Bengal and Assam. Nehru was insisting that India should remain united as a single country – under his leadership – while Jinnah saw that if he agreed to such a solution, his dreams of founding his own country would disappear for ever. Each of these men was as influential and charismatic as the others – and each was determined that, whatever State was formed after the British withdrawal in 1947, he would become its undisputed leader.

By the time of Mountbatten's appointment, his predecessor, Lord Wavell, who had held the post for three years, realized that nothing he could do or say would bring the two sides together. He was the most upright and honourable of men; perhaps that was his undoing. If he had been more devious he might have been able to play the game according to the same rules the others were using. At any rate, both the Hindus and Muslims had lost confidence in Wavell and he, foreseeing the outbreak of violence as inevitable, had initiated a special contingency plan, code-named Operation Ebb-Tide, to evacuate all non-essential British residents from India should the need arise. This was the situation Mountbatten found facing him as he set out to achieve a peaceful settlement.

The last Viceroy arrived in Delhi on 22 March 1947. The Union flag would be lowered by 15 August. If Mountbatten had been reluctant to accept the post, he would soon be delighted by the reception he and Edwina were to be given by the people of India. But not on this first day. There were no crowds waiting at Palam Airport as the Viceroy Designate's aircraft landed in the early afternoon heat. As he was not to be sworn in for another two days, the number one spot was still occupied for the moment by Lord Wavell, whom protocol had prevented from greeting his successor at the airport.

Instead the Wavells were waiting to greet them at the entrance to Viceroy's House, where Lord and Lady Mountbatten bowed and curtsied as they were required to do to the King-Emperor's representative. It was the only time in his life that Mountbatten bowed to a commoner. But even in these closing moments of his predecessor's reign, he rigorously observed every courtesy. Nobody could ever accuse Mountbatten of not knowing how to behave in any situation and he thoroughly approved of protocol being correctly carried out.

The Mountbattens had brought their seventeen-year-old daughter Pamela with them and her year in India was to be the most memorable of her life. Called the Miss-Sahib by the Indians, she became what they described as 'our Princess Margaret' to many of the students who would met her in the coming months. She too would have responsibilities, as Felicity Wavell, one of the departing Viceroy's daughters, explained. Her chief task would be to head the Viceregal School and, with an establishment of several thousand working in Viceroy's House, the school itself was of formidable size. She also had to remember to curtsy to her parents in exactly the same way as every other female did in their presence.

Pamela says the first thing her father did on his arrival in India was to tell Lord Wavell of his dismay at the way in which he had been treated by the Government at home. 'My father thought it was most dishonourable and a disgraceful way to treat someone as distinguished as Lord Wavell, who had had no idea that he was going to be replaced right up to the time of my father's appointment. He was such a straightforward person that the idea of anyone being underhanded just wouldn't occur to him. My father was anxious to reassure Lord Wavell that he had had nothing to do with the intrigue and Lord Wavell told him that he had never believed that he had. It was a great relief. Lord Wavell was a very sensitive person although he couldn't express himself well and he was obviously wounded by Attlee's methods. He and my father had a very emotional meeting on that day, but it cleared the air.'

Once the handover had been completed between Lord Wavell and Mountbatten, the first formal occasion was the swearing-in ceremony held in Durbar Hall, the largest of the state rooms in Viceroy's House. Resplendent in his white dress uniform, plumed hat, ceremonial sword and bedecked with his many decorations, Mountbatten looked every inch the Emperor the people insisted on treating him as. The Vicereine was wearing a gown of ivory silk brocade and her wartime decorations, including the Conspicuous Service Medal, the Grand Cross of the Order of St John and the Crown of India. She did not wear her diamond tiara, though she did put it on for the official photographs afterwards as she sat beside her husband on their gilded thrones.

The Indian people expected their rulers to look like gods and the Mountbattens did not disappoint them. What surprised some of the old hands at the swearing-in ceremony, and confused many of the Indian princes, who were preparing to leave after the brief introductions, was the presence of film cameras and photographers and reporters who were handed a transcript of a speech the Viceroy was making. No incoming Viceroy had ever made a speech at his swearing-in before. It set the tone for the manner in which Mountbatten intended to conduct his viceroyalty. He had learned the importance of public relations in the war and he knew instinctively how to manipulate the media. It was a talent he would continue to use for the rest of his life.

The Mountbattens had been used to staying in some of the finest houses in the world: the vast estates of their multi-millionaire American friends and the castles and palaces of Dickie's relations in Britain and throughout Europe. But all of them, including Buckingham Palace, faded before the glory that was Viceroy's House in 1947. Designed by Lutyens and built to reflect the majesty of an Empire on which the sun never set, the house had so many rooms – 377 – it took the new Vicereine two weeks to see them all and traverse its one and a half miles of corridors. Mountbatten was thrilled to find the house had a private cinema. Set in a park tended by over four hundred gardeners, the house had so many indoor and outdoor servants that even someone with a memory for faces as prodigious as Mountbatten had to give up trying to familiarize himself with them all.

Pamela Hicks says that Viceroy's House was very grand, 'but if anyone had ever been prepared to live in such splendour it was my father. After all, he was a nephew of the Tsar of Russia and nobody did things on a grander scale than they did. Until the age of fourteen, my father lived in some of the grandest palaces in Russia, where the protocol was so rigid it was frightening, so he grew up fully familiar with life in such places. He knew exactly what to expect in Viceroy's House and enjoyed every minute of it.'

Pamela said there were one or two petty irritations which used to infuriate her father. He would become wild with rage because the servants insisted on clearing everything as soon as he left a room. 'He liked to write notes to himself to remind him of a job to do or someone he wanted to talk to. As soon as the servants saw the pieces of paper they would clear them away and he would forget what he had written. It took a long time before he could persuade the Comptroller of the Household to instruct his minions to leave things alone.'

One of the first things that Pamela had to learn was which servants could be ordered to perform which tasks. 'There was such a complicated caste system that one had to be very careful not to ask someone of one level to do something that was beneath them. On one very formal occasion my mother was about to enter a reception at Viceroy's House, when her little Sealyham, Mizzen, who was very old by then, had an "accident" right beside her. It took such a long time to find the right grade of servant to clear up the mess that my mother, in formal long white dress, diamond tiara and elbow-length gloves, got down on her hands and knees and cleared it herself. She didn't care but the servants were horrified.' The Viceroy had his own personal messenger, as did his wife, and these two servants refused point-blank to do any work at all for anyone else; it would have been too demeaning. There were six aides-de-camp, three English and, at Mountbatten's insistence, three Indian, with three on duty at all times. The most senior of the ADCs was attached to His Excellency; number two attended Her Excellency and the third waited on Pamela. As she said, 'It was heady stuff for a seventeen-year-old.'

Pamela was given two exotic pets, a mongoose and a parrot, and she had to be very careful who to ask to clear their cages.' There was no question of my bearer doing it. He wouldn't even consider it and would have been mortified if I had even asked him. It was a servant of a much lower grade who was brought in for such tasks.'

One of the main advantages Mountbatten brought to the role of Viceroy was his royal connection. Many of the Indian princes feared they would be left out of all the political negotiations and they were highly relieved to find that the man they were going to have to deal with was the cousin of the King-Emperor. His royal blood reassured them that he would look after their interests and, as many of them knew him from his tour of India with the Prince of Wales in 1921, they regarded him as an old friend – someone who was going to be on their side. It was probably the only time in his life that Mountbatten's royal relations were to prove a positive help in his career.

Elizabeth Collins was Edwina's personal secretary and she could not believe the splendour of her quarters. 'I was waited on hand, foot and finger,' she recalls. 'I was not allowed to do anything for myself. There was always a servant waiting outside my door night and day and the kitchens could provide anything from a snack to a five-course meal twenty-four hours a day.'

Mrs Collins remembers one occasion when Mountbatten upset the staff by barging into their working area – something no other Viceroy had ever dreamed of doing. It was on a day when a formal function was being held at which Mrs Collins's presence was required. 'Lord Mountbatten was always on time. He hated unpunctuality and on this day I was delaying the departure of the entourage because a belt I wanted to wear had not arrived back from the dhobi [laundry]. They said they couldn't find it. Finally, Lord Mountbatten stormed into my room to find out what was wrong. When I told him the reason for the delay he rushed downstairs and in full dress uniform, plumed hat, spurs and sword, found the laundry and searched until he came up with the belt. He wouldn't leave without me; it would have disrupted his organization and he was not going to have that. The fact that he was the Viceroy – a bit like God to the servants – didn't concern him one little bit. He always said he could do anything better than the rest of us and on that day he proved it.'

One of the things that Mountbatten had always enjoyed when he was Supreme Allied Commander, South East Asia, was being able to jump into a Jeep whenever he wanted and drive off unaccompanied. As Viceroy such privileges were denied him. The only time he was allowed to drive himself was when he and Edwina and Pamela drove to Simla, their summer residence two hundred miles north of Delhi. As Pamela recalls: 'Once we were out of sight of Delhi, he would order the driver to stop and move over so he could take the wheel. He would then drive until we were just outside Simla when the chauffeur would once again take over as it would not have done for the Viceroy to be seen driving his own car.'

Security was a continual problem, not only for Mountbatten but also for his family. Edwina hated the idea of being accompanied everywhere by a carload of armed police and she did everything she could to throw them off her trail. On one occasion, though, she realized that the areas she was travelling through were dangerous and more so when she found she was being trailed back at Viceroy's House she told her husband of her adventure and said that although she hated the idea, she knew now that perhaps she did need some protection. Mountbatten drily explained that she had been protected all along; the cut-throats she was worried about were her personal bodyguard in plain clothes.

Ian Scott (later Sir Ian) had been in the Indian Civil Service and later in the Indian Political Service for fifteen years when Mountbatten was appointed Viceroy. Ten of those years were spent on the North-West Frontier. Immediately prior to Mountbatten taking over, Scott had been one of Lord Wavell's private secretaries. He was asked to continue in this role as Mountbatten's number two (there were three ICS private secretaries altogether).

Scott remembers exactly how long he served under Mountbatten – one hundred and twenty-five days – because this was the number inscribed on a silver cigarette box that the Viceroy gave him as a farewell present at the end of his term of office. Scott's initial impression of his new boss was not favourable, and never altered. 'He invited my wife and me to dinner soon after his arrival. She sat next to him throughout the meal and he spent the entire time telling her how he was the first Viceroy to have been made a Knight of the Garter before taking up his appointment. I am not sure that she knew what KG meant, and certainly found the vanity of this account very boring.'

Scott was an admirer of Wavell and made no bones about comparing the two men: 'Mountbatten had remarkable qualities, but I never liked him as a person. Wavell was more honest and forthright in his dealings with people; Mountbatten was an entirely different animal altogether. He had tremendous skills in persuading and getting people to do what he wanted them to do, but he could not have matched Wavell as a man in a thousand years. Mountbatten's strength was due to the fact that all that mattered to him was success, never mind the means. He was sent out to India by Attlee to do a particular job and he did it. Mountbatten had personal charm and charisma and he could lay it on whenever it suited him. Even Gandhi fell under his spell. During Mountbatten's time as Viceroy we went from one crisis to another (as indeed we did in Wavell's time), and he handled them all brilliantly. There was one occasion when things were looking very serious and there was a real danger of public order breaking down. Gandhi spent three hours with Mountbatten and that evening went on All-India Radio to say that what the Viceroy was trying to do was exactly what he, Gandhi, had been advocating since the twenties. Gandhi was himself something of a charmer when he wanted to be; but on this occasion he was no match for the Viceroy.'

Although Scott did not admire Mountbatten on a personal level, it did not affect his admiration for him as a man who got things done. 'I believe that Mountbatten obtained a settlement in India which Wavell could not have done. It was his great triumph. There was a crescendo of violence in the country which would have become very much worse if Mountbatten had not forced through the settlement in his own way and to his own timetable.'

Scott even believed that Mountbatten should have been given the job, after the independence of India, of sorting out the situation in Palestine: 'He would have managed to get an agreement between the Arabs and Jews, probably the only man in the world who could have done so. After getting the Hindus to agree to the partition of India, the problem of dealing with Palestine would have been relatively easy.' Mountbatten was brilliant in the art of institutional politics; persuading, manipulating and outmanoeuvring the opposition and in reconciling conflicting interests.

In the period of Mountbatten's viceroyalty, India's administration was beginning to disintegrate. As Scott says, 'The nuts and bolts were starting to fall apart.' Britain and its people were tired of Empire. Soldiers who had fought in Burma wanted to go home and the British garrison was leaving at the rate of a division a month. Mountbatten was not only the Sovereign's representative as Viceroy, but head of the Indian Government also. He was ultimately responsible for every item of central administration, every detail of expenditure.

Each day would start with a staff meeting chaired by Mountbatten. 'It would last for one hour,' says Scott, 'out of which he would talk for perhaps fifty-five minutes. That was his preferred method of working out his policy. If someone wanted to make a suggestion he would stop and either adopt it or discard it. One of his great attributes was his ability to make a decision on the spot. If someone came up with a good idea and he did not adopt or discard it at once, he would think about it and some time later it might emerge as one of his own thoughts. But it was as a man that the really less pleasant aspects of his character came out. He was incredibly vain, to a degree that is hard to imagine. And after Wavell, who was a man without personal conceit, it took some getting used to.'

Mountbatten's well-known obsession with honours showed itself when another, equally vain, public figure went out to India on an official visit. Field Marshal Montgomery, the victor of El Alamein, was no shy, retiring soldier but one who thoroughly enjoyed his fame – and relished displaying the decorations bestowed on him by grateful nations. Scott recalls a meeting between Mountbatten and Montgomery (with, of course, a photographer present): 'They were just like two peacocks preening themselves, each one determined to outshine the other. They even counted each other's medals to see who had the most. When Mountbatten found out that Monty had (as I remember the numbers) thirty-three to his thirty-two, he was less than pleased. So he exerted himself to make sure he could get at least one more than his rival. Countries whose armies had been nominally under Mountbatten, even if they hadn't actually fought, were encouraged to offer decorations and eventually he ended up with thirty-four – one more than Monty.'

Mountbatten's ambition after partition was to be appointed Governor General of both India and Pakistan. It would have been another significant first and both Gandhi and Nehru (the Prime Minister-to-be of India) were agreeable. But Mr Jinnah, the leader of what was to become Pakistan, would not hear of it. He believed, as most Pakistanis still do today, that Mountbatten had shown favouritism to the Indian Hindus, and he resisted all efforts to make him change his mind. Scott says, 'We spent three whole days doing nothing but try to persuade Jinnah to agree but he would not move. There was a certain justification in Jinnah's attitude. Mountbatten's sympathies were increasingly with the Hindus, and he was a personal friend of Nehru.'

Pamela Hicks disagrees totally with Sir Ian's assessment of her father's attitude to the Muslims. 'My father found it practically impossible to deal with Jinnah, who was the coldest person you could meet. Of course, my father did not know then how ill Jinnah was, but he was completely inflexible. So much so that my father bent over backwards to accommodate him. The reason why my father wanted to become Governor General of both India and Pakistan was so that he could be seen as being completely impartial. If he held the same position in both countries, no one would have been able to accuse him of favouring one side or the other.' One example that Pamela gives of her father's attempts to placate Jinnah was when he appointed his favourite officer, a Muslim captain, to head the Pakistan Navy. It was a personal sacrifice for Mountbatten who did not want to lose so valuable a friend and aide, but he was prepared to do so to show Jinnah that he was not being treated as second best.

Many of the accusations against Mountbatten were because of his wife's undoubted leanings towards the Hindus. She very quickly became emotionally involved with Nehru and openly admitted her admiration for him. What has never been proved is whether they were lovers. People who were closest to them both at the time say they were not. But whatever the truth may be, Edwina would do anything for Nehru and all her sympathies lay with him and his people.

Pamela says that her mother's involvement with Nehru sometimes made life difficult for her father as she would often ask him to do something for the Indians which he knew he could not do without upsetting the other side. This 'resulted in fearful rows between them'. On the other hand, because Edwina identified so closely with the Indians she was able to tell her husband what their true feelings were about specific subjects and this proved invaluable to Mountbatten in his negotiations.

The personal feelings that Ian Scott had about Mountbatten did not in any way colour his judgement of him as Viceroy, or as someone to serve. 'He was a good boss. He had extraordinary energy and an infinite capacity for hard work. It was simply that his methods appeared at times to be so underhanded. On one occasion a serious situation developed that required a certain course of action. The Private Secretary, Sir George Abell, and I prepared a report with alternative suggestions for dealing with the problem. Mountbatten studied the report and discussed it. He carried on his thinking aloud. Suddenly he looked at us and said: 'I know what you are thinking. You're thinking Wavell wouldn't have opted for this solution because it's not quite cricket. Well I will do it.' That was precisely what we were thinking. That was the difference between the two men.'

Scott also cited another example of the less pleasant side of Mountbatten's character. Scott's brother was a senior member of the Foreign Service, whose last appointment was (unusually) Permanent Secretary at the Ministry of Defence when Mountbatten was Chief of the Defence Staff. One morning Rob Scott found a note on his desk from Mountbatten requesting that the head of Public Relations in the Ministry should be immediately dismissed. The reason given was that he had committed a serious breach of confidentiality by a press release which he had issued after a top level conference at which he had been present.

Rob Scott sent for the officer concerned and showed him Mountbatten's note. He replied that he had told the press exactly what Mountbatten had ordered him to say, using the GDS's exact words. Rob Scott went along the corridor to Mountbatten's office and confronted him with this statement. Mountbatten at first tried to bluff his way out of it, but eventually was forced to admit that he had in fact done what the officer had said. Had he not been challenged at this level on this unsavoury episode, the career of a senior officer might have been ruined. Mountbatten had evidently realized that he had made a mistake in authorizing the press release and tried to shift the blame away from himself.

In the short time that Mountbatten was Viceroy of India he found himself under enormous pressure on all fronts. The political pressure he could cope with quite easily, even though at almost every turn he was confronted by another seemingly insurmountable obstacle. But he loved problems and was never happier than when he was being asked to provide solutions that would satisfy all sides.

However, the job was tiring and at the end of an exhausting day, when all he wanted was an hour or so's relaxation, he suddenly found, to his dismay, that Edwina would demand his urgent and constant attention. She was just starting to experience the menopause and it was a particularly trying time for her and everyone around her. Pamela recalls that her father would go into her mother's room at the end of the day and sit soothing her for two or three hours, as she screamed and ranted. Edwina suffered from violent headaches and other unpleasant symptoms associated with this condition and Pamela says, 'My father would try to comfort her but he couldn't cope with tears and – like a bull in a china shop – he always seemed to say the wrong thing and put his foot in it, when all he really wanted to do was help. There's no doubt that theirs was a partnership and he could not have done the job without her help. But at the same time her problems meant he was in a state of total exhaustion for much of the time when he should have been resting and building up his energy reserves for the following day. I suppose you could say that my mother supported him for three-quarters of the time but the other quarter was completely destructive.'

Edwina used to accuse Mountbatten of ignoring her or deliberately going against something she had said, and Pamela says that while it was true that he did ignore her, it was never deliberate. It was just that he had so much on his mind.

In addition to Mountbatten's duties as negotiator in the run-up to Independence, and in spite of Edwina's unstable condition for part of the time, they were also required to fulfil all the usual roles of a Viceroy and Vicereine. There were garden parties, lunches, dinners, receptions, diplomatic functions to attend, official and social correspondence, exhibitions to be opened, schools to be visited, all while Mountbatten was spending the major part of every day trying to satisfy the Hindus and mollify the Muslims. In preparation for the handover of power on 15 August, less than five months after the Mountbattens arrived in Delhi, many countries were starting to appoint their diplomatic representatives, every one of whom was received personally by the Viceroy. Lunches for fifty people and dinners for over eighty were commonplace and on 18 July Dickie and Edwina celebrated their silver wedding anniversary with a dinner for ninety-five guests, including many of the personal staff of the Viceroy and Vicereine. It was a nice touch as most of the Indian employees, even the most senior, had never before been asked to dine at the same table as their European masters.

As the date for the handover of power grew closer the tempo of life in Viceroy's House increased dramatically. And then suddenly, at one minute past midnight on 15 August 1947, British rule ended in India and Mountbatten's one hundred and twenty-five days as Viceroy came to an end. The Mountbattens spent their final hours as Viceroy and Vicereine watching a film: Bob Hope in *My Favourite Brunette*. Mountbatten had achieved what he had set out to do. India had gots its independence and Pakistan became a separate country.

Viceroy's House became Government House and the last Viceroy was installed as the first Governor General. Mountbatten held his first official reception in his new role that same evening when three thousand guests were received. Two days earlier, he and Edwina had flown to Karachi for a similar duty when fifteen hundred of the country's leading citizens had been invited to witness the foundation of the State of Pakistan.

The bloodshed that followed Partition gave Edwina the chance once more to display her remarkable talents for getting things done. She visited refugee camps and burnt-out villages, offering practical support and help. She organized transport, food, medicines, drugs, and tried to comfort those who had lost husbands, wives, sons and daughters on both sides. For three months the civil war raged with atrocities being committed with equal ferocity by Sikh, Hindu and Muslim.

Edwina became Chairman of the Relief Committee, responsible for providing over a hundred refugee camps with food, water and clothing. She travelled constantly seeing that aid was going where it was most needed. Mountbatten, with his brilliant flair for organization, remained at Government House, where an Emergency Committee had been set up under his chairmanship, though this was kept quiet so that the Indian people would not think that the former Viceroy had taken over once again. Mountbatten had to remind himself – and others – that he was no longer the single most powerful man in the sub-continent, and all his suggestions were intended merely to be helpful to the official Government of India, and not directives to be obeyed without question.

By November events had settled down to a state where Mountbatten and Edwina were able to leave for a short visit to England to attend the wedding of Princess Elizabeth and Lieutenant Philip Mountbatten. Pamela was to be one of the bridesmaids. Edwina had recovered sufficiently to seek the company of one of her boyfriends, the conductor Malcolm Sargeant, and Dickie did not object when she invited him to stay with them on one of the two nights they spent at Broadlands. Perhaps he thought she deserved a reward for her efforts in India.

Returning to Delhi they decided that the situation had cooled enough for visitors to be encouraged once more and the sophisticated mutual understanding they had long had about each other's companions came to the surface once more in their first guest list. Yola Letellier, Mountbatten's girlfriend of many years, joined them, as did Edwina's former lover Bunny Phillips, with his new wife Gina. But it wasn't all sweetness and light. One evening Edwina's unreasonable (in view of her own behaviour) jealousy flared up and there was an old-fashioned row between her, Yola and Dickie. By the next morning it was forgotten.

Malcolm Sargeant took the scenic route from England to Turkey and ended up in India, where any romantic intentions he and Edwina might have had were thwarted when he caught a highly unromantic bout of dysentery. John and Patricia Brabourne also joined the Mountbattens at Government House for a brief glimpse of what life in the former British Raj had been like.

In all, the Mountbattens spent nearly fifteen months in India during which time they witnessed history being made and indeed, in his case, helped to make it. Some critics say that Mountbatten was not the right man for the job; his mind was too mercurial, his decisions made without sufficient thought and consultation. The handover of power needed someone with patience who could deal with the Asian mind in similar fashion. Mountbatten, they claimed, believed speed was of the utmost importance; not that a peaceful solution was the most vital prerequisite. What they do not suggest is the name of the paragon who could have avoided the problems Mountbatten encountered.

It is true that independence saw the unleashing of the worst horrors India had seen in its long history. Hundreds of thousands of Hindus, Sikhs and Muslims tortured and killed for no reason other than that the victims were of the wrong faith. What is not so obvious is what might have happened had Mountbatten not obeyed the orders of his political masters and forced through the handover of power in the time allotted.

The British Government believed that the unrest in India was just 'teething troubles' to be experienced by an emerging nation, and the loss of life an inevitable price that had to be paid. Churchill never changed his mind about India and saw the resulting bloodshed as a complete vindication of his earlier fears. Mountbatten said he viewed Independence Day with 'complete and undiluted pleasure'. With hindsight he might have added, 'and a little foreboding'.

11

CHARACTER

Anybody who's got driving ambition cannot be all that nice.' The words are those of David Hicks describing the character of his father-in-law. 'When he wanted to be he could be absolutely charming, the most amusing company and delightful to be with. But where his career was concerned, nothing else mattered. He could be a complete bastard. Just like me. I have the same driving ambition, the same compulsion to be the best.'

Mountbatten was always fascinated by other people's opinion of him. He was particularly interested in obtaining a secret Gestapo file that had been kept in 1943/44 on the orders of Himmler himself. Part of the file contains a laboriously detailed family tree which had been designed primarily to show conclusively that Mountbatten was a German national. Himmler comments: 'In practice one should call such a man, if he was ever caught, to final account for treason against the people.' The judgement that Mountbatten was a traitor is tempered only by Himmler's observation that the Battenbergs have always behaved 'somewhat peculiarly'. The German view of Mountbatten's importance to the Allied war effort was illustrated by the comment that 'This man plays a decisive part in connection with the establishment of a "second front" in Europe.

Himmler's assistant, Dr Eckhardt, added to the file in April 1943, citing the interrogation of a Canadian officer caught after the Dieppe raid. In his description of Mountbatten to the Gestapo, the officer said, 'You are immediately attracted by the important personality of this man. This in my opinion, is his greatest trump card. Quite candidly spoken I do not believe he has many more trumps. Mountbatten in his office is very much like the Mountbatten in action. He tackles everything with so youthful an enthusiasm that he, no doubt, impresses the less reasonable people. The soldiers adore him and would follow him anywhere. Losses appear to impress him but little provided his aim is attained, and even setbacks to not appear noticeably to damp his burning zeal.'

Eckhardt also added his own assessment of Mountbatten's abilities as a commander: 'Mountbatten owes his rapid career and his important post largely to the fact that he is the grandson of Queen Victoria [*sic*].' Winston Churchill would, no doubt, have been astonished to hear that nepotism was the only reason for his placing the conduct of so vital a part of the war effort in Mountbatten's hands.

The film star Douglas Fairbanks Jr was among the first Americans to volunteer to fight in the Second World War. He was a self-admitted 'hero-worshipper' of Mountbatten, whom he had known all his life. Commissioned into the US Navy, Fairbanks wrote many times to Mountbatten seeking a place on his staff in Britain. Eventually he was successful and enjoyed a short period when he worked fairly closely with his old friend. In letters to Mountbatten, Fairbanks was extremely complimentary, writing: 'Really, Dickie, I've never heard of a man more universally respected and admired.' And in another: 'I take great pride in boasting of you as my friend as your exploits are like legends.'

When Fairbanks was posted, protesting, to a sea-going position, he commented that he did not have the enthusiasm for naval adventure that Mountbatten obviously had. But, in thanking Mountbatten for all he had done for him, he said that his experience of working with him had 'gained me terrific kudos, and after the war I'll reciprocate by giving you a part in a picture'.

The relationship between Mountbatten and Douglas Fairbanks took on the appearance of a mutual admiration society. If Mountbatten wrote to Fairbanks congratulating him on a particular success in a movie role, the reply would invariably be couched in the most glowing terms. And when Mountbatten invited Fairbanks to plant a tree at Broadlands in 1973, 'to commemorate your long friendship and distinguished position in the world', Fairbanks replied, 'You still remain an incomparable "hero" to me, while at the same time being something between a surrogate "father", "brother" and "friend".' He continued: 'Despite many amusing similarities in our characters (of which others often remind me), it is now too late in life to so much as *try* to emulate you.'

Fairbanks's relationship with Mountbatten was one of hero-worship and Mountbatten willingly put up with his attentions, partly because he liked Fairbanks and partly because it suited him to have someone with his international reputation as a film star, as a subordinate. After the war Mountbatten took it upon himself to write to the Earl of Halifax concerning public recognition for Fairbanks, in addition to his DSC, which was for valour. When Mountbatten told Fairbanks of the moves to get him a CBE he 'nearly swooned with excitement'. When the time came for Fairbanks to be posted away from Mountbatten's staff, he (Fairbanks) felt that part of the reason was because his mentor did not relish having someone so glamorous in such close proximity to himself. If ever there was a case of the pot calling the kettle black!

John Brabourne believes that one of Mountbatten's greatest strengths was his ability to make up his mind once he had listened to everybody he thought worth listening to. 'That was the secret of much of his success and also the reason why Peter Murphy was so important to him. Few people actually knew what Murphy's role was in Dickie's life, but his real position was as a sounding board. He was brilliant at spotting mistakes in something that Dickie was planning, and he wasn't afraid to speak up. Dickie would show him a letter he had drafted and Peter would read it and say what he thought the reaction of the recipient would be. He wasn't always right, but he did manage to show Dickie that there were alternatives to the things he proposed. When Peter died, some of us in the family took over the task. It wasn't always pleasant. Dickie didn't like being told he was wrong, but he would, once he was convinced, redraft his speech, letter or whatever it was. But if he thought he was right even after one had pointed out an error, nothing would make him change his mind. He could be inflexible at times. I remember on one occasion when we were in France and he came into the room and showed me a letter he intended to write. I said that it was completely wrong and the letter should not be written. He replied that he had known I would say that and we had a good old stand-up row. But he went away and rewrote the letter and afterwards said he had had second thoughts and perhaps I was right.'

Mountbatten's attention to detail began in his early childhood and remained with him throughout his life. When he was eleven years old and a pupil at Locker's Park preparatory school he developed a tendency to explain and describe things very precisely in his correspondence with his parents. Writing to his mother in September 1911 he tells her that he would like a model torpedo boat for Christmas and then goes on to give a detailed description of the boat, where it can be bought (Harrods

Toy Department) and how much it would cost (£2-18-6d). Realizing that this is rather expensive he explains at length how the gifts of money from his father and an aunt, plus his own savings, can cover the cost exactly. And to make sure there is no possibility of error on his mother's part he encloses a drawing of the boat.

He was extremely protective of his possessions and displayed an untypical business brain when he was given a small portable typewriter. He told his mother that he would not allow any of the other boys to use it but he was prepared to type their letters for them – for a fee!

When Mountbatten went up to the Naval College at Osborne he continued his practice of explaining in precise terms what he wanted other people to do. When he needed a tennis racquet from home he not only described which one he wanted but sent a drawing of the press so that no mistake would be made. He was also very fond of a special prayer book he had used at home and asked his father to buy him an *exact replica* in case the original should be lost.

Similarly, when he wanted a water pistol to use in the 'war against the other dormitory' he specified the exact make and model that was required. He had always been anxious to please those in authority and when he discovered that the furniture polish supplied by the college was not up to the standard he desired to keep his locker looking the best in the room, he again wrote to his parents demanding (as he became older his tone became more imperious) that they send him 'as quick as you can' a special polish which the servants used at home.

In the later years of his life Mountbatten would become known for his insistence on correct forms of dress. His entire day could be ruined if he spied someone on parade sloppily dressed. And this too was something that became part of his life very early on. In 1915 he wrote to his father from Dartmouth for advice on the appropriate medal ribbons to be worn on his uniform, though at that stage of his career he cannot have had too many to worry about.

His tendency to use people included his own family and on one occasion, when he had broken his ankle at Dartmouth, he wrote to his father urging him to use his influence – and rank – to write in turn to the surgeon looking after him, to make sure he could take his examinations in the hospital instead of having to report back to the college where he thought things would be more difficult. It worked.

The boastfulness which characterized much of his life later on also emerged fairly early. But strangely enough it was only on letters to his mother that he liked to show off. When he wrote to his father the letters were more of a routine progress report. There was an easy familiarity in these reports, with no hint of the formality that boys of his generation usually displayed towards their parents, but towards his mother Mountbatten showed deep affection and he appeared to keep nothing from her.

If he had done well in examinations or sport he dwelt at length on every one of his achievements. He was particularly fond of his technical knowledge, which was advanced, even as a schoolboy, and he sent his mother a matchbox he had made himself out of naval brass. He proudly explained that he had invented some valuable improvements on the original design suggested by his teacher and that all the boys in the class were now copying his design. When he was promoted to be a prefect, he explained to his mother the responsibilities the new post entailed. He obviously took the task seriously and talked a lot about keeping discipline. He added, though, that where the younger boys were concerned, he also had to advise them, not just administer punishment.

The letters to his mother were chatty, well written and gave a complete picture of life at boarding school. He loved to include riddles he had learned and in one letter in which he enclosed a riddle in French, he went to some pains to rectify a linguistic error she may have detected in a previous letter. He assured her that a wrongly placed accent was his mistake and not the French master's who had told him the riddle.

The correspondence with his father concentrated for much of the time on the conduct of the war. And as a typical young cadet he showed the usual enthusiasm of youth for action. In writing to Prince Louis, Mountbatten gave the impression that war was terribly exciting, not in the least bit frightening or depressing, and in letter after letter he emphasized how much he wanted to go to sea and take part in the action.

In 1917 the college started a scheme whereby cadets were taken to the front for three days to give them some experience of warfare. Mountbatten was the first to apply and wrote to his mother asking her permission: 'I am just longing to see something of the trenches and it would be quite safe as far as safeness goes. Do say yes please.' He eventually went into the trenches in June 1918 and even here showed how practical he could be as he wrote to various relatives asking for the loan of breeches and other suitable articles of clothing as he did not want to have them specially made for himself 'just for the occasion'.

And when his parents gave him a puppy which was intended for the whole crew, he wrote to tell them that he had bought several items for the dog out of his own pocket but hoped to 'get something back for it some time'.

Cadet Mountbatten was inordinately proud of a magazine he started in August 1917. He sent his parents a copy of the first issue with the news that it had proved to be 'surprisingly popular' and that he expected it to make a profit of at least £11.00.

During this period Mountbatten also showed his concern for his Russian relations, having read about the revolution in the newspapers. Writing to his mother he says: 'How awful about what has happened in Russia . . . I suppose Uncle Nicky [Tsar Nicholas II] is safe, though I can't understand why he has not abdicated if they are not going to form a republic but form a constitutional monarchy. I suppose Alex succeeds and his uncle is Regent. It says Aunt Alix is under guard, so I suppose she is all right also Aunt Ella, and the cousins.'

Throughout his life Mountbatten displayed one characteristic that was regarded as unusual in someone of his generation and background. He was not in the least colour prejudiced. In fact he had only one hatred of a particular people and that was later, against the Japanese. Following the treatment of Allied prisoners of war by the Japanese, Mountbatten found it impossible to forgive them and for the rest of his life he would remain an implacable enemy of all things Japanese. He wouldn't own, or even be driven in, a Japanese car; none of his possessions was Japanese and he refused to attend any functions honouring anyone from that country. He did make one exception and that was when Emperor Hirohito paid a State visit to Britain as a guest of the Queen. Mountbatten asked Her Majesty's permission to absent himself from the State Banquet, which was granted, but he then sought a private audience with the Emperor in order to enlist his support for the United World Colleges. Apparently he was prepared to forgo his own principles if it was to benefit one of his important causes – and in this instance, once again, his plan worked. The Japanese Government provided funds for scholarships to the United World Colleges and today there are a number of students from Japan attending the colleges throughout the world.

Where colour alone was involved, Mountbatten had no such feelings, though he did recognize the problems that inter-racial marriages could bring. In a conversation on the subject with Patricia he said, 'When you think of the difficulties of fitting your life with someone of your own race, upbringing or culture it's hard enough. The further away from home and familiar things you go the more difficult it becomes. It's not because someone is black, brown or whatever. It's merely that their upbringing is different and that's where the problems start.' Lady Mountbatten adds, 'He wouldn't have minded in the least if I had brought home an Indian boyfriend. But he would have been slightly worried if I had wanted to marry one – not because he was Indian, but because he thought I might have problems fitting in. and as far as the reaction of his friends, he wouldn't have thought about that for a moment. If they didn't like it that was their bad luck. It wouldn't have affected his feelings at all.'

As a young woman, Lady Mountbatten experienced what it was like to be the daughter of such a famous man when she joined the WRNS. 'When I went to my first posting, the fact that I bore the same name as my father, who was then Chief of Combined Operations, meant that some people tried to ingratiate themselves, while there were others who went out of their way to distance themselves from me, presumably for the same reasons. One of the things I inherited from my father is the ability to spot a phony, though in his case it didn't always work. He wasn't invariably able to see that somebody wasn't quite up to the mark, but once he spotted that they couldn't match his standards they were very quickly out. He used to say: "Of course one of my failings is that I think I can do it better than anybody else" which he usually could. But his main characteristic, in my view, was his intense loyalty. He was unbelievably loyal to his friends and colleagues, even to those who were not as worthy of it as they might have been.'

Both Mountbatten's daughters are protective of his reputation. Patricia says, 'A lot of people, particularly in his career, were very jealous of him and were far from friendly towards him. What they didn't understand was that the apparent playboy image was a very small part of his life and during the most important part he was a highly professional and competent naval officer. The amazing thing was he never bore grudges, though to be honest he did enjoy getting the better of someone if they upset him. He would not hesitate to use every means at his disposal to defeat them and enjoy doing so. In fact the only person he ever really hated was Max Beaverbrook [the first Lord Beaverbrook, owner of Express Newspapers] with whom he was very, very fed up. Nobody really knows the true story behind their enmity but the most accepted version is the one about the opening sequence to the war-time film *In Which We Serve*. The film opens with a shot of a waterlogged copy of the

Daily Express in the sea showing the headline "There will be no war". Now some people thought my father had engineered that when in fact he had had nothing to do with it. It was all Noel Coward's work and of course he too was disliked by Beaverbrook. Later on Beaverbrook continued his attacks on my father when he went to India, writing articles which said, "Can we risk having this traitor in our midst?" and my father even got to the point where he thought of suing for libel but he decided it would be a waste of time and he just ignored the whole thing. Beaverbrook also blamed my father for the loss of so many Canadian lives at Dieppe and the *Express* sought every opportunity to belittle him. Beaverbrook really was a horrible man.'

Derek Hill is an artist who has painted the portraits of many famous men and women, including several of the crowned heads of Europe. Mountbatten kept a photograph of Hill's portrait of the Prince of Wales beside his bed. Hill knew Mountbatten for most of his life, having lived at Romsey since the age of ten, when the Mountbattens were his parents' landlords. As an adult he was invited to Broadlands many times and also, owning a small house in Ireland near Classiebawn, he frequently spent time at the castle.

When Derek Hill started working seriously as an artist, Dickie and Edwina offered great support and as he says, 'When Dickie decided to help, the whole Mountbatten machinery was switched on.' Mountbatten posed for Hill and their friendship continued until the day of the murder. In fact he had spent the Saturday before the murder at Classiebawn and been invited to go out in the boat but had been forced to decline because of other commitments.

'As a model Dickie was ideal,' says Hill. 'He had almost perfect features and knew what was required as a sitter. He used to sit for hours on end talking about his life and never became impatient or fidgety. And, unlike many of my subjects, he didn't try to tell me what to do. He looked upon having his portrait painted as a duty and you know what duty meant to him. When he saw the finished picture he was reasonably pleased but thought his eyes were too close together. I replied that this was how I saw him and anyway it was a Hesse family portrait. Prince Charles has it as well. The one thing I found out about him when he was sitting for me was his uncertainty. Most people, I know, think that Dickie was bombastic and completely confident. I thought he was very difficult and insecure. He appeared to be an extrovert but inside he was quite inhibited. If he was called away to the telephone he would always come back and say things like, "That was Princess Marina, or Lilibet [the Queen] on the phone." As if I had to be told that it was someone important. He was never terribly interested in jokes, I don't think humour was one of his characteristics. I know that once or twice I had to repeat stories several times for him to get the point. He wasn't very quick on the uptake. I found him to be easy to talk to but he wasn't all that interested in gossip and as far as art was concerned he had no interest at all. You could never describe him as a connoisseur.'

Mountbatten was fastidious to a degree in his appearance. No one ever saw him unshaven, dishevelled or wearing the wrong clothes for the occasion. Hawes & Curtis, one of London's best-known tailors and outfitters, dressed Mountbatten for most of his life and he went to endless trouble to make sure that they obeyed his demands for perfection. In 1955 he wrote to the firm ordering eight suits from thirty yards of a special tweed material and stressing that he wanted them to undertake not to sell the pattern to any other of their clients, 'so that it remains exclusive to Broadlands'. Three months later he wrote again saying he realized that this was not practicable.

His correspondence with Hawes & Curtis reveals the extent of his attention to the smallest detail in his eternal quest to be dressed always in the correct manner. In 1957 his secretary replied to a letter from the tailors with which they had enclosed a sample pair of socks for Mountbatten's attention. The answer stated: 'Lord Mountbatten asked me to say that the socks you have sent him would be suitable for the country but he is afraid they are too vulgar for town. He asks whether you could find him a quiet check which would be suitable for London wear.'

Socks occupied a considerable portion of his attention around this period. He wrote to Stephens Bros Ltd of Regent Street in 1958 about a present he intended giving to the President of the United States. 'I would like to change the half dozen black wool socks for President Eisenhower to half a dozen lisle thread socks, for this is the type he saw me wearing and I am sure he would prefer them.' He goes on to explain that on a recent visit to the White House the President had been great impressed with his Tenova socks. And when the company stopped making his favourite socks he asked them to resume production just for himself. They declined, even though they wrote back thanking Mountbatten for introducing their goods to President Eisenhower.

Mountbatten liked to introduce members of the Royal Family to his outfitters and Hawes & Curtis were suitably grateful when he caused Prince Philip to become one of their customers, especially when His Royal Highness went on to grant them a Royal Warrant of Appointment.

As with everything in his life, Mountbatten was demanding with his tailors. In one letter to them he pointed out several faults in a garment he had purchased: 'The belt is three inches too long and the pockets are too shallow . . . I cannot remember any other occasion with lapses of this sort and felt you would want to know about them.'

David Hicks says that even though his father-in-law was fussy about his clothes the results were usually disastrous: 'He had absolutely no taste at all in clothes. He looked magnificent in uniform and knew without hesitation the correct order for decorations and which uniform went with which occasion, but when it came to civilian clothes he was hopeless.'

During his naval career, Mountbatten was equally concerned with dress. He told Sir Charles Lambe, the Second Sea Lord, in 1956 that 'The design of "our Burberry" would be greatly improved if it had detachable shoulder straps on which could be attached little cuffs bearing miniature rank stripes . . . for there are many occasions in the rain when one would like to know the rank of an officer.'

His preoccupation with uniforms was beautifully illustrated in a comment he made to Field Marshal Sir Gerald Templer following an official dinner they had both attended. 'It was a most memorable occasion and one which made me regret for the first time that I never bought a lieutenant general's uniform (to which I believe I am legally entitled to this day) in order to mingle completely into the wonderful Army background of the occasion.'

Personal comfort was also high on his list priorities. When he was First Sea Lord, Mountbatten instructed his naval secretary to send to the Flag Officer Royal Yachts one packet of Jeyes special toilet paper, 'in case he wants to order it for *Britannia*'.

Forms of address were important both to Mountbatten and to Edwina. They had a private code which started just between the two of them and then was extended to the rest of the family and close personal friends. If a relative or someone equally close wanted to write to him and not have the envelope opened by his private secretary, they would write the words 'For Himself' in a corner, much as personal friends of the Queen put their initials in the lower left-hand corner of the envelope when they are writing to her. Mountbatten was anxious that the privilege of sending him letters in this way was not abused and when a Mrs J.R. Eden of The Children and Families World Community Chest wrote to him using this form of address he was not pleased. Lady Mountbatten told her secretary, Elizabeth Collins, 'As you can imagine, Lord Louis was much put out by the use of this phrase, which you and I know full well is confined to the family and close personal friends only.'

Always interested in anything new, Mountbatten was prepared to test the latest developments in practically any field. When the giant firm ICI sent him a length of Terylene, a new synthetic fabric, with the suggestion that he have it made up into a suit, he readily accepted, though he realized that they had chosen him only because of his publicity value and if he approved of the cloth it would do wonders for their product. Mountbatten sent the fabric to Hawes & Curtis, and received a polite but firm rebuke from this old-established and strictly traditional gentlemen's outfitters. They told him that 'the material is *not* suitable for making suits as the cloth is too light, weighing only 2oz'. When Mountbatten reported this to ICI they in turn suggested that they were not in the least surprised at 'the conservatism of Savile Row tailors' and recommended someone who was prepared to work with Terylene.

Eventually Mountbatten persuaded Hawes & Curtis to make his suit, with some reluctance. They were loath to lose such a valuable and prestigious client – and he did not want to go elsewhere. To mollify Mr E.H. Watson, the partner who dealt with his requirements, Mountbatten sent him a Christmas present that Edwina had brought back from her Far East tour. Watson was thrilled and wrote that he would treat the gift as a 'most treasured possession'. He also added a practical note for Mountbatten's benefit, telling him that the abolition of purchase tax in 1963 meant that the price of 60 yards of Broadlands tweed would now be 5s (25p) a yard cheaper. Nothing could have delighted Mountbatten more as he needed 120 yards of this material every three years to clothe the river, game and forestry staff at Broadlands.

Mountbatten was a tremendous admirer of Chaplin and had been since they first met in Hollywood during Dickie and Edwina's honeymoon. So he was very disappointed when Chaplin declined an invitation to Broadlands, where, no doubt, he would also have been invited to plant a tree, because of filming commitments. Chaplin later made up for the disappointment by spending a weekend at Broadlands – and planting the requisite tree.

When Fairbanks discovered that Mountbatten had used his influence to obtain knighthoods (at different times) for two of his oldest friends, Charlie Chaplin and Noel Coward, he said, 'You are the most wonderful friend and no one can pursue a goal more persistently than you.'

Noel Coward, Douglas Fairbanks Jr and Mountbatten had been close friends for years, and in a cloud of euphoria over Coward's recognition, Fairbanks really went over the top in commenting on Mountbatten's role: 'Probably the most admirable of your many virtues . . . you have never failed to find time to give even more of yourself both to "worthy causes" and, more importantly, to your friends. It is a very unique quality in famous men, most of whom, in my experience, have been so absorbed with their own destinies and ambitions that they were incapable of doing anything more than the minimum to flatter, but there was a certain amount of truth in what Fairbanks had said. Mountbatten may have been in the front row when it came to receiving honours for himself, but he was also completely unselfish about helping others who he believed were worthy of recognition. And, as Fairbanks said, it is an unusual trait in a prominent personality.

Both Mountbatten and Douglas Fairbanks Jr apparently saw themselves as glamorous James Bond-type figures until they were well into middle age and beyond. When Fairbanks saw Mountbatten presenting a sportsman's award on television, he knew exactly the right thing to say, 'You'll be competing with [David] Niven soon – if not already!' This feeling that they were attractive to women lasted, in Mountbatten's case, until he was in his late seventies. In 1978 he told Fairbanks that he was thrilled by the revelation of the former movie star Grace Kelly (later Princess Grace of Monaco), that before she was married she had kept his picture beside her bed. And this was before she had even met him.

Much has been made of Mountbatten's undoubted conceit. But it was a vanity that applied only to his achievements and ability to do things. He was an exceptionally good-looking man yet this was one area where he was completely unaffected. He did not spend lots of time admiring himself before a looking glass, and his daughter Pamela remembers him telling her one day that he intended to go out for a walk on his own. She was surprised because he was one of the most easily recognized figures in the country. He said, 'It will be all right. Nobody will recognize me out of uniform' – a very modest remark from someone with a reputation for having a great opinion of himself.

Mountbatten the perfectionist could drive some of his suppliers to distraction with his demands. In ordering china for Classiebawn from the Crown Staffordshire Company in 1962 he noted that 'the cipher is upside down on the marmalade and jamp pots, and is in a slightly different position on each pot.' That same year Jarrolds of Sloane Street supplied him with a visitors' book which he was most unhappy about: 'the cipher is not correctly positioned as it is . . . canted over to the right by as much as 3 or 4 degrees.' This was the sort of petty detail which could drive him – and others – to distraction. His character was such that he was incapable of giving anything but his full attention to any subject that interested him. In many ways he was a complicated man; in his own view he was the simplest of beings.

James Mooney-Boyle worked for Mountbatten for eight years from the time he retired as Chief of the Defence Staff. Having something of a murky past (he worked in counter-espionage during the war), he is vague about his actual duties but claims he was an unofficial 'aide-de-camp' recruited by the security services to help look after Mountbatten when required. Mooney-Boyle accompanied Mountbatten to many engagements in Britain, and on one visit abroad to see his sister, Queen Louise of Sweden. He says that his old boss did not have a great sense of humour, particularly when the joke might have been on himself, but there was one occasion when Mountbatten was the butt of a story which he told against himself many times afterwards. Standing bemedalled, in full uniform, outside the Ritz Hotel in London, waiting for his car after a function, he was approached by three American servicemen slightly the worse for wear. One of them, mistaking Mountbatten for the doorman, said, 'Will you call me a taxi?' Mountbatten, drawing himself up this full height, replied frostily, 'I am an admiral in the Royal Navy.' Quick as a flash the GI saluted and said, 'In that case, call me a battleship.' Later Mountbatten saw the funny side.

Mountbatten regarded himself as British through and through, yet on both sides his blood was more German than anything else, and one aspect of his character showed the German influence more than any other. He loved to win. Perhaps someone should have explained to him that the British dislike winners and, above all, those who obviously set out to win. When the British do win something they go to extraordinary lengths to conceal the fact, and to make it appear accidental. Nothing infuriates the British people more than the man who sets out to win, plans the way in which he will do it – and then single-mindedly does it, thrusting aside all obstacles. The way in which Mountbatten identified his targets in life and then methodically achieved them one by one was considered by many people to be distinctly 'un-British'.

Towards the end of his life he set out his philosophy. He was asked what he had wanted to do and the reply was: 'I only had one ambition and that was to enter the Royal Navy and spend my entire life in the Service . . . I joined the Royal Navy in May 1913, seven weeks before my thirteenth birthday . . . I continued my active service in the Royal Navy until 1965 which spanned fifty-two years of my life. All of it was happy, exciting and rewarding. I would not dream of going in for any other career if given the choice again.' On the question of his attitude to the monarchy he said, 'I have known our beloved Queen since she was a small child and have always been deeply fond of her . . . So long as we have people of the calibre of our Queen and her heir I don't think you can improve on constitutional monarchy and my loyalty is therefore absolute and complete.' And his final thoughts on his own family were: 'The happiest times of my life have been spent with the family together and the thought about death which saddens me is that I shall miss them all very much.'

12

EMPLOYER

In the fifty-five years that Mountbatten lived as a husband and then as a widower, he employed hundreds of men and women. Not just as Viceroy of India, when there were over a thousand servants at Viceroy's House, or during his time as Supreme Allied Commander or First Sea Lord, when his official duties required him to employ a large staff, but also in a private capacity, as master of Brook House, Broadlands, Classiebawn and all the other homes he and Edwina owned and occupied.

He was thought in the main to be a generous employer and his staff, if they were loyal, received every consideration. Mountbatten believed in looking after their welfare as if they were members of his own family and he enjoyed a paternalistic outlook over those who worked for him. Financial affairs of former servants received the same attention as matters of national importance, and even when the sums involved amounted to only a few pounds, he tried very hard to be as scrupulously fair and attentive as he would if his own fortune was at stake.

When the Dowager Lady Milford Haven, Mountbatten's mother, died, Lord Louis took over responsibility for looking after her long-serving maid, Edith Pye (whom Patricia and Pamela called 'Piecrust'). Both the Mountbattens accorded her special status due to her age and her long and devoted service to Lady Milford Haven. Miss Pye was invited in 1951 to spend Christmas at Broadlands, because, as Mountbatten said, 'She has been longer in the family than I have as she came to my mother in 1900 shortly before I was born.'

Miss Pye had lived with Lady Milford Haven in an apartment in Kensington Palace and Mountbatten arranged that she could remain there after his mother's death, though as a single woman 'she will occupy less rooms and therefore she should be called upon to pay only one ninth of the rates bill'. Mountbatten wrote to Sir Ulick Alexander,

Keeper of the Privy Purse, who allocated grace-and-favour apartments on behalf of the sovereign, asking that Miss Pye should be found suitable accommodation. A smaller flat was eventually found and then Mountbatten arranged for a covenant in her favour which allowed her an income of five pounds a week. Mountbatten noted in his file at the time that Miss Pye also received an annuity from his mother of fifty-two pounds a year, an old age pension of seventy-six pounds a year and private means which brought in another twelve pounds a year, giving her a total annual income of four hundred pounds.

When another of Mountbatten's employees, a Mr Bell, died in service, his pension of ten shillings a week was given to his widow. And in a letter to Commander North at Broadlands, Mountbatten took him to task for not paying one of the outside staff a five shillings a week raise that had been agreed. North was instructed to 'pay it by the weekend, including all backdated pay'.

Both the Mountbattens readily assumed responsibility for the wellbeing of a number of people who had not worked directly for them, but for their parents or grandparents. In 1950, Lord and Lady Mountbatten not only agreed to continue paying money towards the living expenses of a Private Karpitchkoff, a former servant of the Battenberg family, who had been invalided out of the army in the 1914–18 war, they increased the sum from twenty-six pounds to thirty-six pounds a year, which was paid to the Russian Benevolent Society. It may not seem like a large amount these days but in the 1920s and 1930s it could have meant the difference between starvation and survival.

No sum was too small to be looked at by Mountbatten and no job too menial for his personal attention. The man who tended his late father's grave at Whippingham on the Isle of Wight was paid two pounds a year for his trouble. In 1950 Mountbatten decided to double the sum (his mother was also buried there) and took out a covenant for seven years in the name of the recipient, Mr C. Kelleway. Payments usually took the form of covenants as they minimized exposure to income tax, a legal ploy used by many people when paying allowances to others.

If an employee left Mountbatten on amicable terms, there were few lengths to which Mountbatten would not go in his efforts to secure alternative employment for him. In 1952 a private secretary named Brice was responsible for organizing the London office. When Mountbatten was posted abroad he no longer needed a fully staffed office at home and Brice had to go. Mountbatten used all his contacts to try to find him another job, writing to the chairmen of a number of prominent companies such as British European Airways, extolling the virtues of his private secretary. And it also seems that a number of these close aides never hesitated to approach Mountbatten if they needed help on private family matters. Brice turned to Mountbatten for advice on the predicament facing his parents during retirement. His father hated inactivity and neither parent liked the place where they were living. Mountbatten was asked if he could help find them employment as live-in housekeepers. He was then asked if he would act as guarantor for an overdraft facility of fifty pounds at Brice's bank. Mountbatten agreed immediately and in his reply to Brice he offered to establish a covenant in favour of Brice's mother for two hundred pounds for seven years. And in a gesture that was devised to preserve his former private secretary's pride, he offered the money subject to Brice returning to work for him at some future date. He also suggested that if Brice wanted to discuss the matter privately he should telephone him at Broadlands, reversing the charges – but stipulated that it should be in the cheap period.

Mountbatten's offer was not accepted, either for the covenant or for Brice to return as private secretary, as the one-time employee knew his own value and he believed that Mountbatten was trying to get him back on the cheap. Brice indicated in a further letter that Mountbatten was not the most generous of employers in salary terms, stating that he could not afford to work for less than his present salary which is 'rather more than I should be worth to you'. Mountbatten was not about to be fooled by that one and his reply showed an equally astute knowledge of the going rate for private secretaries, saying that no one knew better than Brice that he (Mountbatten) could not afford to pay a private secretary seven hundred pounds a year 'however good'.

When Elizabeth Collins was working for Mountbatten's secretary in London, he was Chief of the Defence Staff. His office was in Whitehall from where he would telephone her several times a day at her office a couple of miles away at his home. On one occasion Mrs Collins remembers she was having a particularly busy day with the telephone ringing constantly. Suddenly she heard a ring at the front door bell and when she went to answer it she found a uniformed army despatch rider who handed her an envelope marked 'URGENT'. Inside a message which read, 'Ring me immediately – Mountbatten of Burma.' She did so straight away only to find that her employer merely wanted to know why he had been unable to contact her earlier. Where Mountbatten was concerned, immediately wasn't soon enough. Everything had to be done yesterday.

Vice Admiral Sir Ronald Brockman was on Mountbatten's staff for longer than most, serving under him as secretary for nearly thirty years. He says that Mountbatten was at times an infuriating boss, 'whose main fault was his inability to delegate. He would often instruct you to do something and when you got around to it you found that he had already done it himself. Everything was urgent in his book and nobody could work faster than he could himself. Another of his irritating traits was his habit of looking over a typist's shoulder when one of his letters was being typed. He would nearly always make changes as he went along and it's surprising that anything ever got finished. But in fairness, when somebody did something that pleased him he would always show his appreciation. Conversely, if things did not go according to his plan, he would blow up in a violent temper. But they never lasted. He was not one to sulk.'

Major General Sir Simon Cooper KCVO is Master of the Queen's Household with responsibility for all the eighty or so functions that are held every year at Buckingham Palace. He has total control over all the domestic staff in the Royal Household and is one of Her Majesty's most senior advisers. His military pedigree is impeccable: his father was also a General, and from joining the Life Guards as a national serviceman in 1955 Simon Cooper rose to command the regiment in 1974. In between came tours of duty in Aden, Germany and several in Northern Ireland, and he was also Commandant of the Royal Military Academy at Sandhurst for two years. In 1965, holding the rank of Captain, he was Adjutant of the Life Guards, the senior regiment of the British Army, whose Colonel in Chief was Earl Mountbatten of Burma. Sir Simon was invited to become Mountbatten's aide-de-camp at Whitehall where he was Chief of the Defence Staff. It was an invitation that was difficult to refuse.

'My first impression, which never changed, was that he had a very short fuse, did not suffer fools gladly but that if he believed you were in the right, he would back you to the hilt. I had to go through an interview with Lord Mountbatten and it seemed to me that what was most important in his view was that one fitted in. He chose his personal staff with some care and insisted that we operated as a team. If you were the odd one out, you didn't stay. It was as simple as that.'

Sir Simon goes on to say that nobody ever won an argument with Mountbatten, even if it was proved that he was in the wrong. He always had the last word. But if as a boss he was demanding of his staff, he was no less demanding of himself. He worked extraordinarily long hours and never seemed to tire. 'He thought nothing of working throughout the day, attending a function in the evening, and then going back to the office at midnight for a couple of hours' more work. His energy was amazing.'

According to some members of Mountbatten's family he was always rather mean with money, complaining about the cost of things and easily angered if a possession of his was lost or broken. As an employer though, he was both generous and loyal. When one of his Irish staff died in 1965, he immediately wrote to his agent Gabrielle Gore-Booth asking her to tell the family that he would pay for all the funeral expenses and also to let the man's wife know that she could stay in their cottage as long as she needed. In addition, Mountbatten lent the widow £300 interest free, which she repaid at £2 a week, and told his agent that in future the lady in question was to be provided with timber for her house at wholesale prices. But he drew the line at paying for the drink at the wake!

Miss Gore-Booth wrote to thank him for allowing her to pay herself a £5 bonus at Christmas, which was not as miserly as it sounds, as Mountbatten had already given her two handsome Christmas gifts of spurs and expensive riding boots.

His loyalty was shown to good effect when he backed his servants against a family of well-connected French tenants at Classiebawn, who found fault with just about everything and everybody. First, they did not approve of the butler, Peter Nicholson, wearing the Mountbatten livery and insisted that he wear plain white jackets of their choosing. Mountbatten was having none of this and the livery stayed. Then the tenants wanted the widow of the dead servant and her children to vacate their cottage – they remained. They were highly critical of the staff who had served Mountbatten for years and told Miss Gore-Booth to get rid of them all. Mountbatten was incensed over this high-handed attitude and refused absolutely to countenance the sacking of 'his employees' by people who were merely renting his house. The agent thought that these measures by the French tenants were a ploy to get their rent reduced. Mountbatten wrote to her, 'I have little doubt that when they realize on what intimate terms I am with General de Gaulle, with whom I am having a tête-a-tête luncheon in June, and how well I know Mr de Valera [the President of Ireland], they won't try any funny tricks with me.'

These same tenants caused Mountbatten a lot of trouble and threatened a rife between him and his agent when she paid a number of food and drink bills on their behalf. Mountbatten admonished her: 'You have no authority to pay bills of this sort out of my money ... if it should happen again you will have to find the money yourself.'

As a long-distance employer Mountbatten was called on to resolve many staff problems by letter. But this did not in any way diminish his patrician attitude. With the wisdom of Solomon he wrote to Miss Gore-Booth when she had been unable to settle a dispute between two long-serving members of the domestic household. Mrs Kennedy refused to drive home with Paddy Duffy if her own son, Paddy Joe, was not available to drive her. Mountbatten said, 'If this is the case she will have to walk, since what I am not prepared to do is engage a taxi or go to any expense in getting her to and from work if Paddy Duffy is available and Paddy Joe is not.'

Mountbatten liked his Irish staff very much but he was also aware of their limitations. When the seventeen-year-old Prince Carl Gustaf of Sweden was planning a visit to Classiebawn, Mountbatten wrote to Carl Gustaf's mother, Princess Sibylla, to warn her what to expect: 'The servants are all fairly primitive Irish folk and we live all in any old rough clothes ... For dinner we usually put on collar and tie and any odd day suit (never dinner jackets).' In 1963 Mountbatten informed prospective tenants of Classiebawn of the wages per week he paid his staff and which he expected them to match:

The Agent	£8.00
Steward and wife	£12.00
Cook	£7.00
Assistant Cook	£5.00
Retired Butler (from English Estate)	£6.00
Head Housemaid	£5.00
Under Housemaid	£3.10
Parlourmaid	£3.10
Chauffeur Handyman	£7.00
Skipper of Boat	£8.00
Total	£65.00

Elizabeth Collins says that after Edwina died and she went to work full time for Mountbatten, he became a very considerate employer, choosing birthday and Christmas presents with great care. He also spent more time with his staff than previously, obviously looking for companionship as well as attention.

Ronnie Brockman won't hear a word said against Mountbatten. 'Nobody could have had a more loyal friend and employer. He would stand up for you against anyone, if he thought you were in the right. But if he knew you were in the wrong, he would give you the most fearful rollicking in private.'

Although there were other servants such as Charles Smith the butler and one or two at Broadlands who served Mountbatten for longer, John Barratt was the man closest to Mountbatten during the last ten years of his life. 'He never went anywhere without me. I chose his clothes, his food, drove him to and from all his engagements and listened to his tales over and over again. We were more like companions than master and servant and when he went I missed him more than I could ever realize.'

Barratt believed he would be looked after financially by the family of Lord Mountbatten for the rest of his life. When Lord Romsey told him, two days before Mountbatten's funeral, that there was no future for him at Broadlands, he was devastated. He said that Mountbatten would never have acted in such a fashion and he believed he should have made his wishes known before his death.

Lord Romsey, and the Broadlands records, tell a slightly different story. Barratt was not told to go. What Lord Romsey did say was that he did not anticipate carrying out the same kind of public duties that his grandfather had always done, so it was unlikely that he would have need of a private secretary. Barratt was not shown the door unceremoniously the moment the funeral was over. He remained at Broadlands for a further three months because there was a tremendous amount of work to clear up after Mountbatten's murder and even then, great efforts were made to get him another job.

He was given the post of Director of the Mountbatten Memorial Trust, a post he held for a year before resigning. And when a book of Mountbatten's life in pictures was published, John Barratt was allowed to keep 80 per cent of the royalties. He then joined the household of Prince and Princess Michael of Kent. Eventually, however, he ended up working as a street cleaner in London. His fortunes ebbed even further and at one time he was reduced to living off the charity of friends and was seen in the crypt of St Martin-in-the-Fields Church in Trafalgar Square receiving free meals. Patricia Mountbatten tried to contact him to offer help but he did not respond and when he died, in November 1993, he had still not had any contact with the family for whom he had worked for so many years. His old employer would have been deeply sorry to see him in such reduced circumstances; perhaps Barratt never did recover from the loss. Certainly the rest of his life was one long decline and his final days were light years away from the glamorous lifestyle he had enjoyed with one of the world's superstars.

Mountbatten loved having a large staff around him. He enjoyed empire building in every job he took on and the remarkable thing is that almost without exception, his staff, even those who could not stand him personally, all said that he was an excellent boss. He was demanding, impatient and at times drove them all to distraction, but the fact that so many of his staff remained with him for years on end must say something in his favour.

13

FAMILY MAN

If there was one image that Mountbatten liked to portray above all others it was of himself as a family man. Even when he and Edwina were going through the worst moments of their marriage, with the possibility of a permanent split being discussed, he preserved to the outside world, and this included his own relatives, the illusion that all was well and his domestic life was perfect. His granddaughter Joanna said, 'Throughout our lives we were all conned into believing that Grandpapa and Grandmama had an ideal marriage and a perfect relationship. It was almost as if there was a conspiracy to prevent us knowing the truth.'

Mountbatten's daughters had known from an early age of their parents' problems. The present Countess Mountbatten recalls when she was eight or nine years old being hidden behind a curtain in her mother's boudoir when the both came into the room. 'I remember clearly hearing my father say to my mother; "You're breaking my heart, you know." It was the first indication I had that anything was wrong and, although I didn't fully understand what they were talking about [it was Edwina's revelation of one of her extra-marital love affairs] I knew it was serious because my father was so upset.'

The relationship between Mountbatten and his elder daughter was extraordinarily close by any standards, so much so that they had to disguise the fact from Edwina because of her jealousy. She knew her husband loved his first child with an intensity she herself was unable to feel, but she had little idea of the real strength of the bond between them.

Mountbatten simply doted on Patricia. She became the most important person in his life, occupying a position that few children have ever achieved with a parent. It began when she was a child. Her mother was always too busy with social events to bother with a small girl. Patricia says, 'I have this early memory of my mother's footsteps coming towards my bedroom door in the evening, and then passing right on by. And I can still hear the clink of her jewellery as she walked along the corridors at Brook House.' Patricia's father, on the other hand, was never too busy to spend time with her. No matter what time of day or night he arrived home, the first thing he always did was go to her room to tell her of the day's happenings and listen to her account of her day. He wasn't just acting the part of the doting parent, he genuinely loved being with her, reading stories at night and playing games until he was called to go out for yet another dinner, dance or theatre engagement.

It was almost as if he knew that Edwina could not adapt to being an affectionate mother and he became both mother and father. Patricia says he was never impatient with her, never shouted or lost his temper: 'The thing I most looked forward to was him coming home. It was the highlight of every day.'

The relationship that began in the nursery never faltered. It was undoubtedly the most constant factor in his life and the love he felt for Patricia was returned in full. Even her marriage to John Brabourne did nothing to intrude on the special intimacy that existed between father and daughter and this was one image he did not have to work at. It was entirely private, of no concern to anyone else and one of the main reasons why Mountbatten never remarried after Edwina's death in 1960 was because he was determined that his title should go to Patricia and her alone. The possibility of his remarrying, with his second wife becoming Countess Mountbatten, and having a son, who in the normal course of events would have succeeded to the earldom, was something Mountbatten would not countenance. He wanted no one but Patricia to become the next Countess Mountbatten of Burma – he got his wish.

Patricia Mountbatten has of course many fond memories of her father but the earliest goes back to when she was four or five years old and the family were living at Adsdean, the house they rented near Portsmouth for fifteen years. It was also one of the few occasions when Mountbatten became really angry with his daughter. They were attending a meet of the local hunt and although Mountbatten did not regularly ride to hounds, preferring to keep polo ponies which were rested during the winter, he had on this occasion rented an enormous hunter for the day. Patricia was alongside on her tiny Shetland pony when she thought,

'What fun. I'll ride my horse under his. With that I did just that. He had the most awful fright, thinking his horse could have reared and kicked me doing terrible damage, and he was very, very cross. "What a stupid thing to do," he yelled. I was more surprised than frightened because he never lost his temper with children, but of course, he was really frightened of what the consequences might have been.'

Another early memory was of when they lived at Brook House, which was pulled down in 1936. It was Patricia's fifth birthday and she was brought down from the nursery to the dining room where her father was lying full length on the floor hugging something to his chest. 'I was curious to know what he had hidden and then suddenly he held up the most beautiful dachshund puppy, which was my birthday present and my first dog. His name was Don and I was enchanted with him and kept him until I was evacuated to New York in the Second World War, when he died.' Lady Mountbatten has remained faithful to the dachshund breed ever since and she is still accompanied everywhere by the latest addition.

Mountbatten introduced both his daughters to the pleasures of reading aloud. He used to march up to the nursery before bedtime and read the *Just So Stories, The Jungle Book*, a great favourite, and *Emil and the Detectives*. And also, rather surprisingly to the children, because he was not a religious person, he felt it was important for them to get to know the Bible. He bought a children's version with a picture on one side of the page and a story on the opposite side. This was obviously a success as Pamela and Patricia followed the same pattern, with the same book, with their own children when they were young.

Although Mountbatten himself did not regularly attend church, he insisted on his daughters being baptized and confirmed. As children they were taken to church with their governess, walking a mile in both directions to the village church in Sussex where they lived, carrying their prayer books and 'wearing gloves as our governess reckoned young ladies should not only attend church on Sunday mornings, but be dressed appropriately also'.

Mountbatten appeared to take a humanist approach to religion and, as with his attitude to most things in life, he tended towards the practical in his beliefs. Patricia Mountbatten says they discussed religion and its meaning when she was quite young and he said, 'Some people think of God as an old man with a beard sitting on a cloud and if you aren't good he will punish you. But I don't think that. I believe that you should behave well because if you don't you will make people unhappy, and you will end up being unhappy yourself.'

He was equally practical about things like stealing and telling lies. Lady Mountbatten recounts the story of when she was about ten and she and a cousin took some cigarettes from the house. 'We went into the bushes in the garden and smoked and of course, we were caught and sent to bed. When my father came home, details of the crime were given to him and he brought us downstairs to face the music. But instead of shouting at us he just said, "This is very stupid of you. If you wanted to try smoking I would have given you a cigarette, all you had to do was ask, and apart from anything else people who do this sort of thing and then lie about it are invariably caught out, and once other people realize that you don't tell the truth you'll never be trusted again."' As a result of that minor sermon, Lady Mountbatten has never smoked to this day and she is also regarded as a stickler for the truth.

When Lady Mountbatten talks about her parents the conversation naturally focuses on her father who was quite obviously the biggest single influence on her life. She says about her mother: 'She was sweet and nice but one never felt frightfully close. She found it impossible to just sit down and relax and talk over any worries or difficulties. She couldn't do it with her husband and certainly not with her children. She wasn't the person I would have gone to with a problem. It was always my father who I turned to. We had the sort of relationship where there was nothing we couldn't talk about – literally anything from religion to sex.'

Mountbatten came to rely on his elder daughter more and more. She replaced Edwina in his affections with a love that became almost an obsession. 'There wasn't a day in my life when we didn't talk. If he was away he would ring up, sometimes very late at night, but he never missed. It became so much a part of my life that it never occurred to me that there was anything unusual in it. There was a small gap when I first married and I remember being worried when I came back from my honeymoon and didn't hear from him for several days. Finally he did ring up and when I asked what was wrong he said, "Well, now you're married Mummy told me that I must not be so possessive." I replied that I hoped things were not going to alter just because I was married and after that we went back to as we were before.'

As a parent Mountbatten anticipated the difficulties which his family would face if the Germans had landed in Britain during the war. So, against Edwina's wishes, he decided to send his daughters to America. Lady Mountbatten says, 'He was well aware that with our Jewish ancestry we would have been in the ovens and he said to my mother, "I can't concentrate on fighting this war if I'm worrying all the time about what is going to happen to you and the children if the Germans come." My mother had no intention of leaving but Pamela and I were not consulted, we just went where we were told. It was typically far-sighted of our father to look that far ahead. So, in July 1940, we sailed on the last American ship to leave these shores. We were landed, literally, on Mrs Cornelius Vanderbilt, an extraordinary, old New York Society hostess, who was one of the few people they knew well enough, and who was rich enough to have us without feeling imposed upon.'

Mountbatten's younger daughter Pamela stayed for only eighteen months, as it was felt by then the main danger had passed in Britain and it was safe for her to return home. Patricia stayed on to graduate from high school. When she too came home she had grown from a child into a young woman of eighteen – with a slight American accent which both intrigued and amused her father.

Shortly after returning to Britain Patricia joined the WRNS and this was when her relationship with her father really took off: 'He started to treat me as an adult and this occurred at a time when his marriage was going through a sticky patch. So my mother became very jealous of my relationship with my father, particularly when she realized that he was enjoying spending evenings or weekends with me more than he would with her. The only reason was that he found it difficult to get close enough to her at this point, so I naturally became his closest companion. We had been closer than the average father and child even before I went to America but it was later, when I could accompany him as an adult, that her jealousy really showed itself.'

Somewhat surprisingly, Mountbatten was never jealous himself over Patricia's boyfriends. His wife was consumed with jealousy over everybody she knew; he, on the other hand, was in Patricia's words 'totally unjealous'. Father and daughter even discussed what would happen if she had an affair with someone. 'He was the sort of person who would have thrown up his hands and said, "What a terrible thing to do." His line was more likely to be, "Have you thought this through?" The only advice he gave me about sleeping around – and this was in the 1940s when the opportunities were not so available and sex wasn't anywhere near as commonplace as it has become today – was that if you jumped into bed with all and sundry, it soon got around. And when you did eventually meet someone with whom you wished to spend the rest of your life, you would perhaps regret not having waited.'

In 1946 John Brabourne, at the age of twenty-one, proposed to Patricia Mountbatten. In fact he did so several times, with what he says was monotonous regularity, until finally she said yes. She had her doubts and told her father about her fears: 'Subconsciously I suppose I was worried by the fact that my parents had had a difficult marriage for many years and I did not want the same thing to happen to me. I desperately wanted a marriage that would last and certainly I did not want to get married thinking that if it didn't work out we could simply get divorced, which is just what happens a lot of the time now. Once I had agreed to marry John I suddenly got cold feet. So I went to my father and told him what was troubling me. I said, "I don't know how you are supposed to feel about someone you are about to marry. I do love him and like him very much but I don't feel I am absolutely madly, head over heels in love. What's going to happen if we do marry and then in a few years' time I meet someone and I do fall madly in love?" And he said, "Don't worry, I know you well enough to know that even if that happened your sense of duty would not let you do something stupid. Everything is going to be all right." Which turned out to be wonderful advice because he knew John better than I did and he realized what the basis of a good marriage was, even if he didn't have one himself.'

Some years before her marriage, Patricia received a letter from her father in which he set out to reveal his feelings for her:

Physical attraction (by no means unknown to Freud between parents and children) has hardly ever entered into our remarkable friendship . . . the attraction which you have had for me from the day I first saw you in April 1924 was an almost mystical feeling that you were really part of me living on in the world . . . You know how basically fond I am and always have been of Mummy, you know pretty well about my girlfriends, but none of them have the magic 'something' which you have . . . I have grown so fond of Pammy, few fathers could be fonder of a daughter or miss her more than I miss her now, but the mainspring of my love is that she is your sister and you love her . . . There is always one woman in a man's life and darling – she is you. Bless you always.

You'll never really know how much I love you.

It is a remarkable letter that was first shown to Pamela Hicks when Philip Ziegler discovered it while researching his official biography of Mountbatten. She was naturally hurt at finding out that she had always been second best in her father's eyes, but she said there had never been the slightest indication of such a feeling during his lifetime. She knew that Patricia was special – the whole family did – but never once was she given the impression that her father's feelings for her were anything less than those he felt for her sister. Perhaps that tells us something extra about Mountbatten's character; that out of consideration for his younger daughter, he never once indicated his true feelings.

Although she admits that her father was the greatest single influence on her life, Patricia Mountbatten never, consciously at any rate, compared her husband with her father. 'It never even occurred to me to compare my husband, or anyone else, with my father. I knew from about the age of eighteen that he was different from everybody else. He was such an extraordinary person; a law unto himself, that it was no good expecting – or even wanting – anyone to be like him. Anyway, as much as I loved him, he really was a very demanding person and very tiring to be with all the time so I wouldn't have wanted a husband who was like that as well.'

For Lord Brabourne, the transition from aide-de-camp to son-in-law was fairly straightforward with only one slightly tricky moment. 'I didn't know what to call him at first,' he recalls. 'After all, for years he had been "Sir" and it seemed a bit ridiculous to go on calling him that when he was my father-in-law. He solved it by saying, "I don't expect you to call me 'Sir'. On the other hand you can't go from calling me 'Sir' to Dickie overnight. So why don't you call me nothing for a while and then gradually start calling me Dickie?" 'That's what I did, and it worked very well.'

David Hicks was already a world-famous designer when he joined the Mountbatten family by marrying Pamela, Mountbatten's younger daughter. David is an extrovert who, on his own admission, enjoys the limelight, or as he puts it: 'I've always been confident and the idea of occupying centre stage appeals to me enormously. So when I suddenly found, on my wedding day, standing at the top of the aisle in Romsey Abbey, that 2,500 people were staring at me, I only had a moment's stage fright. It was slightly daunting to see Queen Elizabeth the Queen Mother and Princess Margaret there, plus the entire Royal Family of Sweden. Our own Queen could not attend because she was due to give birth to Prince Andrew within two weeks. But I must say I enjoyed the whole thing tremendously; much more than Pamela did.'

During their courtship David Hicks not only had to seek the approval of the Mountbattens, but also of the Queen. In the time-honoured fashion, he wanted to go down on one knee to propose and then formally request Pamela's hand in marriage from her father. 'It was a bit like a scene from a movie. We were at Broadlands and in front of the house is a large pond which has a fountain. I knew how to turn it on, so I did so thinking it would be more romantic to propose in this setting. Anyway I was just getting started when Dickie came storming out of the house yelling, "Who the hell's turned that bloody fountain on? We can't waste water like that." I said, "I'm afraid I did, sir," and Pammy scurried inside. So we walked up and down the lawn as though we were on the foredeck and I said, "I would very much like to marry Pammy. May I?" And he said, "Yes, of course." It was as easy as that. But I had to go through the motions. If I hadn't he would have been very annoyed. He was quite a frightening man until one got to know him. Actually, both he and Edwina were quite relieved that Pammy was getting married. She was thirty and Patricia had already been married for eight years when she was that age, though Pammy had refused proposals from nine other men before me and her parents were wondering if she would ever say "Yes".'

Much more nerve-racking than seeking the approval of his fiancee's parents, though, was the occasion when David was asked to dine with the Queen. Ostensibly the reason was that Her Majesty was going to Broadlands for a shooting weekend and she likes to get to know her fellow guests beforehand. But the real reason was that David had to be paraded for royal approval. 'One day Pammy rang up and said, "The Queen wants to meet you and we've been asked to dine the day after tomorrow." I replied, jokingly, "Well as it happens I'm free." So we duly turned up at Buckingham Palace and I must admit I was a little nervous but there was no need. The Queen had arranged everything beautifully with the other guests all being old friends of mine so I was able to relax immediately. Thankfully I didn't have to sit next to Her Majesty which would have been a bit daunting, but there was no interrogation and I was swept off my feet by her charm and charisma. It was a wonderful introduction to royalty.'

When the wedding plans were being prepared Mountbatten attempted to take over the entire organization as he did almost everything with which he was associated. But he had come up against a future son-in-law who was also a great organizer, and who insisted on being present at all the planning meetings. David Hicks says, 'I gave way to him of course in the matter of protocol and which members of the various European royal familes should sit where, but Pammy and I knew the sort of ceremony we wanted and in the end everyone was happy. One thing we couldn't plan, however, was the weather and on the day there was a great snow storm and I actually ended up being taken to church in a police car.'

At least David managed to get into the church, which John Brabourne had not been able to do at his own wedding in 1946. Tickets had been allocated to all guests on Lord Mountbatten's instructions, with no one allowed inside without one. The only person who had not been given a ticket was the bridegroom and the police refused him entry for about five minutes until someone in authority arrived to identify him and let him in. Mountbatten's reputation as someone whose word was to be obeyed to the letter was so well known that the police officer on duty at the church door was going to make no exceptions. And when Mountbatten was told of this minor hiatus after the ceremony he remarked, 'Quite right too.'

It was the only hiccup at Patricia's wedding. The ceremony had been planned for months with Mountbatten in his element as supreme. He set up committees to supervise traffic arrangements for the 370 'intimate' friends and relations who were invited to the wedding breakfast at Broadlands, plus another 700 guests at a reception in the Crosfield Hall at Romsey. The invitation lists received his closest attention as he weeded out those not considered essential and he personally saw the Archbishop of Canterbury who agreed to officiate. Drafts of his own speeches – and those of everyone else who was due to speak – were worked and reworked until they received his full approval and meetings were held with his future son-in-law's trustees to ensure that Patricia was going to be kept in the style she was used to.

Mountbatten similarly involved himself in every aspect of the Hicks' wedding and when they left to drive to Southampton to board the liner *Queen Elizabeth* at the start of their honeymoon, they found that here too the magic of the Mountbatten name had worked wonders. They were allowed into their suite on board the night before all the other passengers. So they were the sole occupants of a ship designed to accommodate a thousand passengers and they had 950 crew to look after their every need – surely one of the most glamorous beginnings to any marriage!

Not long after the wedding David Hicks had a taste of what life was going to be like as a member of the Mountbatten family. He and his father-in-law were going to the theatre in London and they arrived half an hour early so David suggested that they slipped into the pub next door for a quick drink. 'As we walked into the bar everybody turned and applauded. Dickie was instantly recognized and he gracefully acknowledged the applause. It was nothing new to him; it happened all the time, but it gave me an insight into how much of a hero he was in his lifetime.'

Mountbatten liked to claim that he had been instrumental in obtaining lots of work for David Hicks, and there's no doubt that wherever he went he tried very hard to introduce David's name to prospective clients. Perhaps he overestimated his own influence, but David says that he cannot recall a single instance when a job came his way through his father-in-law. While this may be the case, it would be reasonable to assume that when Hicks was commissioned to redesign the interior of the Prince of Wales's apartments at Buckingham Palace, a contract that received tremendous publicity and, no doubt, enhanced Hicks's already well-established reputation, the initial contact was made because Prince Charles knew of the designer's Mountbatten family connection.

Mountbatten's sons-in-law disagree about the extent of the division in the family caused by Edwina's jealousy. David Hicks says that there were definitely two camps with himself and Pamela on Edwina's side and his brother- and sister-in-law supporting Lord Mountbatten. John Brabourne, however, insists that there were never two camps, just Edwina alone against everyone else – and that only in her own mind. None of the others was against her as such. It was all in her imagination and nothing they could do would persuade her that they cared for her and did not want to exclude her. 'Nobody kept her out of anything,' says Lord Brabourne, 'she kept herself out of it. She was, unfortunately, on her own. We did everything we could to keep her happy. If she started a relationship, such as the one with Sir Malcolm Sargent, we used to everything possible to try to make it a happy relationship. And my father-in-law would also help. He wasn't particularly fond of Sargent, who was actually rather boring, but he put himself out to make life as nice as possible for his wife, and if that meant having someone there whom she had a thing for, then Dickie would try to make things as easy as he could.'

Mountbatten actually went to some lengths to accommodate Sargent in order to please Edwina. In 1953 he used his influence to get the conductor's name on the annual Navy List as Official Musical Adviser and later that same year, professed himself 'bitterly disappointed' when he was too late to secure a Coronation Medal for Sargent. Mountbatten's mother, the Marchioness of Milford Haven, did not care much for Sargent. The family didn't know if it was deliberate or not, but she seemed never to remember his name and referred to him as 'the Bandmaster'.

If there was a division within the family, it did nothing to drive a wedge between Patricia and Pamela. They were and are the closest of companions, as they have been all their lives.

John Brabourne's relationship with his father-in-law was probably closer than that of practically any other son-in-law in history. Mountbatten had always wanted a son, which partly explains the closeness that developed between him and his elder daughter, Patricia. She became the son he never had and all the ambitions he would have had for his son devolved on her. When she married, part of that responsibility was assumed by her husband, whom Mountbatten then treated like a son. John Brabourne could do no wrong in Mountbatten's eyes. He was exactly the sort of man Mountbatten would have chosen as a son for himself, and the fact that he adored Patricia as much as Mountbatten himself forged an even closer bond between the two men.

But John Brabourne is very much his own man and was one of the few to stand up to Mountbatten, which may explain part of their mutual respect. If Mountbatten knew he could browbeat someone he would do so. With his son-in-law, he found a man with tremendous ability – and a business brain that was to be the saviour of Mountbatten's fortunes. 'We had tremendous rows,' says Lord Brabourne, 'real stand-up shouting matches which might end up with one of us storming out of the room, but usually it was all over in five minutes or so. I never gave way to him if I believed I was right, and to his credit, if he saw the sense of an argument he would eventually come round and never sulk.'

With David Hicks the relationship was more delicate. Hicks was already a famous name when he came into the family and Mountbatten was not all that keen on competition. He liked David well enough and told his friend, the artist Derek Hill, 'I admire David so much because everything he's got he's achieved on his own – just like me.'

The year before he was killed, Mountbatten took two of his grandchildren, Norton and Joanna, to Egypt. It was intended to be a holiday and nothing more but, as Joanna recalls, when Mountbatten was involved nothing was quite what it seemed. 'Grandpapa never went anywhere purely as a tourist. He was always on the job, always trying to persuade people to do things they didn't really want to do and give money to things they had never even heard of. So when we went to Egypt, the President, Anwar Sadat, had to be informed and when we visited the Pyramids, our personal guide asked us to wait a moment while he sorted out the other tourists who were inside. With that he disappeared and by the simple expedient of turning off all the lights inside he cleared the Pyramids in minutes so that we could enjoy them by ourselves. My grandfather thought this was all perfectly normal; he expected paths to be smoothed in front of him and all lights to turn green. He saw nothing out of the ordinary in people putting themselves to enormous trouble on his behalf. He loved to travel in great style and he was completely unaware of the anomaly of trying to be democratic while at the same time enjoying the utmost luxury. He used to tell us the story of Gandhi who used to insist on travelling around India in the lowest class transport – fourth or fifth class on trains and so on, but his followers made absolutely sure that their leader had some degree of comfort. No other passengers were ever allowed near Gandhi and Grandpapa used to say that it took an incredible amount of organization and lots of money to make sure that Gandhi could travel in abject poverty. He never saw the irony of himself telling the story.'

Writing in his diary about this particular trip, Mountbatten somehow gave the impression that there were just the three of them, travelling purely as tourists and making all their own arrangements. Not according to Joanna: 'We were accompanied everywhere by John Barratt, Grandpapa's secretary, and we were aware of the smooth machine that was operating in the background, making sure that nothing ever went wrong with the transport or accommodation. On the odd occasions when something did not go as planned there would be huge explosions from my grandfather. He wasn't a man who tolerated mistakes.'

One thing that all the members of Mountbatten's large family are agreed upon is that nothing was too much trouble for him. He relished dealing with other people's problems and in the family he was regarded as the one person they could all go to, and the one person with whom they could discuss any topic. He never talked down to his grandchildren and they were never aware of the huge generation gap. His love of his family and the affection in which they all held him were probably the most outstanding successes of his life. Few things mattered more to Mountbatten than the happiness of those closest to him, and if he interfered a little to much in their private lives, it was done with the very best of intentions. And when they told him, as some of them did in no uncertain terms, that his advice was not always welcome, he accepted the rebukes with good grace. He was the head of a remarkable family and when they stood up to him, as his eldest grandson Norton did over his relationship with the future Lady Romsey, Mountbatten did not sulk. He thought he was right and nothing Norton said persuaded him otherwise, but he took defeat in this case with good humour.

Joanna feels one of the nicest things about her grandfather was his pride in all his grandchildren: 'No matter whether some of us were geese; we were all swans to him.'

Edwina Brudenell remembers here grandfather as two very different peole:'He was this very cosy family man, head of this huge family, loving to organize us all and take charge of everything, and then there was this super-hero figure all dressed up in these amazing uniforms, weighed down with medals, being saluted by all and sundry. He used to take us to the Royal Tournament when we were small and we would follow him, looking about seven feet tall, down the red carpet to the saluting base, and we felt terribly proud. And of course when we went to the Trooping the Colour, we would have a police escort for the car and seats in the best positions. It was all very exciting – and very different from the Grandpapa we saw at home. He had the most appalling table manners. He loved to have messy puddings like chocolate mousse and hold his spoon high above the table and then suddenly let it all splash down all over the plate and elsewhere. Our parents hated it but as grandchildren we thought it great fun. He was a man who took over everyone and everything – very bossy, even down to deciding what everyone was going to have for breakfast. Not that we always took notice of him.'

When Mountbatten's grandchildren went to school they were warned that some people might try to get to know them because of their famous grandfather. Edwina says, 'One or two people were a bit crawley but we soon learned to see through it and in fact I was proud when people asked me about him and it wasn't until later that I had short periods when I covered up slightly about being related to him – and about having a little bit of money.'

On the question of Mountbatten's reputation for interfering in everyone's lives, Edwina is defensive. 'He was concerned about one's boyfriends and used to talk about the sort of man one was going to marry. In my case it was far into the future because I was younger than my cousins, but he did like to know something of the background of one's friends and I think that when the time came for me to marry he would have liked someone appropriate. I think he would have accepted whoever I chose, but if it had been someone from another culture or background, he would have worried about it. The one piece of advice he gave me about a husband was "never marry a sailor" but he never said anything about actors and that's what I married. I think he would have approved.'

Another of Edwina's memories is of the small things that Mountbatten taught her as a young girl. 'When we were at Classiebawn, at the end of dinner he would teach me how to select a cigar and smell it and cut it and hand it to him. Lighting his cigar was a great favour and all the grandchildren used to take it in turns, and to sharpen his pencils. He used to pretend he was a king and I learned how to curtsy to him. He made it into a game and that's how I learned some of the things I know now. He also showed me how to choose his ties and which ones went with a particular outfit. To me he was that special person a grandfather should be, slightly removed from your own parents and someone to whom you could go and discuss anything with. That was his real secret; the ability to talk to you about anything under the sun: love, sex, school, nothing was taboo and he never talked down. He fulfilled a very special role for me. I miss him terribly and still see him sometimes in other people. He gave our family any grandeur we might have. It was all down to him and he included all of us in his triumphs. There was a definite sparkle around when he was present and that's something that can never be replaced. Sometimes I cannot believe that he's gone. His presence is all around me and at other times I ache with sadness because I can't speak to him.'

Edwina's brother Ashley was equally devoted to his grandfather but he has a slightly more detached view of Mountbatten. 'He certainly wasn't the central figure in my life. My father occupied that role. But as a family we were very regimented and I suppose that was as a result of Grandpapa's influence. Our lives were very patterned: Broadlands for

Christmas, and again in the summer for the Romsey Show. Then the Bahamas for part of the winter and the South of France in July and Classiebawn in August. He was always there, we were always doing the same thing and year after year it was very much the same. On our side of the family he was in the unique position of being our only grandparent – my cousins had Doreen, Lady Brabourne, but we had no grandmother – and as my grandfather had two daughters who had both married men who had lost an older brother in the war, and had no other siblings, it was the perfect situation for someone who wanted to express himself as a family man. Grandpapa absolutely adored the family image bit and he carried it off brilliantly.'

Ashley first became aware of his grandfather's fame when he was a very young boy. 'I was at my prep school in Oxford when I was about eight and one day, feeling a bit sorry for myself, I was walking by the river when one of the groundsmen came up to me and introduced himself. He said he had been a sergeant in the Army and had served under Lord Mountbatten in Burma. It was the first time I have ever encountered anyone in this way and it's stuck in my memory ever since.'

Ashley recalls that his grandfather was a great one for making the children work, 'which was always very nice. Much less boring than simply having a grandfather who sat around telling stories. At around eleven o'clock in the morning I'd make him an egg nog or port flip and because I was supposed to be the artistic one in the family I'd be made to bring out my paints and repair the standard if it was a bit weatherbeaten. He also had a pair of slippers with his own crest on them and I drew the crest for him to make sure it was all correct. Then we had something called the Imperial Spy Command, a small private army in which he was the only grown-up. We were all given code names, his was Mammoth, and he organized everything on military lines.'

As a grandfather Mountbatten could be intimidating and occasionally frightening. 'He tended to shout rather a lot,' says Ashley, 'but once we realized that it was all bluster we soon got his measure. There was only one time when I was really frightened and that was at the thought of what he might do, not what he actually did do, which was very little. We were at our house in the Bahamas and we had borrowed his alarm clock without his permission for a project of our own. Well, of course, we broke it and all of us were terrified of his reaction. Actually our parents were much angrier than he was but that was the only time he really frightened me. He hated anyone taking something of his without his permission. Since he's died, however, I've met people who worked with him and they've told me what he was like if things went wrong. His anger was awesome.'

When he died Mountbatten left to each of his grandchildren a number of boxes into which he had placed over the years various personal items. Among Ashley Hicks's inheritance are navigating instruments from Mountbatten's yacht in the 1930s, his naval Morse-code kit and his compass and sextant from his days as a serving officer. Everybody received a copy of the ingenious and complicated family relationship tables Mountbatten compiled over the years and Ashley also has an English translation of an account of a visit to *The Mikado*, written by Prince Louis of Battenberg during a visit to Japan in 1881. Mountbatten was scrupulously fair in dividing his goods among the grandchildren and, as with everything else in life, lists were made to see that each of them received an equal share.

One effect that Mountbatten had on his grandchildren, whether planned or not, was that they all felt a pressure to achieve. Michael-John, who is now a successful film producer in his own right, says, 'Being the grandson of a famous international figure made me feel that one had to live up to certain standards because of the family background, and in the early days I sometimes used to ask myself why somebody might be interested in me. But I no longer have this feeling. I don't worry now about my background.'

Mountbatten had always been a great storyteller and his grandchildren were fascinated by his tales of derring-do in the war. And, strangely, for someone who had the reputation of being the vainest man in the world, many of his best stories were against himself. He would often cause great merriment among his grandchildren by starting off a story about what brave and extraordinary exploits he had been involved in – all true as it happened – and then the punch line would show how he had been made a fool of in the end.

His humour was childlike. Michael-John recalls that his grandfather 'had the most wonderful giggle and he would love to sit with us and watch a Charlie Chaplin or Buster Keaton film. It didn't matter that he had probably seen it before dozens of times. He loved slapstick and Laurel and Hardy were also two great favourites. In fact he was fascinated by the whole film world and when I became involved in movies he always wanted to know all about the latest technology, cameras and sound systems.'

Mountbatten often said that he would have liked to work in the film business and his family agree that he would have been a natural, but not as a director. Michael-John says, 'He did not have the disciplined, creative mind a director needs. I think he would have made a better cameraman.' John Brabourne, the most successful film-maker in the family, feels his father-in-law would have been a good producer, 'Because a producer needs to be able to persuade other people to put up the money and he could always do that, and also choose the right people for various jobs, and he was pretty good at that also.'

Lord Brabourne owes much of his early success in films to his father-in-law's support. Mountbatten gave unstintingly of his time and energy to further the careers of his family and when John Brabourne decided that the film world was where he wanted to make his mark, Mountbatten brought his considerable talents as a 'fixer' to bear. Coming from a family which personified the traditional values of the English and Irish upper class – his family had owned and farmed land in Kent and Ireland for more than five hundred years – John Brabourne could reasonably have been expected to continue this way of life. His wife was independently wealthy, and the expectation of more to come on the eventual death of her parents. He enjoyed a substantial income from his own family trusts, so there was little reason for him to embark on a career in what is rightly regarded as one of the most risky businesses in the world. However, he was determined to get into films, and once Mountbatten had done what he thought was the right thing by warning him of the risks, he then did all he could to promote John's career.

Mountbatten himself had always been fascinated by the film world; he was even offered a job as head of sound at Warner Brothers Studios at one time. His contacts in Hollywood, or elsewhere, were at the highest level, and continuing his belief that if you want to get anywhere you should always start at the top, he began by introducing John to one of the most powerful men in the film industry, Spyros Skouras, the President of Twentieth Century Fox. That first meeting produced positive results as Skouras went on to support Brabourne's first project – a film entitled *Harry Black* starring Stewart Granger.

Skouras wrote to Mountbatten admitting that it was through his introduction that he had decided to help Brabourne and stressing the opportunity being offered: 'I am just as delighted as you are about the fact that our conversation in New York resulted in the present negotiations with John and his group regarding *Harry Black*.' Skouras eventually provided Brabourne with £325,000 to finance the film – a substantial amount in the 1950s.

Having made the initial introduction, Mountbatten was not a man to let matters rest there. He pressed his son-in-law to cement the relationship with Skouras saying, 'I have advised him [John] that if he finds another story which he feels might interest you, to send it to you.' And he continued, 'If ever you want a competeur and keen young man to produce another of your British quota films in England, I heartily recommend John!!!'

Brabourne himself was fully aware of the advantages of having a father-in-law who could pull such strings and he was not above asking Mountbatten to intervene on his behalf. When he needed assistance in producing a film in India, he suggested that Mountbatten should write to Skouras, even saying that it would be helpful if Mountbatten did not mention the fact that he [Brabourne] knew of the approach.

Lord Brabourne always knew what his father-in-law was up to because he was sent copies of every letter that mentioned him. The relationship between all three men was further improved when Mountbatten invited Skouras to a magnificent, formal function in the splendour of the Painted Hall at Greenwich. The American was suitably impressed and afterwards said he was tremendously honoured to be Mountbatten's personal guest on such a memorable occasion.

John Brabourne has gone on to become, with his partner, Richard Goodwin, one of the film industry's most successful filmmakers with a string of outstanding critical and box office hits. No doubt he would have achieved this success even without the help of his father-in-law who played no part in any further productions. And movie moguls are not philanthropic sentimentalists who throw their money around simply because they are impressed by titles or claims of friendship by the great and the good. They are hard-headed businessmen who demand value for money and no matter how famous Mountbatten might have been, if John Brabourne had not had the talent to produce the goods at the right time – in other words, to show a profit – no amount of fixing by his father-in-law would have persuaded the man of the stature of Spyros Skouras to back him.

Nevertheless, it was Mountbatten who opened the door for his son-in-law. And no one was more delighted and proud that once again his judgement had proved correct. If he had not believed that John Brabourne had the talent and determination to succeed, he would not have wasted his time in the first place. The final outcome was that Mountbatten had managed to do something positive for a member of his family and nothing gave him greater pleasure.

Mountbatten's eldest grandson, Norton (Lord Romsey), says that if there was ever a special relationship in the family, apart from that between his mother and her father, is was the one shared by Mountbatten and Prince Charles. Charles absolutely revered Mountbatten, whom he called Uncle Dickie, but whom he referred to as 'my honorary grandfather'. From an early age the young Prince relied heavily on Mountbatten's advice and counsel and they saw each other at least once a month. When one of them was abroad, they would correspond frequently in lengthy letters telling each other what they had been doing, who they had met and where they had been.

At Gordonstoun, Charles was a contemporary of Norton Knatchbull and he became friendly with all Mountbatten's family. He was particularly close (and still is) to John Brabourne and Patricia, who is his godmother, and would often spend holidays at their home on the Caribbean island of Eleuthera.

As early as 1965, when Charles was just seventeen, Mountbatten was invited to take part in an important meeting to discuss the Prince of Wales's future. It took place at Buckingham Palace where a small number of the great and good including the then Prime Minister, Harold Wilson, the Archbishop of Canterbury, Dr Ramsey, the Dean of Windsor, and the Chairman of the Committee of University Vice-Chancellors, Sir Charles Wilson, joined the Queen and Prince Philip around the dinner table to map out the development of the 'King-in-waiting'.

After they had all had their say, Mountbatten spoke. He had already decided the only route the Prince should take and he made his ideas sound as if there was no alternative. He suggested that Trinity College, Cambridge, was where Charles should study for his degree (as the place where the last Prince of Wales had continued part of his education). Then Charles should be entered for the Royal Naval College at Dartmouth and, finally, a spell as an officer in the Royal Navy. History has recorded that all his suggestions were agreed to immediately and that was the path followed precisely by Prince Charles, until he retired from the Navy in 1976.

Mountbatten later told Prince Charles, 'There is no more fitting preparation for a King than to have been trained in the Navy.' Once His Royal Highness had completed his initial training Mountbatten even advised on his various postings to make sure he gained all-round knowledge as a naval officer. Prince Charles has since said that almost everything he learned as a young man he learned either from, or because of, Lord Mountbatten.

Mountbatten's affection for his great-nephew knew no bounds. He would put himself out on any occasion if he thought it was what the Prince wanted or if it would benefit him in any way. When Prince Charles graduated from Dartmouth, Mountbatten learned that Prince Philip was going to be abroad and would therefore be unable to attend his son's passing-out parade. Cancelling all other engagements that day, Mountbatten commandeered a helicopter which flew him to Dartmouth where he represented the family. Afterwards he took Charles with him back to London where they joined the Queen at Buckingham Palace for lunch. Prince Charles has never forgotten that on one of the biggest and proudest days of his life, Lord Louis was there at his side. And again, on 11 February 1970, when the Prince of Wales was formally introduced into the House of Lords, Mountbatten (along with Lord Snowdon) was in the Chamber to lend his support.

Broadlands became a second home to Prince Charles during his naval service. He had his own room where he kept a spare set of clothes and, apart from Mountbatten's clumsy if well-meaning attempts to match him with his granddaughter, Amanda, he knew that here he could relax and do just whatever he liked. There was no pressure and when he needed a sympathetic ear, his honorary grandfather was always on hand, prepared to listen. Charles once said that what he liked most about Mountbatten was that he could tell him anything without fear of being ridiculed or laughed at. For most of his life Prince Charles has been a solitary figure, a loner who finds it difficult, because of who he is, to interact with others. It is arguable that the nearest he ever came to having someone to whom he could confide anything and everything was Mountbatten.

Certainly Mountbatten, for his part, regarded Prince Charles as someone very special. The biggest compliment he felt he could pay him was to treat him as one of the family, for in Mountbatten's eyes no one was more important.

CONCLUSION

In the latters years of his life, Mountbatten's role as self-appointed champion of the Royal Family consumed more and more of his time. He took up cudgels on their behalf on many occasions, believing that the self-imposed royal rule of 'never answering back' did not apply to him. When a television reporter, in an attempt to offer Mountbatten a somewhat back-handed compliment over his role in India, said he had done 'an extraordinary job of political manipulation without knowing anything about politics . . . In fact, he is the only royal who has ever done a constructive job,' Mountbatten not only rejected the accusation that he knew nothing about politics, but took much greater exception to the implied criticism of his royal relations.

Mountbatten never tired of assuring various members of the Royal Family of how useful they were and how worthwhile were their contributions to national life. And if the Queen disregarded many of his suggestions if they involved political or State affairs, she took full advantage of his superlative skills in public relations on matters of personal family business where his avuncular advice was frequently sought. Mountbatten had an unerring intuition for correct public behaviour. He knew instinctively how the Royal Family should react to any issue of national interest. In this area he was invaluable to, among others, Prince Philip, whose own natural inclinations might occasionally lead him to behave in a manner which could attract criticism. One such occasion was when Prince Philip decided he was going shooting on the day after Winston Churchill's death. Mountbatten counselled strongly against doing so and refused to take part himself as a mark of respect. Prince Philip eventually decided, with, no doubt, some gentle persuasion from the Queen, to abandon his plans for that day. It was not a matter of momentous importance, but typical of the help Mountbatten was able to offer the Royal Family.

Similarly, he anticipated by at least fifteen years the eventual furore that would be caused over the Queen's wealth. He knew that some day uninformed speculation over the size of her fortune would lead to trouble – and he was right. His advice was to plant a responsible, authoritative article on the subject in a serious newspaper and thereby nip any future trouble in the bud.

Mountbatten was a firm believer in using the media to get across his own views and no one was more adept at manipulating the press. He had a number of favoured journalists to whom he would leak stories and, of course, he also enjoyed the friendship of not only their editors, but in most cases the men who owned the newspapers. No one needed a press officer less than Mountbatten.

By any standards his achievements were remarkable. To become an Admiral of the Fleet and First Sea Lord in a naval career that was twice seriously interrupted was outstanding enough. When placed in the context of his other roles – Chief of the Defence Staff, Viceroy and Governor General of India, Governor of the Isle of Wight, Chief of the Combined Operations and Supreme Commander, South East Asia – the sheer man-hours involved are staggering for one person. There are those, who claimed he wore his public offices as a woman wears her handbag – as a useful adornment, but whose prime purpose is to enhance the wearer's overall appearance to the outside world.

Mountbatten was not a modest man. No one, not even his greatest admirers, could ever claim he was not vain – and he himself cheerfully admitted that he liked to blow his own trumpet. It wasn't a pleasant trait, and to some people, not all of whom could be considered enemies, it was extremely unpleasant – and very un-British.

If his public life was a brilliant success, his marriage was, in the main, a sad failure. In the thirty-eight years he was married to Edwina, they were both desperately unhappy for far more of the time than they were happy together. He learned to accept his wife's many lovers with a sophistication that was never natural to him. He also accepted the humiliations she heaped on him, and forgave her every time. A smile or kind word from her could make his day, while to her he was, at times, an irritation and a bore. Yet she gladly accepted the reflected glory that being married to one of the most successful men in the world brought. Edwina was a complex character. She genuinely wanted her husband to succeed and she was pleased and proud when he did. But it did nothing to stop her flaunting her relationships.

If he looked elsewhere for comfort it was never with the same success. Superficially he was a man of the world; underneath he was a betrayed husband trying hard to conceal his unhappiness. None of his extra-marital affairs meant anywhere near as much to him as his marriage, but even when he tried to explain this to Edwina he was ham-fisted and clumsy. What he really wanted was for her to care for him as much as he did for her. It was never to be.

The one true love affair of his life (in the purest terms) was with his daughter Patricia, to whom he dedicated his achievements and from whom he received admiration and love in equal measure. With the exception of his wife, Mountbatten's family was the one side of his private life that left him completely fulfilled. He loved nothing more than the companionship of his daughters, grandchildren and sons-in-law, and until the day he was killed, they enjoyed him to the same extent. In their eyes his stature was never diminished.

Mountbatten was outrageous; a man who shaped the truth to fit his own version of events and who glossed over facts and incidents that showed him in an unfavourable light. Yet when he was caught out in a blatant lie he would own up with good humour which itself was a ploy because in that way he could usually disarm his accusers. Most of the time it worked.

He attracted tremendous loyalty and undying hatred – there was very little indifference. He could be the most courteous of men and the most infuriating. He was brilliant at picking other people's brains and never hesitated to hi-jack another's ideas, which he would then proceed to produce as his own. He was aware of his lack of formal qualifications and suspicious of his intellectual superiors, yet his brain was formidable, clear, concise and analytical. No one could identify targets more clearly, or reach his objectives more ruthlessly. His path was littered with the blighted careers of those who had the temerity to disagree with him or prove him wrong. He seemed always to be see his own role in terms of confrontation: of battles to be won and enemies to be defeated.

Mountbatten was a one-off. A workaholic who was brave, generous, vulnerable and affectionate. A loyal friend and considerate lover, royal snob and super-efficient officer. If only he had been able to organize his private life like his public life, he would have been a completely happy man.

The private Mountbatten was troubled, insecure, constantly worried about money – without ever needing to be – and desperate for affection and attention. He hated to be alone, found it difficult to relax and impossible to take second place. His lineage meant he was always destined to be on the fringes of royalty, yet never fully a member. If only he had been able to understand that his achievements placed him in a unique category, way beyond anything any member of the Royal Family could reach.

There are plenty of princes around – there was only ever one Mountbatten.

BIBLIOGRAPHY

Barrat, John and Ritchie, Jean, *With the Greatest Respect*, Sidgwick & Jackson.

Evans, William, *My Mountbatten Years*, Headline.

Franklyn, Noble, *Prince Henry – Duke of Gloucester*, Weidenfeld & Nicholson.

Hoey, *Invitation to the Palace*, Grafton.

Holman, Dennis, *Lady Louis*, Oddhams.

Hough, Richard, *Louis and Victoria*, Hutchinson.

Hough, Richard, *Mountbatten – Hero of our Time*, Weidenfeld & Nicholson.

Masson, Madeleine, *Edwina*, Robert Hale.

Morgan, Janet, *Edwina Mountbatten*, Harper Collins.

Mountbatten – Eighty Years in Pictures.

Pattinson, William, *Mountbatten and the Men of the Kelly*, Patrick Stephens.

Poolman, Kenneth, *Kelly*, William Kimber.

Rose, Kenneth, *King George V*, Weidenfeld & Nicholson.

Smith, Charles, *Lord Mountbatten: His Butler's Story*, Stein & Day.

Terraine, John, *Life and Times of Lord Mountbatten*, Hutchinson.

Windsor, Duke of, *A King's Story*, Cassell.

Ziegler, Philip, *Mountbatten – The Official Biography*, Collins.

Zeigler, Philip (ed.), *The Diaries of Lord Louis Mountbatten*, Collins.